Gert-Jan Hospers, Sebastian Amrhein (Eds.)

Coping with Overtourism in Post-Pandemic Europe

Regionen in Europa/ European Regions

herausgegeben von

Prof. Dr. Helmut R. Ebert
(Universität Bonn)

Prof. Dr. Karl Eckart
(Universität Duisburg-Essen)

Prof. Dr. Gert-Jan Hospers
(Radboud-Universität Nijmegen)

Prof. Dr. Hartmut Kowalke
(Technische Universität Dresden)

Band 7

LIT

Contributors

Sebastian Amrhein, Rhine-Waal University of Applied Sciences, Germany

Martijn Duineveld, Wageningen University & Research, The Netherlands

Florian Eggli, Lucerne University of Applied Sciences and Arts, Switzerland

Eva Erdmenger, Wageningen University & Research, The Netherlands

Huib Ernste, Radboud University, The Netherlands

Robert Fletcher, Wageningen University & Research, The Netherlands

Roos Gerritsma, Inholland University of Applied Sciences, The Netherlands

Sina Hardaker, Julius Maximilian University (JMU) Würzburg, Germany

Gert-Jan Hospers, Radboud University, The Netherlands

Tom Jakobs, Municipality of Deurne, The Netherlands

Andreas Kagermeier, University of Trier, Germany

Ko Koens, Inholland University of Applied Sciences & Breda University of Applied Sciences, The Netherlands

Lola Kuenen, Netherlands Enterprise Agency RVO, The Netherlands

Moritz Langer, Ludwig Maximilian University (LMU) Munich, Germany

Miroslav Roncak, Palacký University Olomouc, Czech Republic

Guido Stompff, Inholland University of Applied Sciences, The Netherlands

Fabian Weber, Lucerne University of Applied Sciences and Arts, Switzerland

Acknowledgements

This book and the editorial work to prepare it were financially supported by Stichting Stad en Regio, The Netherlands. Most chapters are edited papers presented at a workshop on overtourism held in Kleve (Germany) and Nijmegen (The Netherlands) at 10 and 11 November 2022. The workshop took place at the premises of Rhine-Waal University of Applies Sciences (Kleve) and Radboud University (Nijmegen). Thanks are due to both institutions for their hospitality.

Introduction - The return of overtourism on the policy agenda

Gert-Jan Hospers & Sebastian Amrhein

Traditionally, the Italian city of Venice has been a tourist magnet. In the late eighteenth century, residents were already complaining about visitors creating nuisance in the public space of the canal city. In the last two decades, tourism in Venice has exploded (Nolan & Séraphin, 2019). During the corona period, when tourism in Venice came to a sudden halt, many residents hoped that their city would become less crowded after the pandemic. But anno 2023, Venice's popularity is once again undiminished among vacationers. Although the influx of tourists is less than before corona, the city is again sighing under the large number of visitors, especially in the high season. On busy days, some 120,000 people visit downtown Venice (Simmons, 2023). In addition to tourists staying in Venice for several days, the city is confronted with many day-trippers, including cruise ship passengers and vacationers staying elsewhere in the region.

Venice's tourist popularity is having a major impact on the city. For example, ever more residents are moving out of the centre to quieter places in the surrounding region. As a consequence, the inner-city of Venice is shrinking dramatically in demographic terms: the downtown population fell from some 157,000 in the early 50's to slightly more than 50,000 in 2021 (Allaboutvenice.com, 2023). This population decline is not only the result of rising prices in the local housing market, but also has to do with dissatisfaction. More and more residents think negatively about tourists and feel that their daily living environment is being taken over. Indeed, mass tourism is damaging Venice's lagoon, canals and historic heritage. Paradoxically, tourism is destroying the very thing that travellers come for (Hospers, 2019). The Venice city government increasingly recognizes the downsides of tourism and tries to act against it. For example, the municipality fines tourists who do not behave in public space and even charges an entrance fee to day-trippers visiting the centre.

The situation in Venice is an extreme example of what is known as 'overtourism', which Koens et al. (2018) define as the "excessive negative impact of tourism on the host communities and/or natural environment" (p. 2). Apart from Venice other European cities are struggling with the downsides of mass tourism, including Berlin, Rome, Lisbon, Prague and Amsterdam. Smaller European cities with an attractive tourist profile – think Porto, Palma de Mallorca and Dubrovnik – also suffer. Even villages are confronted with overtourism, such as Giethoorn (The Netherlands), Hallstatt (Austria) and Cinque Terre (five fishing villages in the Italian region of Liguria). And, what applies to Venice can be seen in other destinations as well: the corona crisis has not caused tourists to reconsider traveling less. Even if tourist numbers still lag behind pre-corona levels, many destinations in Europe are overcrowded again. Some authors even talk about the trends of 'revenge travel' or 'catch up travel' after COVID-19, exacerbating the problem of overtourism in some popular destinations (Pasquinelli & Trunfio, 2022; Vogler, 2022). In short, overtourism has returned on the policy agenda – also in post-pandemic Europe it remains a relevant issue.

The set-up of this book

Given the ongoing relevance of the topic after the corona-period, this edited volume brings together a number of theoretical, empirical and policy perspectives on overtourism in Europe. The book starts with thought-provoking reflections on the phenomenon from a social constructivist respectively philosophical viewpoint. In **chapter 1**, Eva Erdmenger demonstrates in an original way why the term 'overtourism' has a right to exist. She does so by analysing how residents of Copenhagen and Munich, two popular tourist cities, describe the effects of tourism on their living environment and construct their reality of overtourism. In **chapter 2**, Huib Ernste enriches the debate on overtourism by introducing the concept of 'atmosphere', a new-phenomenological conceptualisation of embodied touristic experiences. Researching atmospheres gives us a more comprehensive view on the core of touristic activities and situations and thus is a useful way to get a better understanding of how overtourism 'feels'.

Part I of the book discusses approaches that decision makers in attractive tourist European destinations have followed to cope with overtourism. In this respect, it makes sense to distinguish between different types of destinations, as Fabian Weber and Florian Eggli argue in **chapter 3**. They convincingly show how, among other things, approaches to handle overtourism differ between urban places, coastal and island destinations as well as rural and mountain areas. As an example of an urban destination, Lola Kuenen, Robert Fletcher and three of their (former) colleagues discuss the case of Amsterdam in **chapter 4**. They argue that COVID-19 created a sense of urgency in the Dutch capital to change the perspective on urban tourism. This was not just words, action was also taken: the resulting Amsterdam 'Tourism in Balance'-approach integrates aspects of both pro-growth and degrowth agendas. In **chapter 5,** Miroslav Roncak gives a detailed account of how Prague has dealt with tourism after the corona crisis. Of particular interest is the city's guiding principle of 'cultural sustainability', i.e. the preservation and promotion of the city's rich cultural heritage while ensuring that tourism development aligns with the interests of local communities.

Overtourism may have implications for local policy domains that, at first glance, are not directly related to tourism, such as a municipality's overall sustainability ambitions and its handling of citizen participation. In this regard, Part II discusses experiences gained in towns that are part of the Cittaslow-network as well as in the tourist hotspots of Barcelona and Amsterdam. In **chapter 6**, Gert-Jan Hospers and Sebastian Amrhein describe mini-cases to assess the value of Cittaslow-membership in attempts to prevent overtourism. Even if it always depends on local conditions, they argue that Cittaslow can be a useful concept for destinations seeking a balanced tourism development. In **chapter 7**, Moritz Langer points to the precarious labour conditions of many tourism workers in Barcelona. According to the participants in the focus group he spoke with, there is a pressing need for degrowth and more economic democracy in Barcelona's tourism sector. Also Roos Gerritsma and Guido Stompff plea for a better insight in the position and the role of stakeholders in cities that are confronted with overtourism. They do so in **chapter 8** by asking the intriguing question 'who is at Amsterdam's tourism policy making table?' Their research reveals a rather scattered landscape with in- and excluding mechanisms, giving reason for the City of Amsterdam to think about the set-up of alternative participatory design methods.

Part III of the book ends with challenges in the field of overtourism, both for destinations dealing with this phenomenon and for researchers that examine its underlying mechanisms. In **chapter 9**, Andreas Kagermeier makes clear how important it is to look for ways to reconcile the interests and needs of residents with the promotion of tourism activities. Bringing about such a reconciliation is not easy, he fears, since it implies a fundamental shift in the role played by DMO's and their willingness to take the concerns of citizens seriously. In **chapter 10**, Sebastian Amrhein builds on sociological approaches and research on social movements to challenge the so-called 'support narrative'. He illustrates how the COVID-19 pandemic has made the dependencies of locals in tourism hotspots visible and, as a matter of fact, reinforced their insecurities. Thus, the pandemic can be considered an obstacle to profound change rather than a catalyst. In **chapter 11**, Sina Hardaker calls for comprehensive research on the role of digital platforms (e.g. Airbnb and Uber) in the overtourism debate. Based on an impressive literature review she reveals the multiple and intricate ways in which these platforms are linked to overtourism. Hardaker comes up with a detailed research agenda. Implementing this research will ask for an interdisciplinary perspective, which, in our view, is also needed for research on overtourism in general.

Literature

Allaboutvenice.com (2023). *Venice population and why we are so few*. [Online] Available at: https://allaboutvenice.com/

Hospers, G.J. (2019). Overtourism in European cities: from challenges to coping strategies. *CESifo Forum, 20*(3), 20-24.

Koens, K., Postma, A. & Papp, B. (2018). Is overtourism overused? Understanding the impact of tourism in a city context. *Sustainability, 10*(12), 4384.

Nolan, E. & Sépharin, H. (2019). Venice: capacity and tourism. In R. Dodds & R. Butler (Eds.), *Overtourism: Issues, Realities and Solutions* (pp. 139-151).

Berlin: De Gruyter.

Pasquinelli, C. & Trunfio, M. (2022). The missing link between overtourism and post-pandemic tourism: framing Twitter debate on the Italian tourism crisis. *Journal of Place Management and Development, 15*(3), 229-247.

Simmons, J. (2023). Overtourism in Venice. *Responsible Travel*. [Online] Available at: https://www.responsibletravel.com/copy/overtourism-in-venice

Vogler R. (2022). Revenge and catch-up travel or degrowth? Debating tourism Post COVID-19. *Annals of Tourism Research, 93*,103272.

Chapter 1 - Reasons why the term 'overtourism' has a right to exist: the social constructionist perspectives of urban citizens

Eva Erdmenger

Introduction

According to media, *"mass tourism is destroying the planet"* (Spangler, Darbha & Lay, 2019, n.p.). Following Haase's (2021) framing analysis, media articles frame overtourism almost exclusively negatively and compared it with war scenarios and the (neo)colonization of destinations. Especially in times of the fast world of social media, media reports with a sensationalist propaganda about tourists invading destinations mobilised followers strikingly quickly. Ultimately, social movements were formed, and residents started to protest against tourism because it "means local people can't buy homes" (Palmer, 2021, n.p.). For those working in the tourism industry, such as Clemens Baumgärtner, the Head of Munich's department of Labor and Economy, overtourism is

"one of the most awful words to me; I'm happy about every tourist who comes. And will I never become tired of telling everyone I don't want to scare people off with the word 'overtourism'. That applies to us in Munich, and this even applies for the surrounding mountain regions, where some people say, "now it's getting too much!" I think that's a signal to our guests, who have a lot of money and a lot of reputation to bring to us." (Tourismus Oberbayern München, 2021, TOMCast #2, 25th June, 2021; translated from German).

From a more scientific understanding, overtourism is *"the excessive growth of visitors leading to overcrowding in areas where residents suffer the consequences of temporary and seasonal tourism peaks, which have enforced permanent changes to their lifestyles, access to amenities and general well-being"* (Milano, Cheer & Novelli, 2019, p. 1). In line with this understanding, most scientific definitions somehow refer to a volume of tourism which exceeded an undefined and largely varying carrying capacity and tolerance limit of a destination. Thus, concepts like the limits to growth of the Club of Rome and tourism carrying capacity became on vogue again. While some researchers claim that the neologism overtourism would be old wine in new bottles (referring to the debate about mass tourism), Dirksmeier and Helbrecht (2015) argue that now the emphasis would be on the quantitative dimension of urban tourism. Baumgartner (2020) in turn highlighted that mass tourism led to a nature-oriented debate while overtourism became a resident-oriented discussion, which goes beyond the debate of the scientific research community. Some researchers, as well as industry stakeholders, prefer to use less emotionally loaded terms such as imbalanced tourism or reduce the social phenomenon to the specific negative effects like overcrowding (Vagena, 2021). Although a couple of (scientific) definitions are recited more often than others, there is no official or agreed-on understanding of overtourism.

What becomes clear from the differing perspectives on overtourism as cited above, is that overtourism polarises. While scientists and industry shareholders often roll their eyes when they hear the word overtourism, media and the broad society generously use this word to express their growing anti-tourism sentiments. Nonetheless, overtourism was indeed one of the most prominent topics in tourism research around 2017-2019 and thus also leading debates at the ITB Berlin 2018. Scholars were collecting empirical data of case studies like Barcelona, Venice, and Amsterdam to analyse what hides behind the phenomenon overtourism which was pressing in those cities. Table 1 gives an impression of the increase of publication about overtourism in broader media reports compared to scientific articles. Considering that the multi-stage publication process of scientific articles usually takes at least one year, the number of scientific publications is slightly delayed compared to fast daily media with lower publication barriers. Table 1 discloses that despite the outbreak of the COVID-19 virus in 2020, the overall number of publications about overtourism remained at a high level with only a small decrease of publications.

Year (Jan. 1st - Dec. 31st)	Number of hits for the keyword search "overtourism" (with quotation marks)		
	Google News	Google Scholar (excluding citations)	Web of Science
2016	459	7	-
2017	498	32	1
2018	1,560	288	12
2019	3,470	1,110	77
2020	2,460	2,050	112
2021	3,540	2,390	97

Table 1 *Number of publications about "overtourism" between 2016 and 2021. Source: Own research as indicated by Google News, Google Scholar, and Web of Science*

The fact that this supposedly irrational, over-simplifying term (Milano, Novelli & Cheer, 2019) gained such a broad recognition, justifies that we pay close attention to it – no matter if we like the term or not. However, what does *not* become clear from the previous citations is how citizens, who live in popular destinations and must cope with the negative effects of tourism, perceive, define, and describe (over)tourism. Indeed, anti-tourism sentiments go beyond overcrowding as previous research disclosed (Koens, Postma & Papp, 2018). Instead, residents' complaints rather deal with the unsustainable transformation of their living environment – which is catalysed and visualised by tourism. Various researchers hence agree that the multiple negative effects, which come along with overtourism, are to a large extent influenced by or even rooted in the long-term development of the globalization and urbanization (Bello et al., 2017; Tschöll & Költringer, 2019). Nonetheless, the majority of overtourism perception studies is based on standardised quantitative (online) surveys (Almeida-García et al., 2021; Arif et al., 2019; Kim et al., 2020; Namberger et al., 2019; Szromek, Kruczek & Walas, 2020; Tichaawa & Moyo, 2019; World Tourism Organization (UNWTO) & IPSOS, 2019; Zucco et al., 2020; etc.). However, Oskam and Wiegerink (2020) have lamented that "residents' dissatisfaction [is] more than an onedimensional quantitative problem, to be solved by bringing numbers down to a measureable threshold" (p. 112). In fact, various researchers concluded their overtourism studies with a call for more qualitative studies (cf. Almeida-García et al. 2021; Gannon et al. 2021). Even before the advent of the overtourism phenomen, Moufakkir and Reisinger (2013) criticized in their anthology that "host gaze studies have been confused with residents' attitudes surveys, where locals' perceptions are quantified, and simplistically (though not simplified) examined" (p. xiii).

What is missing is an analysis on how citizens construct the phenomenon overtourism from their point of view but going further than just visual perceptions of tourism. As an example, Bouchon and Rauscher (2019) discussed in their conceptual paper, which is based on a qualitative approach, that overtourism is a notion constructed from various aspects, such as the urban morphology. Nonetheless, the duo motivates for further reflection on feelings and perceptions of parties that are being impacted by overtourism. Likewise, Egresi (2018) concluded, based on his qualitative content analysis of newspaper articles and their reader comments, that most residents complains are not (only) about overcrowding but a complete transformation of their place from a residential neighbourhood into a tourist-oriented area. In summary, up until now there is a dearth of qualitative research following a social constructionism epistemology (explanation will follow) to unveil the complex process of perception which decides upon residents' attitudes toward tourism.

Therefore, to complement previous research results with further in-depth qualitative data, the study presented in this chapter analyses how residents of two urban tourist destinations in Europe describe the effects of tourism on their living environment and, based on that, construct their reality of overtourism. To get an understanding of citizens' emotions towards tourism, which are usually neglected in surveys, Doxey's (1975) four-parted Irritation Index (short: Irridex) offers a basic model to measure residents' attitudes toward tourism. The index differentiates between euphoria, apathy, annoyance, and lastly antagonism. The fact that the Irridex was developed almost fifty years ago shows very well how old the debate about residents' tolerance toward tourism actually is. According to Doxey (1975), host community's sentiments about tourism change with the perceived costs and benefits of the local tourism development, which is why many previous studies were framed in the social-exchange theory. Previous studies concluded that overtourism emerges when residents' have more costs (negative effects) from tourism than benefits and thus emotionally pass the threshold from annoyance to antagonism (Martín, Martínez & Fernández, 2018; Szromek, Kruczek & Walas, 2020). To test if this assumption proves to be right, the Irridex was also used in this study to categorise the attitudes of the study participants while they were describing how tourism affects their living environment and personal lives.

Based on the state of the art and the outlined gaps of understanding, the guiding research questions for this study are:

RQ1: *How do residents (socially) construct the phenomenon "overtourism"?*

RQ2: *Which perceptions of tourism pass residents' tolerance threshold and cause feelings of antagonism?*

The methodology that has been deployed to collect data in two case studies, namely Copenhagen and Munich, will be presented in the next section. Following, the empirical evidence about citizens' constructions of tourism in their living environment and their understanding of overtourism will be disclosed. Finally, a discussion and conclusion will round the chapter off.

Methodology

Social phenomena like overtourism are constructed through language and texts, such as non-neutral products of media (Couper, 2015; Sandu & Unguru, 2017). For instance, narratives like *"overtourism in Venice means local people can't buy homes"* (Palmer, 2021) influence citizens' perception of and sentiments towards tourism. People become more sensitive and aware of tourism and its effects in their living environment than they used to be. Push notifications, pictures of tourism crowds, and various media channels on our mobile devices shape our picture of the world at minute intervals. Hence, this complex and strongly influenced construction of realty cannot be ignored when analysing social phenomena like overtourism. That is why this study has been conducted following the epistemology of social constructionism. Social constructionism, which dates back to Berger and Luckmann's (1967/2011) 'The Social Construction of Reality', is based on the idea that social processes define our knowledge and understanding of the world (Couper, 2015). Michael Crotty (2015) defined social constructionism as *"the epistemological view that all knowledge, and therefore all meaningful reality as such, is contingent upon human practices, being constructed in and out of interaction between human beings and their world, and developed and transmitted within an essentially social context"* (p. 6).

Like interpretivism, social constructionism describes that meaning is created by human actors, however, it puts a stronger emphasis on language, culture, and interaction of a collective (Gray, 2018). In the context of tourism geography, the social constructionist approach challenges the traditional conceptualization of a 'simply existing' tourism space, also 'the destination', by highlighting that sociocultural practices define (tourism) space (Iwashita, 2003). This approach thus helps to detect individual meanings of social roles (tourist, resident, etc.), places (urban, destination, etc.), and perceptions (too much tourism) (Butowski et al., 2021). Taking on this epistemology, the purpose of this study is to raise awareness for residents' reality and thereby challenge the academic positivist facticity (Couper, 2015) about the disliked media buzzword overtourism.

To conduct a first exploratory field research, two research projects with master students who studied Applied Human Geography at the University of Trier have been realised in Munich in 2018 and in Copenhagen in 2019. Preliminary data has been collected through resident surveys (Munich = 84; Copenhagen = 129), additional key informant interviews (Munich n = 4; Copenhagen n = 3) and various observations of the impacts of tourism on the respective city and its inhabitants. After the data collection, the author analysed the data to explore potential directions and methods for the following comprehensive research project.

The exploratory data confirmed previous research conclusions, which criticised that standardised questionnaires are not fully sufficient to uncover residents' socially constructed viewpoints on overtourism. Therefore, this study is thus based on a mixed method of focus groups with local citizens (Barbour, 2017) and a photo elicitation (Harper, 2002), which will be referred to as image-based focus groups. The method has been pre-tested in Munich in December 2019. Based on the pre-test results, the focus group participants of the main data collection in 2020 received the instruction to prepare two pictures for the focus group discussions: (1) something in the city that is important for their lives and (2) something that is typical for tourism in their city. These photographs have then been exchanged among all participants at the beginning of discussions to trigger memories and emotions as well as to support the articulation of unconscious thoughts (Harper, 2002).

To disclose rather opposing and diverse perspectives, the compilation of the focus groups was purposive (Flick, 2019) based on the living area of the citizens. To achieve that, the online and offline advertisement for the focus groups invited everyone over the age of 18 who has lived in one of the two case studies for at least one year. To ensure anonymity of the participants, they have been anonymised as M-RES (RES= resident, M=Munich) and C-RES (C=Copenhagen) throughout this study.

To analyse the qualitative data of the image-based focus groups, Braun and Clarke's (2006; 2021) reflexive thematic analysis (TA) has been applied for two main reasons. First, TA is especially useful in heterogeneous group discussion about diverse topics (Barbour, 2017; Braun & Clarke, 2006). In this study, it allowed categorization of residents' understanding of overtourism or tourism in their city in general. Second, TA is particularly suitable for the interpretation of both written (focus group transcriptions) and visual data (photographs) (Walters, 2016). Therefore, the six-step process as proposed by Braun and Clarke (2006) guided the TA of this study:

1) Familiarization with the data
2) Generation of initial codes
3) Search for themes
4) Review of themes
5) Definition and naming of themes
6) Production of the report

The transcriptions, the coding process as well as the in-depth analysis and interpretation have been executed with MAXQDA 2020 software. Especially the visual and analytical tools of this computer-assisted qualitative data analysis software enabled the researcher to structure and portray the main research findings. Thereby the rigor, validity and reliability of this highly qualitative data set could be increased (Schreier, 2014).

To ultimately complement the citizen-focus data set, 37 key informant interviews have been conducted between 2019 and 2022. Nonetheless, in this contribution the focus will be on the image-based focus groups. Further information on the complementary data can be found in Kagermeier and Erdmenger (2019), and Erdmenger and Kagermeier (2022).

Findings: residents' construction of overtourism

While in Copenhagen in February 2020 (pre-pandemic) 22 people participated in five image-based focus groups, the data collection in Munich in September 2020 encompassed five personal and two virtual focus groups with 24 study participants in total. The socio-demographic profiles of both participant groups can be found in Table 2.

	Copenhagen (n=22)	Munich (n=24)
Gender	Female: 64%	Female: 50%
	Male: 27%	Male: 45%
	Diverse: 9%	Diverse: 5%
Age	18-30 years: 18%	18-30 years: 12%
	30-40 years: 14%	30-40 years: 21%
	40-50 years: 18%	40-50 years: 0%
	50-60 years: 23%	50-60 years: 63%
	61+ years: 27%	61+ years: 4%
Level of education	No degree: 5%	No degree: 0%
	Secondary education: 0%	Secondary education: 8%
	Higher education: 18%	Higher education: 13%
	University degree: 77%	University degree: 79%
Work (in)directly related to tourism	Yes, (in)directly: 14%	Yes, (in)directly: 50%
	No: 86%	No: 50%

Table 2 *Socio-demographic profiles of focus group participants. Source: Own research*

Although representativeness is not a goal of qualitative research, large distortions can impact the findings and thus meriting a brief mention. Due to the global travel restrictions during the data collection in Munich in September 2020, a strikingly large number of tour guides were interested in participating in the focus groups. Furthermore, in both study locations a very high proportion of participants has a University degree. It can be assumed that firstly people with a (very) high education level feel more comfortable in a discussion group invited by a University researcher. Secondly, as the discussions in Copenhagen took place in English, participants did not only need language skills but also to feel comfortable to discuss in English. Such a distortion is a common weakness of research methods that rely on voluntary participation and needs to be taken into consideration.

Copenhagen: how misbehaving crowds disturb a hygge lifestyle

The study participants in Copenhagen repeatedly described tourism in their city with examples like people with maps in their hands, large cameras, pull-along suitcases on cobblestones, double decker sightseeing buses, crowds of people in narrow streets, rental bikes, and *"sulfate yellow clouds"* (C-RES12, 2020) from cruise ships. Furthermore, the focus group participants reported that they identify tourists' nationality by certain patterns of clothing or moving. Overall, many, but not all, citizens were certain to be able to differentiate locals and visitors, for instance as C-RES4 explained (2020): *"It's a bigger city, so you'll expect crowds too. But suddenly you have clumsy crowds, and that is the difference"*. Indeed, tourists' behaviour was one of the main discussion topics. As another example, C-RES17 (2020) tried to elaborate at which point tourists' behaviour starts to be problematic:

"So, I think when I told you before that I actually love meeting the tourists in the church Absalon because they sort of blend in with the local community how it lives and how we live. Then, I think it is very positive. But when they enter as tourists and make noises and also because of the increase of tourists and tourism in general, lots of more bars and restaurants has opened. And that makes a lot of noise and in that way, especially in the summertime, I am affected by that. But I like it when they come, you know, by bike, on foot, like we do, like the locals do."

In the statement above, the resident clearly differentiates what kind of tourists' behaviour (s)he loves and likes, and when (s)he starts to feel negatively affected by the impacts of tourism. The description is very emotionally charged (indicated with continuous line), based on real experiences and results with concrete demands on tourists' behaviour (indicated with double continuous lines). Furthermore, this person describes visual (outstanding behaviour) as well as audible (noise) tourism indicators (indicated with dashed line), which both disturb this person (indicated with wavy line). Lastly, the person uses descriptions, which indicate a quantitative increase of tourism volumes (indicated with dotted line). Similar expressions and wording can be found in various focus group passages. As another example, C-RES9 (2020) explained:

"But I see more tourists when I come from work. I have certainly observed an increase, an intense increase of tourism. And in the special areas around Nyhavn, around the little mermaid, along Langeligne, the streets around there and the increase of busses, tourist busses, which are driving around on roads that are actually not made for that kind of big busses. And that affects you not directly, but indirectly. You feel that the traffic and the number of people, of tourists is reaching a point where it is difficult to operate as if you were in real Copenhagen."

Further crowding-related statements were about cruise tourists, who arrive in *"big waves of people"* (C-RES20, 2020) and walk like *"herds of cattle"* (C-RES12,

2020). In relation to that C-RES17 (2020) explained: "*I never go to Nyhavn because it's packed with tourists. I don't feel like it's my place anymore.*" These examples clarify that sensory, mostly visual or audible, perceptions of tourists define how residents conceptualise tourism. Crowds of busses or people are two very easy to spot scenarios that are not at all uncommon in large cities. Albeit, tourist busses and rental bikes are usually labelled as such and thus easy to identify as presumably touristic infrastructure.

Furthermore, crowds are mostly perceived as a problem because the hinder residents in their experienced daily activities. Consequently, many focus group participants explained that they avoid certain popular or crowded places. Nevertheless, almost all residents agreed that taking detours would not lower their quality of life as long as there are alternative routes, which is mostly the case in large cities. Besides spatial encounters in busy urban hot spots, residents also reported about an increase of tourists walking around in or close to private space, such as open backyards. According to the residents, a similar increase can be observed in formerly unknown public shared spaces like parks in the city. This became obvious when the focus group participants showed their pictures of something important for their lives in the city, which depicted many leisure and green spaces. In fact, very many participants presented photographs of natural areas and described these with words like "*peace,*" "*quiet,*" "*escape,*" and "*oasis*". To summarise, residents of Copenhagen feel that the increasing number of tourists, which they see and hear due to outstanding behaviour, does affect them and the life in the city to an extent that their popular Hygge lifestyle, which means to "*enjoy the good things in life with good people*" (Visit Denmark, 2021, n.p.), is intensively disturbed depending on time and place.

Munich: how urban growth affects the urban everyday life

Residents in Munich described their perceptions of tourism similar to the results in Copenhagen which led to a fast saturation of data. Also, the perception of an increasing tourism volume or intensity has been confirmed by the people living in Munich. Thus, the following quotes will again be underlined to highlight emotions (continuous line), demands on tourists' behaviour (double continuous line), sensory indicators (dashed line), disturbances (wavy line), and increasing tourism volumes (dotted line). For instance, M-RES11 (2020), who works as an official city tour guide, explained (translated from German):

"It kept getting fuller every year […]. I do guided tours in various districts besides the city centre [as part of a campaign called 'Viertelliebe'] because the city centre just became too much. So, the topic of overtourism is certainly relevant. Especially for residents of Munich, I think many residents avoid the city centre at some point."

Moreover, also tourists' behaviour played again a major role in the focus group discussions in Munich. This topic has often been illustrated with examples and photographs from the world-famous Oktoberfest. In addition to that, M-RES17

(2020) explained, addressing a tour guide in the focus group, that bad tourists' behaviour can be influenced through educational tours if they do not behave appropriately on their own account (translated from German):

"I think the behaviour of the tourists is very important, the crowds. That [behaviour] depends either on their own consideration or through the steering of the tour guide. But, of course, there are situations where the tour guide walks with a megaphone and makes a lot of noise, which is unpleasant if you are nearby. Either you don't want to hear anything or want to talk to someone else. Or you are on your way through the city and a group is completely insensitive to the environment and blocks your path. But I haven't had any negative experiences with it so far, so mostly I haven't had any negative experiences."

Strikingly, M-RES17 felt the need to underline that (s)he did not gain (m)any negative experiences in Munich yet and that the scenarios outlined above are just hypothetical. Indeed, many study participants in Munich agreed that there are no major issues in Munich due to tourism in contrast to destinations, which they visited for their vacation, such as Prague, Milano, and Amsterdam or read about in the media. Because of these problematic, direct or indirect, overtourism experiences, most residents in Munich were however sensitised for potential negative impacts of tourism that might affect their city as well. In contrast to Copenhagen, the debate in Munich was much more centred around the city's basic functionalities and its infrastructure. As an example, M-RES2 (2020) explained (translated from German):

"I wouldn't like to tell anyone where to go. That's why I would never say, we should actively try to minimise the number of tourists so that public transportation works again or that there is enough housing. But I believe that you have to, and can, and should go other ways in order to guarantee that for example living space and public transportation are available to residents."

In summary, the results of the thematic and emotional analysis of this study disclose that overtourism is certainly visualised but not limited to overcrowding perceptions. Instead, it is a phenomenon that is rooted in a complex human-environment interconnectedness that is observed or experienced in various ways. Nevertheless, residents in Munich underlined more often, that issues in their urban everyday life are not caused by tourism, but further fostered by it. In contrast to residents in Copenhagen, the study participants of Munich felt less negatively affected in their personal lives and were thus less negatively emotionally charged during the discussions.

The threshold from annoyance to antagonism

The analysis of both cities and their respective codings about "tolerance limit" showed that a few perceived tourism impacts are prominent in both cities as illustrated in the code cloud in Figure 1. The larger the word in this illustration, the more often has this code been used in all focus group transcriptions.

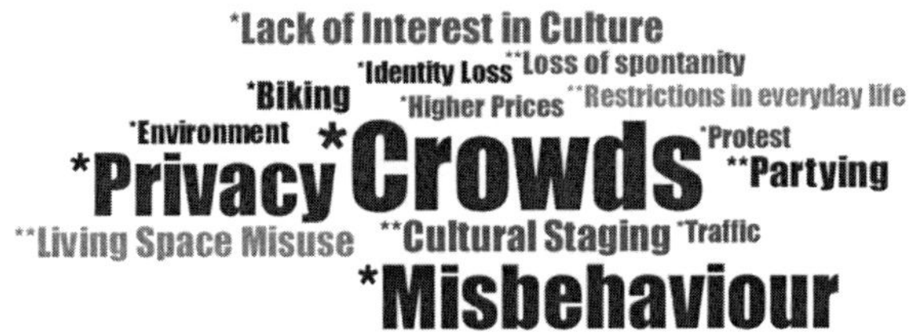

Figure 1 *Code cloud of all codings in the category "tolerance limit" of all image-based focus group discussions. Source: Own research visualised with MAXQDA 2020 (*first coding cycle, **second coding cycle)*

Besides the code frequency, a cross table of the perception codes contrasted with residents' expressed emotions following Doxey's Irridex in Figure 2 shows more clearly, what residents like and dislike about tourism.

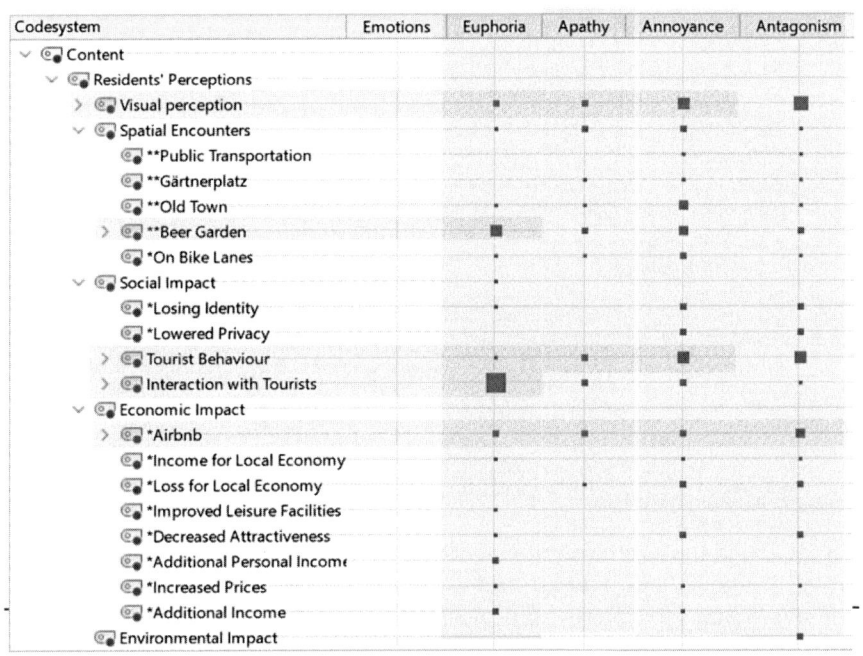

Figure 2 *Cross table of code category "residents' perceptions" of tourism with codings of residents' sentiments as shown during the discussion. Source: Own research visualised with MAXQDA 2020 (*first coding cycle, **second coding cycle)*

It can be seen that the positive feeling euphoria overlaps the most with interactions with tourists. Short encounters where residents could help strangers to find their way around or to buy a parking ticket were often appreciated and caused good feelings among the residents. On the contrary, the most negative feelings were shown when residents talked about various visual perceptions of tourism as well as tourists' inappropriate and alienating behaviour, as outlined in the findings above.

To identify even more specific when and why residents do or could imagine passing the threshold from annoyance to antagonism, another category labelled "tolerance limit" has been coded as illustrated in Figure 3. The coding results depicted support the previous assumption that tourists' behaviour is highly critical to residents' perceptions of tourism. As a matter of fact, it is visitors' behaviour that supports a perceived loss of local identity, the building of crowds in streets or public transportation, the misuse of living space, and the lack of privacy. Thus, tourists' behaviour, and not the amount of them, is the crux of overtourism.

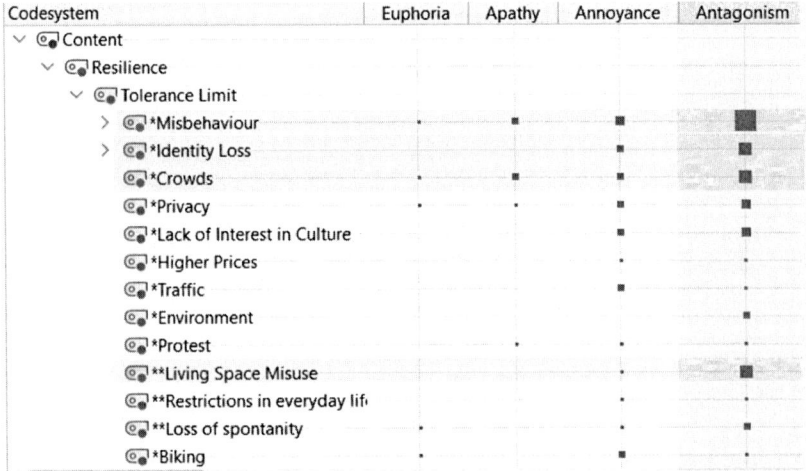

Figure 3 *Cross table of code category "tolerance limit" of tourism with codings of residents' sentiments as shown during the discussion. Source: Own research visualised with MAXQDA 2020.*

Discussion of the findings

In order to avoid the repetition of anti-tourism protests among urban residents, it is pivotal to understand how citizens construct tourism in a certain (negative) way. The vast majority of previous quantitative studies on residents' perceptions of overtourism does yet not go beyond short-sighted descriptive impacts of tourism. This qualitative study in turn reveals more in-depth how residents construct their understanding of overtourism. The image-based focus group discussions enabled the researcher to analyse if citizens base their perceptions on media reports, friends' story-telling, passive observations or active experiences in their own or visited cities. Furthermore, the emotion coding through Doxey's Irridex disclosed which tourism perceptions bother residents the most. Thus, this study displays not only what residents perceive, but also how they do that and why they evaluate these perceptions as good or bad. Figure 4 illustrates these three steps that build up on each other.

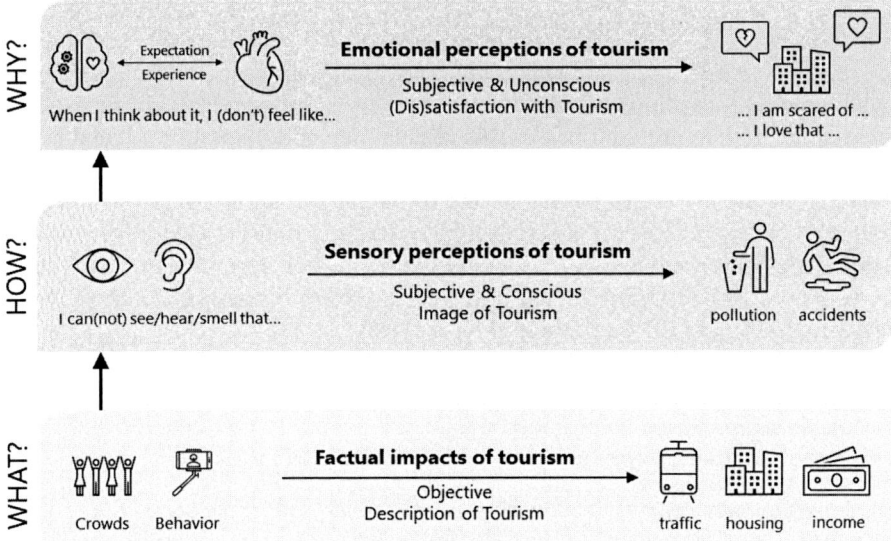

Figure 4 *Process of residents' factual, sensory, and emotional perceptions of tourism. Source: Own research*

On the first level residents explain what they see and how this objectively influences the city. These short-sighted descriptions usually initiated the focus groups discussions which then moved on to the second level: sensory perceptions. In contrast to closed survey questions, the discussions revealed how residents get to know about the factual impacts of tourism. As underlined in the findings, citizens almost exclusively see or hear tourism in their living environment. This leads to the fact that invisible, positive as well as negative, effects of tourism are commonly not known by residents – besides a positive economic effect for the city. At this stage of reflection, residents explained more subjectively that pollution or crowding in public transportation, for instance, jeopardise their needs for safety, freedom, or privacy. The study participants' statements got more detailed and also emotional the longer they discussed such examples. Moving away from objective, factual descriptions, the citizens started to express their feelings about how tourism affects them, what they like and dislike. This was often a reflective process which resulted in an aha-moment among the participants. On the emotional level, experiences about cultural dissimilarities, spatial proximity, risks to personal safety, invasion of privacy, and the disturbance of daily routines were discussed. Many times, the study participants did not connect this reported scenario with tourism at first. Hearing the stories and perceptions or others as well as seeing their photographs about tourism, triggered subconscious perceptions of residents that have not and cannot be(en) elevated in quantitative studies. Based on these empirical results it can now be understood how residents construct their reality of overtourism and why they perceive it as a problem or a potential threat for their urban everyday life. Therefore, the two research questions can be answered as follows.

RQ1: *How do residents (socially) construct the phenomenon "overtourism"?*

Residents construct their understanding on overtourism based on things they see (which includes reading) or hear. It is thus a very sensory process at first. Nonetheless, the human mind processes this sensual perception, assesses it and evaluates if it poses a threat to our needs or not. If media reports are not objectively written, but already highlight threats and problems in a stimulating way, the consumer receives and internalises this subjective information. This information is than revaluated based on own experiences (at home and abroad) as well as stories from people we trust. The image-based focus group discussions were in fact a small reproduction of the process how residents socially construct their understanding and judgement of overtourism based on stories they hear and pictures they see. An in-depth analysis of this highly psychological process, in which media plays an immense role, goes beyond the scope of this chapter and offers ground for an interdisciplinary research approach in the future.

RQ2: *Which perceptions of tourism pass residents' tolerance threshold towards tourism?*

The discussion about residents' limits of tolerance towards tourism revealed that further increasing crowding, tourists' misbehaviour, the lack of housing, tourists causing safety risks, a lack of interest in the local culture, and the alienation of the local identity irritate residents of Copenhagen and Munich the most. Overall, if tourism directly threatens peoples' personal needs, the tolerance limit is or will be exceeded. Nevertheless, it must be underlined that these opinions differed widely within the studied community, depending on the individuals' cultural backgrounds and their amount of interaction with foreign cultures.

Conclusions

To conclude, the term overtourism is used to summarise perceptions and feelings of non-tourism-professionals towards a, for them, hard-to-explain phenomenon. That is why the author claims that the term overtourism, as emotionally-charged, imprecise, and unscientific as it is, has a right to exist and should be taken serious. People living or dwelling in cities, who do not work in or related to tourism, usually do not reflect on how and why they like or dislike the experienced tourism development unless we invite and assist them to do so. And that is what broad (social) media reports did in contrast to most politicians, planners, and researchers who focus on objective, factual, and positivist aspects. The author of this chapter agrees with scholars' and tourism stakeholders' statements that the term overtourism is a sensationalist propaganda. Yet, this study is a plea to look into the phenomena hiding behind this accessible term to understand how we can tackle the therein embedded social, environmental, and economic issues. Lastly, not only sensation seeking journalists have the power to spread appealing buzzwords and to sensitise for tourism. It is on us, people who are educated about tourism, to rewrite the headlines and to collaborate with mass and social media to our society's advantage. These findings can thus support policy-makers, politicians, and tourism planners to implement measures against the advent of overtourism 2.0 in a post-COVID world.

Literature

Ali, R. (2018). The genesis of overtourism: why we came up with the term and what's happened since. *Skift.* Available at: https://skift.com/2018/08/19/genesis-of-overtourism-and-5-other-tourism-trends-this-week/

Almeida-García, F., Cortés-Macías, R. & Parzych, K. (2021). Tourism impacts, tourism-phobia and gentrification in historic centers: the cases of Málaga (Spain) and Gdansk (Poland). *Sustainability*, *13*(1), p. 408.

Arif, A. M., Ullah, S. & Samad, A. (2019). Problems caused by tourism in Kaghan Valley, Pakistan: a study based on local community perception. *Global Social Sciences Review*, *IV*(III), 284-291.

Barbour, R. S. (2017). *Doing Focus Groups* (2nd ed.). Los Angeles: Sage Publications.

Baumgartner, C. (2020). Nachhaltiger Tourismus vs. Overtourism. *Tourismus Trendforum*, 20 November. Fachhochschule Graubünden. Available at: https://www.fhgr.ch/fileadmin/events/veranstaltungsreihen/Tourismus_Trendforum/05_Sustainable_Tourism_vs._Overtourism.pdf

Bello, F. G., Carr, N., Lovelock, B. & Xu, F. (2017). Local residents' perceptions of socio-cultural impacts of tourism in Mangochi, Malawi. *Advances in Hospitality and Tourism Research*, *5*(1), 1-22.

Berger, P. L. & Luckmann, T. (2011). *The Social Construction of Reality: A Treatise in the Sociology of Knowledge*. New York: Open Road Media Integrated Media.

Bouchon, F. & Rauscher, M. (2019). Cities and tourism, a love and hate story; towards a conceptual framework for urban overtourism management. *International Journal of Tourism Cities*, *5*(4), 598-619.

Braun, V. & Clarke, V. (2006). Using thematic analysis in psychology. *Qualitative Research in Psychology*, *3*(2), 77-101.

Butowski, L., Kaczmarek, J., Kowalczyk-Anioł, J. & Szafrańska, E. (2021). Social constructionism as a tool to maintain an advantage in tourism research. *Tourism Geographies*, *23*(1-2), 53-74.

Couper, P. (2015). *A Student's Introduction to Geographical Thought: Theories, Philosophies, Methodologies*. Los Angeles, CA: SAGE Publications Inc. Available at: https://sk.sagepub.com/books/a-students-introduction-to-geographical-thought

Crotty, M. (2015). *The Foundations of Social Research: Meaning and Perspective in the Research Process*. London: SAGE.

Dirksmeier, P. & Helbrecht, I. (2015). Resident perceptions of new urban tourism: a neglected geography of prejudice. *Geography Compass*, *9*(5), 276-285.

Doxey, G. V. (1975). A causation theory of visitor–resident irritants, methodology and research inferences: the impact of tourism. *Travel Research Association, 6th Annual Conference Proceedings*, 195–198.

Egresi, I. (2018). "Tourists go home!" - Tourism overcrowding and "tourismophobia". *European Cities*, 701-714.

Erdmenger, E. & Kagermeier, A. (2022). When the tourists flew out: a study on residents' perception of tourism before and since the COVID-19 pandemic. In A. Trono, T. Duda & J. Schmude (Eds.), *Tourism Recovery from COVID-19: Prospects for Over- and Under-Tourism Regions* (pp. 247-259). World Scientific Publishing Company.

Flick, U. (2019). *An Introduction to Qualitative Research*. Los Angeles: SAGE.

Gray, D. E. (2018). *Doing Research in the Real World* (4th ed.). Los Angeles: SAGE.

Haase, C. (2021). Framing Overtourism: Medien - Macht - Meinungen. *Jahrestagung Arbeitskreis Tourismusforschung. Junge Perspektiven der Tourismusforschung*. 28 October, Berlin, Germany.

Harper, D. (2002). Talking about pictures: a case for photo elicitation. *Visual Studies*, *17*(1), 13-26.

Iwashita, C. (2003). Media construction of Britain as a destination for Japanese tourists: social constructionism and tourism. *Tourism and Hospitality Research*, *4*(4), 331-340.

Kagermeier, A. & Erdmenger, E. (2019). Overtourismus. *Zeitschrift für Tourismuswissenschaft*, *11*(1), 65-98.

Kim, M., Choi, K.-W., Chang, M. & Lee, C.-H. (2020). Overtourism in Jeju Island: the influencing factors and mediating role of quality of life. *The Journal of Asian Finance, Economics and Business*, *7*(5), 145-154.

Koens, K., Postma, A. & Papp, B. (2018). Is overtourism overused? Understanding the impact of tourism in a city context. *Sustainability*, *10*(12), p. 4384.

Martín, J. M. M., Martínez, J. M. G. & Fernández, J. A. S. (2018). An analysis of the factors behind the citizen's attitude of rejection towards tourism in a context of overtourism and economic dependence on this activity. *Sustainability*, *10*(8), p. 18.

Milano, C., Cheer, J. M., & Novelli, M. (2019). Overtourism: an evolving phenomenon. In C. Milano, J. M. Cheer & M. Novelli (Eds.), *Overtourism: Excesses, Discontents and Measures in Travel and Tourism* (pp. 1-17). Abingdon: CABI.

Milano, C., Novelli, M. & Cheer, J. M. (2019). Overtourism and tourismphobia: a journey through four decades of tourism development, planning and local concerns. *Tourism Planning & Development*, *16*(4), 353-357.

Moufakkir, O. & Reisinger, Y. (Eds.) (2013). *The Host Gaze in Global Tourism*. Abingdon: CABI.

Namberger, P., Jackisch, S., Schmude, J. & Karl, M. (2019). Overcrowding, overtourism and local level disturbance: how much can Munich handle? *Tourism Planning & Development*, *16*(4), 452-472.

Oskam, J. A. & Wiegerink, K. (2020). The unhospitable city: residents' reactions to tourism growth in Amsterdam'. In Oskam, J. A. (Ed.), *The Overtourism Debate* (pp. 95-118). Emerald Publishing Limited.

Palmer, S. (2021). Overtourism in Venice means local people can't buy homes. *euronews.travel*. Available at: https://www.euronews.com/travel/2021/09/17/overtourism-in-venice-means-local-people-can-t-buy-homes

Sandu, A. & Unguru, E. (2017). Several conceptual clarifications on the distinction between constructivism and social constructivism. *Postmodern Openings*, *8*(2), 51-61.

Schreier, M. (2014). Varianten qualitativer Inhaltsanalyse: Ein Wegweiser im Dickicht der Begrifflichkeiten. *Forum Qualitative Sozialforschung*, *15*(1), 18.

Spangler, C., Darbha, V. & Lay, J. (2019). Mass tourism is destroying the planet. *The Atlantic*. Available at: https://www.theatlantic.com/video/index/603451/overtourism/

Szromek, A. R., Kruczek, Z. & Walas, B. (2020). The attitude of tourist destination residents towards the effects of Overtourism-Kraków Case Study. *Sustainability*, *12*(1), p. 228.

Tichaawa, T. M. & Moyo, S. (2019). Urban resident perceptions of the impacts of tourism development in Zimbabwe. *Bulletin of Geography. Socio-economic Series*, *43*(43), 25-44.

Tourismus Oberbayern München, 2021. Der Tomcast. TOMCast #2 Zu Gast: Clemens Baumgärtner. [Online]. Available at: https://top.oberbayern.de/inhalte/marketing/tomcast/

Tschöll, P. & Költringer, C. (2019). How to manage the threatening phenomenon of 'overtourism'? Early detecting measures in Vienna. In H. Pechlaner, E. Innerhofer & G. Erschbamer (Eds.), *Overtourism: Tourism Management and Solutions* (pp. 174-185). (Contemporary geographies of leisure, tourism and mobility). London: Routledge.

Vagena, A. (2021). Overtourism: definition and impact. *Academia Letters*, p. 6.

Visit Denmark. (2021). What is hygge? [Online]. Available at: https://www.visitdenmark.com/denmark/highlights/hygge/what-hygge

Walters, T. (2016). Using Thematic Analysis in Tourism Research. *Tourism Analysis*, *21*(1), 107-116.

Zucco, F. D., Flores Limberger, P., de Souza Farias, F., Foletto Fiuza, T. & Morgana Boos de Quadros, C. (2020). The relationship of subjective well-being in residents' perceptions of the impacts of overtourism in the city of Blumenau, Santa Catarina, Brazil. *Sustainability*, *12*(5), p. 1957.

Chapter 2 - How overtourism feels: conceptualising the atmosphere of overtourism

Huib Ernste

Introduction

Tourists are seeking experiences, which are different from their everyday experiences. They might want to have a time-out from their daily routines, and they might want to be distracted from their daily sorrows and stress. They might look for a different kind of excitement, or relaxation and recuperation. Or they might seek new horizon-widening views of strange and far-away places, or search for the fascination for the aesthetics of other cultures, or for the mood which specific places evoke. Experiences are at the core of the tourist industry. However, tourism is not just an industry or a profitable business. Regular recreation, relaxation, and refuelling oneself with new energy, but also with new ideas, new perspectives, new motivations and fascinations, are essential for having a fulfilled life and making sense of daily life. Experiences like these are therefore crucial in any circumstance and are of all times.

However, in today's world, with its many restrictions, functional demands and economic rationalities, the central role of experiences is often neglected or only addressed in a rather one-sided way. Even in an industry like tourism, where touristic experiences are the core element of the business, we notice that experiences are often only addressed from the perspective of the tourist, especially in times of overtourism and the wish to search for more sustainable forms of tourism. The perspective of the people living and working at the places the tourists visit are at least as important. Even if one would give attention to both (opposing) perspectives, this might not be sufficient. Much more attention should also be given to the direct interaction between and the inter-relatedness of these experiences. Experiences are however not easily understood and conceptualised from a scientific point of view. We can distinguish several approaches or attempts, which all have their advantages and disadvantages.

In this contribution, I would like to discuss one of these approaches, which seems to be a promising way forward to understanding touristic experiences under the circumstances of overtourism and sustainable tourism. In general theoretical conceptualisations of these kinds of rather fundamental relationships are highly abstract and therefore not very popular for more applied research in the field of tourism. Therefore, it seems worthwhile to try to bring these complex concepts back to our everyday experience and understanding, so that more researchers may delve into the empirics of these phenomena and come up with crucial new insights that are beneficial also for the tourism sector.

The behavioural approach to touristic experiences

The traditional way of looking at how people experience places is through the eyes of the behavioural psychologist. How a person experiences a place and what kind of affective and emotional relationship that person feels for that place, is thus seen from the perspective of the person, which is confronted with the stimuli from the outside world and expresses her feelings in some way or the other, for example by behaving in a certain way. These expressions and behaviour are seen as the response to the stimulus the person was confronted with at a specific place (and at a specific moment in time). The more general term used in the literature to describe these affective relationships with places is 'place attachment' (Altman & Low, 1992; Lewicka, 2011; Dwyer, Chen & Lee, 2019).

What all contributions to this approach have in common, is that they stick to the original stimulus-response model (Figure 1) and search for the general lawlike relationships between certain utter attributes of a place (as stimuli) and the behavioural response. Even though the focus on place-specific attributes gives the impression that the thus-produced insights are very contextual and take the place context as well as the specific attributes of the person involved into account, these differences are seen as variations of more general variables. These insights, therefore, are nevertheless seen as more general and not situation-specific causal relationships. To be able to set up research for this purpose, one still needs to abstract many contextual and maybe even unique aspects of places, people and situations. An example of a typical result of this kind of research is displayed in Figure 2. This shows the limitations of the behavioural conceptualisation of touristic experiences. This, however, certainly does not disqualify the value and potential of this way of conceptualising touristic experiences.

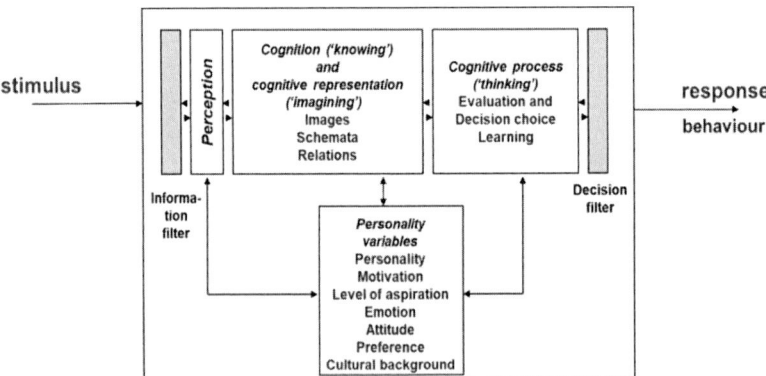

Figure 1 *General behavioural approach towards experiencing places*

The figure furthermore shows that it is certainly not the whole story to be told about touristic experiences of places. Hence, it might be useful to have a look at some alternative approaches. This is what I intend to do in what follows in this contribution in as-simple-as-possible terms.

As a side remark, I want to point to the fact that these alternative approaches, happen to be inspired by continental European philosophy. As this edited volume is focussing on European cases of overtourism, it makes sense to look at European philosophy, thus acknowledging the geographical fact that phenomena are situational and contextual, and cannot easily be addressed from a universalistic point of view. This is, as this contribution also shows, not just an empirical fact, as overtourism turns out to vary from place to place and is also experienced differently from place to place, or from situation to situation, and from person to person. Related to these contextual differences are also different ways of thinking about these kinds of phenomena. Even though this chapter is about how to theorise touristic experiences, it also shows, that there is a cultural geography of different schools of thinking. I do not deal with specific European empirical cases, but I address the theorising of touristic experiences from a specifically continental European perspective, which acknowledges – in a typically European way – the diversity and situational contingency of these touristic experiences in a much more sophisticated way than in the above-mentioned mainstream behavioural approach that the Anglo-Saxon dominated scientific community applies.

The (new) phenomenological approach to touristic experiences

Since we are talking about touristic experiences[1] it is common sense that these experiences, affects, feelings and emotions are highly subjective and individual. We do not just follow a universal pattern of reactions to situations, but we have our very individual judgment, valuation and response, which is also the reason why we usually tend to say that 'one cannot argue about matters of taste'. The approach, which takes this subjectivity as a starting point for gaining knowledge about the world around us is the phenomenological approach. This approach assumes that it is not possible to come up with an objective description, categorisation and qualification of the place or situation, (which in the behavioural approach was seen as the stimulus). Nor is it possible to describe and qualify the response to those stimuli objectively. The real world, according to this phenomenological approach, only appears to us not as reality but as a phenomenon, an appearance, which is to a large degree determined by our subjective look at these things. The key term used for this subjective look is 'intentionality'. For example, if a person likes mountaineering and climbing – with this intentionality, one almost exclusively sees mountains and rocks when traveling through the country – being hardly interested in any other aspects. Therefore, this may serve as an example of how we look with intent. For me, from the Dutch flatlands, this would never be a

---

[1] Although my spelling checker relentlessly tries to tell me that the right spelling of this term would be 'tourist experiences' I deliberately use the broader term 'touristic experiences' to avoid the misunderstanding that this is only about the experiences of tourists, while I explicitly also want to include the experiences of the people living and working at the places the tourists visit, as well as the experience of the relations between them.

category of any importance. I therefore could not even be positioned on the scale for attraction to mountains, which probably would be assumed to universally exist by the behaviourists I was talking about in the previous section of this chapter. For me, other affective elements would probably be more important for the way I would feel at these places. This intentional way of experiencing touristic places is therefore the core aspect of the classical phenomenological approach, which takes conscious intentionality as a starting point to investigate how we experience places and situations and how this determines the meanings and sense we allocate to places, situations and to the related actions (see Figure 2).

If we want to understand the complex phenomenon of touristic experiences, we therefore might need to take a phenomenological perspective at touristic experiences. In this respect, several questions pop up. How are these subjective feelings structured? How did they emerge, how do they vary and change from situation to situation and from person to person? And how do one's feelings and emotions affect those of others? These questions become very pertinent in situations which we tend to qualify as situations of overtourism.

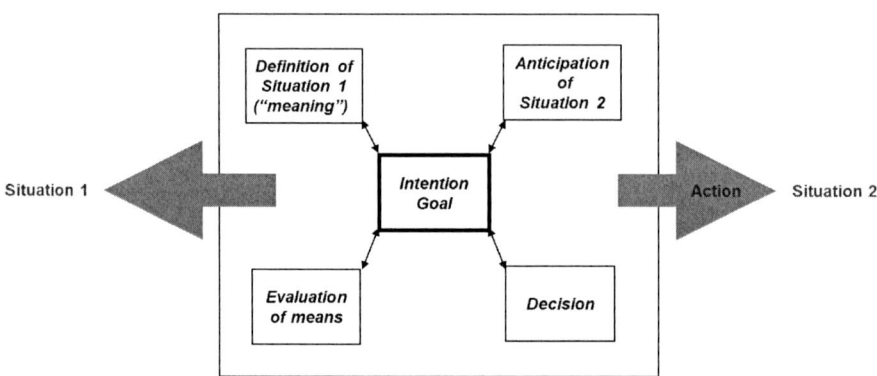

Figure 2 *Example of the phenomenological approach*

But maybe my feelings for a specific place or my experience of that place when I am physically there, cannot even be put in words or expressed in a technical term or as a variable. I might not be able to think about it cognitively, as I may feel it through my body, without being fully aware of it. Of course, I could, nevertheless, attempt to talk about it, but it would probably only result in a rather clumsy and incomplete oral circumscription. As we often also experience in our love for our partner, our body language, a brief touch, embracement or kiss, might say more than a thousand words could ever tell. These kinds of affective relations cannot easily be measured on a scale from 0-100 and probably also have different meanings for you and me. These experiences can be described as truly embodied experiences. You feel it even if you cannot describe it. The same is true for many touristic experiences. The embodied character of these touristic experiences is, by the way, also the main reason why we need to travel, to move our bodies, and to physically immerse our bodies in these touristic places and situations. Travelling enables the full experience of these places. Embodiment is therefore also a core element in the tourist industry (Everingham, Obrador & Tucker, 2021).

This also implies that the traditional phenomenological approach might not suffice to get a good grasp of these touristic experiences, and we might need to come up with a new kind of phenomenology (Simonsen, 2012). The traditional phenomenological approach can be traced back to the work of Edmund Husserl who with his version of transcendental phenomenology focuses very strongly on the conscious intentionality of the person as a structuring principle of how she experiences her surroundings. Husserl describes his version of phenomenology as transcendental phenomenology because it takes consciousness as the starting point while investigating how one can transcend consciousness to get an idea of the outside world.

Following this approach one does not take one's observations as objective facts, but rather investigates the subjective conditions that must be satisfied to count as real. "When we adopt the (transcendental) phenomenological attitude, we do not turn our attention away from the world and towards our own experiential life, we do not turn the gaze inward to examine the happenings in a private interior sphere. We continue to be concerned with the worldly object, but we now no longer consider it naively; rather, we focus on it precisely as it is intended and given, i.e. as a correlate of experience" (Zahavi, 2018, p. 38).

While Husserl's approach focussed mainly on individual subjectivity, it was foremost philosopher and sociologist Alfred Schütz (1967) who extended these ideas into the realm of inter-subjectivity. Through this lens, touristic experiences need to be seen, not as objective facts, nor as subjective construction in the individual mind of the experiencing person, but as reflexive social constructions. In this version of phenomenological analysis, the focus is still rather primarily on the consciousness-related constitution of the meaning of experiences in social reality. One may question, however, especially when we speak of emotions and affects, if this covers and grasps all aspects of these phenomena. Especially feelings are probably not always or not fully consciously and intentionally experienced and often not easily consciously intelligible.

	Old Phenomenology	New Phenomenology
Philosophical Reference Author	Edmund Husserl	Hermann Schmitz
Kind of Phenomenology	Transcendental Phenomenology	Realist (empirical) Phenomenology
Social Apriori	Consciousness	Felt body (affective involvement)
Concept of Subject	Actor (intentional-reflexive action)	'Patheur' (embodied pre-reflexive [pathic] action)
Concept of Sociality	Inter-Subjectivity	Felt-Bodily Communication
Ontology	Thing-Ontology (Constellationism)	Situation-Ontology (Situationism)
Socio-ontological Basis	Lifeworld	Joint Situations
Methodology	Methodological Individualism	Methodological Situationism

Table 1 *Comparison between old and new phenomenology (adapted from Gugutzer, 2019, p. 197)*

This is where the alternative New Phenomenology (see also www.gnp-online.de), suggested by Hermann Schmitz (2019), comes in. Schmitz criticizes the 'old'-phenomenology's psychologistic-reductionist-introjectionist objectivation of experiences (Gugutzer, 2019, p. 186). According to Schmitz, this dissects human beings into a body and consciousness, and the world into an inner world comprising one's mind and personal experiences, and an outer world comprising the places and situations the person is confronted with.

However, this old approach tends to lose sight of one's involuntary, unintended experiences. Schmitz, therefore, designs a different kind of phenomenological approach, which does not take the subjective conscious experiences but rather the subjective embodied experiences as a starting point (see Table 1). He states that when we experience a specific place or situation, we first need to be affected by that place or situation before we consciously develop a certain intentionality towards that place or situation or can reflect on our experiences. We can easily imagine how we are confronted with the material aspects of these situations and by the embodied presence of others in these lifeworld situations, and therefore immediately become aware of our relationship with and attitude towards these places or situations. This, however, is much more difficult to imagine for the kind of emotional ambience such a place constitutes and radiates. These ambiences are no 'things' and also do not have a clear beginning or end or a clear demarcation. Instead, they are inherent in the situation as a whole.

Hence, Schmitz (2005) tends to distinguish between the constellations of mutual positioning of things and persons on which the old phenomenology focuses and the more holistic situations including their ambience he is mainly interested in from the new-phenomenological perspective. This distinction is in our colloquial understanding maybe not obvious and mainly serves an analytic purpose. Until here I have used these terms inter-changingly as is common in more everyday ways of speaking. For Schmitz, however, the more comprehensive view of situations is rather crucial, as it allows him to look beyond the obvious materialised and embodied things – intentionally "ready-to-hand", as Heidegger would refer to it (Heidegger, 1962, p. 135 ff.) – in a situation, and to include the less obvious but not less evoking elements or aspects.

For Schmitz, for example, we become aware of the presence of an ambience of a place, once we are affected, touched or moved by it, without necessarily intending it. Schmitz describes this as affective involvement (in German: *affektives Betroffensein*). In this way, not just material aspects or other persons, but also the ambience of a specific situation or atmosphere, as Schmitz (2012) calls it, is perceived. The atmosphere or ambience is not just a mental or social construction but also has a reality of its own, which we subjectively experience as a subjective fact (in German: *Sachverhalt*). Hermann Schmitz, therefore, describes these atmospheres as 'half-things' or 'quasi-things'. My affective involvement is something I experience and feel in my body before I can even think about it or might intend it. But I nevertheless clearly notice that these are my feelings. It is even through these affective involvements with the environment that the 'I' of my feelings and thinking is constituted. It is not just any body, through which I experience these feelings, nor is it an objectified body as it can be observed from the outside. Instead, it is my felt body[2]. While the old phenomenological approach suited the conceptualisation of how human beings consciously allocate meaning to places and situations and design their deliberate actions accordingly, the new phenomenological approach addresses much more the pathic reactions to a specific place or situation.

When atmospheres are conceptualised as half-things, which are experienced pre-consciously, the affective involvement is not limited to the individual person but is shared with others in that same situation or place. As such, it also creates a relational basis for felt-bodily communication and may serve as a primordial concept of sociality (Gugutzer, 2019; Julmi, 2018) and joint social understanding. This kind of felt-body communication can vary from excluding antagonistic, via agonistic to all-inclusive solidary affects or incorporations (in German: *Einleibungen*) as Schmitz (2011, p. 33) tends to call them. In this way, a kind of embodied dialogue may take place, through the dynamics of mutual affective involvements or incorporations.

When we describe atmospheres as half-things, which are to a certain degree independent of the person experiencing them, one may ask how to describe the way we individually and personally experience these atmospheres. In many cases, this is described as a feeling or emotion or some-times also as a mood (in German: *Stimmung*). However, this sometimes also causes a bit of confusion as different

---

[2] In German language, in which Hermann Schmitz wrote, the objectified body (*Körper*) is distinguished from the lived or felt body (*Leib*).

authors use these terms in slightly different ways (Griffero, 2019). An atmosphere is seen as something we experience as 'out there', as something, which is 'in the air', in the place or situation we happen to be at. At the same time, we experience it as something, which touches us and affectively involves us and provokes corporeal resonances. 'You step into a Romanesque church and feel the sublime silence of the dark, cool hall; you immerse yourself in the noisy gaiety of a fair or feel the oppressive sultriness over the landscape before an approaching thunderstorm'. These resonances almost demand a corresponding reaction. In the Romanesque church, the solemn silence involuntarily muffles the voice and the steps. At the fair, the relaxed or cheerful environment makes us smile and stroll, and the upcoming thunderstorm makes us shiver and hide. These resonances thus have a certain power over us and can be seen as a field of forces we are subject to (Fuchs, 2000, pp. 213-215). They tend to densify and become more directional and concrete, once they affect us and become part of us.

To denote these unidirectional forces Schmitz (2007. p. 576) introduces the term 'mood' (in German: *Stimmung*). He describes two basic moods, one being 'despair' and the other 'satisfaction'. In both cases, they are experienced as rather basic and general feelings, which can hardly be linked to something specific. When they become more directional he calls them emotions (in German: *Erregungen*). This directionality can take different forms. It can be one-directional or all-directional, centrifugal or centripetal, lifting or depressing. Gloom and sorrow, for example, have a depressing impulse, joy, on the other hand, has a lifting one. Longing is a centrifugal force that pulls us into the distance and shame or anxiety is a centripetal force (Schmitz, 1990, p. 299). When they also become focussed on a concrete element, he designates them as a centred feeling (in German: *zentrierte Erregung*). For example, in advance one may have a diffuse feeling of anxiety about an exam. But as soon as one sees the real examination questions this may turn into a concrete fear to fail the exam. Or if one, after a longer period of longing for a new love relationship, finally is concentrated on a specific person and evokes the experience of real love (Gugutzer, 2013, p. 308). This also shows that we should be careful with identifying atmospheres with the way we sense them through our senses. Atmospheres are more than what we concretely sense through single senses because as a whole, they are more than the sum of their parts or expressions.

We are not necessarily immediately fully taken over by the atmosphere we experience. The degree to which we are affected by them may vary, and also depends on our attitude and receptibility with which we experience the atmosphere. It may very well be, that in a specific situation and moment, we sense an atmosphere at that place and are to a certain degree affectively involved, but still experience it from a rather distant point of view, without being carried away by the atmosphere towards active participation (or resistance), which may be the case, when it turns into a centred feeling, as Schmitz would probably call it. We then also feel, how we, as individuals, feel the atmosphere, which then may evoke the intention to react.

When we follow Jürgen Hasse's interpretation, we get a slightly different view of the role of moods. Hasse (2012, p. 19) regards atmospheres as an impersonal reality and moods as a personalised reality. Atmospheres are related to specific situations or events, by which the person is at that moment and in that situation affectively involved. These atmospheric feelings are therefore rather elusive and may disappear as soon as the situation changes. However, when they persist for a longer period of time or repeatedly occur, these atmospheric feelings can also settle deeply in the person and can form the basis for a personalised mood. Others have denoted these personalised moods as attitude (in German: *Haltung*) (Demmerling & Landweer, 2007; Slaby, 2008). In this way, feelings also lose their tight connection to the specific situation and become the basic personal toning of how the person encounters specific atmospheres. This personal and individual mood can determine how far we open ourselves to the affective involvement of an atmosphere, or how we might resist this affective involvement. Moods determine the self and therefore also the sensitivity and perception of atmospheres. The moods that form the basis of our being are co-causally related to the experience of atmospheres. In this way, personal moods can explain the above-mentioned different degrees to which we are receptible to atmospheres.

Atmospheres, therefore, induce our experiences from the outside to the inside whereas moods do so from the inside to the outside (Fuchs, 2000, p. 215). While Schmitz uses the concepts of moods, emotions and centred feelings as degrees and forms of affected involvement by atmospheres exclusively and therefore tends to underestimate the intentional subjectivity of this involvement, Hasse uses the concept of mood to describe the inherently personalised way in which we experience situations and places. This allows more room for the subjectivity of affective involvement. This also creates the basis for performative expressions of feelings and motivates certain deliberate actions attempting to influence and construct atmospheres. In this way, atmospheres are not just phatically experienced but at the same time actively co-constructed.

This also brings us closer to the popular conceptualisation of affective atmospheres by Gernot Böhme (1993). He is very sympathetic to the conceptualisation of Hermann Schmitz, but also diverts from this position, as he does not think of atmospheres as half-things, but as spaces characterised as constellations of things and human beings and by emphasising the possibility to actively and practically construct and configure these atmospheres (Runkel, 2016, p. 8 ff.). To avoid falling back into a duality of object and subject he uses the concept of aura[3] as coined by Walter Benjamin (2008 [1936], p. 23), the aura which the things radiate or breath. "This breathing means that it is absorbed bodily, that it enters the bodily economy of tension and expansion, that one allows this atmosphere to permeate

---

[3] Aura as a concept is often seen as the predecessor of the concept of atmosphere.

the self" (Böhme, 1993, p. 117). The term used for this radiation is the ecstasies[4] or specific aesthetics of the things and persons out of which the atmosphere is made. The atmosphere of a place or situation can then be defined as the sum of the ecstasies radiated by the different things or persons in that place or situation. Not each thing or person will have the same effect. Some will be more dominant than others and some might cancel out others, leading to the tonality of that place or situation. Böhme (1993) thus defines atmospheres as spaces insofar as they are "tinged" by the presence of things (p. 121 f.), people or environmental constellations. Atmospheres are felt in the bodily presence of people. According to Böhme, atmospheres are created by objective means, like geometry, proportion, size, light, colour, acoustics, smell, etc.

Researching atmospheres

Atmospheres as conceived by Schmitz and Böhme in the framework of this new-phenomenological approach seem to be convincing and can easily be associated with several everyday examples. However, they stay rather vague or unclear when we try to empirically 'measure' or 'assess' them. Several attempts and suggestions have been made to operationalise the basic dimensions and elements of these affective atmospheres. It is beyond the scope of this more conceptual contribution to discuss them in detail. Here, we suffice with some hints about these methodological attempts. Shanti Sumartojo and Sarah Pink (2019) describe that the concept of atmospheres implies that wherever we are and what we do, we are always in an atmosphere (see also Pink, 2015). "Following this understanding, the atmosphere is something that we are in the flow of, rather than something that we are researching from the outside, or that it would even be possible to step out of and observe" (Sumartojo & Pink, 2019, p. 36).

This has repercussions for how we conduct our research while being in an atmosphere, through which we therefore also inherently help to configure and participate in. So this is what Sumartojo and Pink call developing knowledge in an atmosphere. For instance, they suggest an autoethnographic methodology in which one engages in a dialogue with the atmosphere. In the same vein De Matteis et al. (2019) report that "Olivier Gaudin and Maxime Le Calvé advance drawing and writing as ethnographic tools to describe atmospheres. In this sense, they argue that drawing is both a field note and an image that can support the presentation of the ethnographic experience" (p. 10).

---

[4] Ecstasies in this sense is what transcends the materiality of a thing. It is not what that thing is in itself, but what that thing is for others.

Thibaud (2001) has suggested the joint strolling and walking 'interview'[5] as a technique in situ to analyse these kinds of atmospheric involvements.

In contrast, "knowing about atmospheres suggests methodologies for examining it after the moment of its emergence, attempting to understand its configurations, the conditions that allow it, the effects and impacts that it might have and what else it makes possible" (Sumartojo & Pink, 2019, p. 41). Again, this requires specific methods. But this is also the realm of knowledge where many different methods are available. From the perspective of architecture and urban design, biophysical methods for registering where people look at or give attention to when they move through urban space have been suggested (see e.g. Richter & Goller, 2008; Gifford, 2016; but also the recent project on eMotional Cities: https://emotionalcities-h2020.eu/), even though they are not based on a true phenomenological approach.

For the latter purpose, the techniques used in Interpretative Phenomenological Analysis (IPA) (Smith, Flowers & Larkin, 2009) can be of use. Michels (2015) also provides further hints and Mădălina Diaconu (2012) offers a broad overview of methods for the multi-sensory exploration of the affective meaning of urban places. Abusaada (2020) on the other hand comes up with a methodological approach explicitly dedicated to the new-phenomenological approach. Furthermore, Jürgen Hasse (2012) provides ample examples of the application of new-phenomenological analysis of urban places, which he describes as micro-logic descriptions. Hasse as well as Andreas Rauh (2012) have also explored the use of visual data (photographic images) to analyse the affective aspects of places and situations beyond the 'here and now'. Ben Anderson and James Ash (2015) in a volume edited by Vannini (2015) discuss atmospheric methods as a version of non-representational methods. Besides the above-mentioned visual methods, Andreas Rauh (2012) also developed a more systematic methodology for collecting qualitative data on how the affective aspects of atmospheres are perceived, which he then applies to experiencing the Museum Island Homboich as well as to the Cathedral of Cologne.

As a third category of methods, or mode of knowing, Sumartojo and Pink speak about "knowing through atmospheres" (Sumartojo & Pink, 2019, p. 44). This addresses the politics of atmospheres and the way that atmospheres deliberately or unconsciously influence others and other situations, especially because it is also in atmospheres that we encounter each other. This latter category of knowing through atmospheres also addresses the design of atmospheres, which coins methods of research through design. Research through Design can lead us to a

---

[5] I put 'interview' here between quotes, because the term implicitly seems to suggest a specific positionality of both the interviewer and the interviewee, which is specifically in relation to these phenomenological approaches not justified, as it is also about the joint experience of the atmosphere.

better understanding of how people think, feel, and act, and how to carry forward design-driven change in places and situations (Roggema, 2017).

What needs to be noted here is, however, that the techniques suggested in these sources are not always developed strictly from the new-phenomenological perspective. They always need adjustments concerning the themes, dimensions and variables addressed in the interviews or observation protocols, etc. (Christensen, 2017). These possible adaptations also touch on a plethora of different techniques for collecting data on affective atmospheres as well as manifold techniques for expressing the results of the analysis of these data beyond the classical language-oriented scientific media. These kinds of methods are nowadays often denoted as creative methods (Benzon et al., 2021) even though that is a bit of a well-selling fashionable label and does not imply that there is much new under the sun. But it does point to the collection of multi-sensory data and possibly multi-modal ways of expressing atmospheres that can 'affect' and 'involve' the audience in the dissemination of the results of the phenomenological analysis.

Conceptualising overtourism from an atmospheric perspective

Having an impression of how touristic experiences are conceptualised from a phenomenological perspective, we should return to the topic of overtourism. The irritation and annoyance that overtourism at some destinations causes can be seen as an atmospheric effect of that specific situation. These kinds of affects are not just due to the functionality of a place or to the physical arrangement of that place. As we have noted above it is always a combination of factors. Especially it is an affective involvement radiating from the toned atmosphere, which is felt in a specific way. By now, this insight has been well-received in tourism research (Volgger & Pfister, 2019), but strangely enough it has been almost exclusively applied to the experience of tourists and not to the experiences of the inhabitants or other users of the destination places. It neglects that this is a shared atmospheric place and a place of encounter, a place, which may contain different competing atmospheres or an atmosphere which at least is ambivalent in the way it affectively involves people.

Every touristic experience as well as the experience of tourism at these places is based on an encounter. This can be either an encounter of the tourist with the atmosphere the destination breathes or an encounter of the local people with the many tourists visiting that place and the related atmosphere which they are taken by. It has to be recognised that similar kinds of material and aesthetic arrangements can be experienced in very different ways. Sometimes, for example, we seek the crowds, and travel far to be part of them, like in the case of a music festival, and enjoy the density, the loudness, the collective movements, the bad food and sleepless nights, while we completely go out of our minds. The atmospheric contagiousness is essential for this feeling. It is a joint feeling and a feeling of being part of a collective. On other occasions, with the same degree of crowdedness, and even almost the same kind of joint collective movements and gesticulations, we feel pressured, hindered and disturbed and would like to flee as quickly as possible after we have taken a half-ruined picture (so that we at least have a partial remembrance of the beauty of the visited place).

These atmospheres are not thing-like objective situations but at best half-things, and according to Böhme partially even makeable (Edensor, 2001). Solving the problem of overtourism might be possible by rearranging and restaging the touristic experiences at these places. Research into the intricacies of our atmospheric touristic experiences might help us in doing so. Without prematurely anticipating the results of this research, we could speculate a qualified way about how these rearrangements could look like. Venice is thinking about introducing an entrance fee for tourists and has banned the huge cruise ships from the city, which might reduce and redistribute the crowds (Edensor, 2015). This adds up to a substantial rearrangement of the physical bodies in the city and to a different atmospheric feeling, without creating a Covid-19-like atmosphere of complete void and rather depressing urban spaces. Where and to what degree this can be done, and where the close togetherness, e.g. in the Venice Opera, is still to be seen, on the bases of a thorough assessment of the affective meaning of these rearrangements. Avoiding these excessive crowds may also allow the introduction of other atmosphere-relevant elements, like street art performances, or a more relaxed atmosphere on the terraces and a general slowdown of the urban rhythm. The feelings of these places are complex, multidimensional, subjective and rather intimate and need further research (Edensor, 2012).

We should of course avoid the mistake to look at the affective involvements only from the perspective of the individual tourist or the individual inhabitant of these tourist destinations. These are shared spaces, and collectively intentionally or unintentionally co-constructed (Kolehmainen & Mäkinen, 2021). Julmi (2016) has addressed how people also communicate with each other through their affects. This opens up a still largely neglected field of research focusing on the affective interaction between tourists and inhabitants at touristic places. Interesting in that respect is, for example, the initiative of Airbnb to enrich the touristic experience by hosting tourists in the apartments of local inhabitants allowing them a unique insight into the authentic daily life of the host. These places indeed breathe another kind of atmosphere than a standardised hotel room of a globalised hotel chain. But if one wants to take also the affective communication between guest and host to a new level, they have introduced the Airbnb experiences, designed as a co-production (Correia et al. 2017) of and encountering experience for both hosts and guests.

This initiative of Airbnb is of course only an example, and in this case an example of a company which has lost a lot of credit concerning their role in the problem of overtourism. Nevertheless, it shows that there is still a world to win, in these respects, also for tackling the problem of overtourism by taking into account how overtourism feels and how to carefully construct affective places and the atmosphere of the interaction between tourists and inhabitants. This focus on pathic relations does not exclude or replace the traditional action-oriented focus but adds a realm of hitherto neglected creative possibilities (Ahmed, 2014; Bens et al., 2019; Kleres & Albrecht, 2015; Albrecht, 2017)[6].

This last remark is rather crucial. The last thing this chapter intends to do is to suggest, that over-tourism can be solved by just looking at the experiential side of overtourism. That is just exchanging one reductive approach with another. That would be a big mistake. There are many direct material and functional aspects related to overtourism, like capacities, local ecologies and authenticity, which is also shown in the other chapters in this edited volume. Addressing these issues without beating about the bush is essential. But, on the other hand, it would also be a mistake to neglect the experiential aspect of overtourism, as shown in this contribution. What is seen as obvious facts like a '(social) carrying capacity', or what is accepted as bearable, or what is calculated as a 'profitable effect' are again very much influenced by the subjective experiences. They are not obvious at all, and often also depend heavily on which subject, stakeholder or community we are talking about.

It is also not sufficient to only include the experiential side of the tourists and touristic entrepreneurs. In that sense, it is stunning that in the recently published *Routledge Handbook of Tourist Experience* (Sharply, 2022) one exclusively looks at that one side of the coin and grossly neglects the experience of the local residents. How these situations of overtourism are experienced is related to many actors and is a part of a multi-factor relational network and much more subjective than the traditional universalistic behavioural and reductionist approaches would suggest (Jordan, Lesar & Spencer, 2021). Reality is indeed much more complex than we believe it to be. Developing sophisticated and effective policy measures against overtourism, therefore, demands a much closer look at touristic experiences, next to the many other material and functional aspects. There are diverse ways to go about this. In many cases it demands a concerted and delicate combination of many different measures simultaneously to make sure that it has a substantial and sustainable effect, which does not unintendedly create too many new problems at the same time.

Without going through all possible measures, in my view, one approach stands out as a good candidate to integrate the experiential dimension of overtourism in

---

[6] Although Ahmeds work (2014) is written from the background of queer and feminist theory, it is fundamental for the political aspect of emotions. And while Albrecht's PhD thesis (2017) is not written from the perspective of touristic experiences but from the perspective of migration, when it comes to processes of affective dialogue it is very telling. Bens et al. (2019) focus specifically on the situation of formal politics, but derive the proposition for how to integrate the emotional dimension into everyday political deliberations. Emotions and affects are indeed everywhere, and much can be learned from these other realms for the field of touristic experiences in case of overtourism.

a sophisticated and situational way. This approach would be the concept of community tourism. Community tourism unites the multi-sensory experiences and valuations of both the tourist and the local inhabitants, and the mutual exchange about them, and is usually developed in a highly participative way (see also Ghidouche & Ghidouche, 2019; Saltık & Turgut, 2021; Kim & Kang, 2020). But also community tourism is not a concept to be applicable from the shelve on the affective and emotional aspects of overtourism. Until now, community tourism research is very much biased towards cases in the Global South, even though, in principle, it is as much applicable in the Global North.

This bias is probably not intended, but an outcome of a still lasting inherent paternalistic colonial view, on positionality and community, as if there is only a real need for community tourism in underprivileged and disempowered communities (Horvath & Carpenter, 2020). Many of the most prominent cases of overtourism are, however, to be found in the Global North. In places coping with overtourism community tourism is very often still underdeveloped, although especially in those cases a participatory approach of collaborative tourism-making could better address the problems induced by overtourism (Phi, 2023). Part of overcoming or decolonising this still rather paternalistic view on communities could be the intention to create a more sustainable and (affectively) balanced form of tourism. This implies that one should not just concentrate on the tourist experience, but also explore possibilities for co-productive contributions by residents. However, developing such a community tourism programme dealing with overtourism from a more experiential and affective perspective should start with a more detailed phenomenological knowledge of the respective touristic experiences.

Conclusions

In this contribution, I have attempted to provide a brief summary of a new-phenomenological conceptualisation of the affective dimension of touristic experiences. This new-phenomenological conceptualisation of embodied touristic experiences provides us with a much more comprehensive view of the core of touristic activities and situations and can better explain why it may stay relevant to travel to places, experience them, meet strangers at these distant places, and share our embodied experiences with them. It also gives us a much richer dimensional framework for analysing and evaluating the atmospheric quality of situations, places and destinations. This conceptualisation does not reduce the affective quality of a place to only individual subjective and therefore rather arbitrary emotions, but enables the design of the affective aspects of places in a way which allows non-arbitrary collective experiences. It also opens up a new way to look at the phenomenon of overtourism and guides us in how to analyse these situations and come up with new ways in helping to solve the problem of overtourism.

Literature

Abusaada, H. (2020). Strengthening the affectivity of atmospheres in urban environments: the toolkit of multi-sensory experience. *International Journal of Architectural Research*, *14*(3), 379-392.

Ahmed, S. (2014). *The Cultural Politics of Emotion*. Edinburgh: Edinburgh University Press.

Albrecht, Y. (2017). *Gefühle im Prozess der Migration. Transkulturelle Narrationen zwischen Zugehörigkeit und Distanzierung*. Wiesbaden: Springer.

Altman, I. & Low, S. M. (Eds.) (1992). *Place Attachment*. New York: Plenum Press.

Anderson, B. & Ash, J. (2015). Atmospheric methods. In P. Vannini (Ed.), *Non-Representational Methodologies: Re-envisioning Research* (pp. 37-50). Abingdon: Routledge.

Anderson, B. (2009). Affective atmospheres. *Emotion, Space and Society*, *2*(2), 77-81.

Benjamin, W. (2008 [1936]). *The Work of Art in the Age of Its Technological Reproducibility, and Other Writings on Media*. Cambridge: Harvard University Press.

Bens, J., Diefenbach, A., John, Th., Kahl, A., Lehmann, H., Lüthjohann, M., Oberkrome, F., Roth, H., Scheidecker, G., Thonhauser, G., Ural, N. Y., Wahba, D., Walter-Jochum, R. & Zik, M. R. (2019). *The Politics of Affective Societies. An Interdisciplinary Essay*. Bielefeld: Transcript.

Benzon, N. von, Holton, M., Wilkinson, C. & Wilkinson, S. (2021). *Creative Methods for Human Geographers*. London: Sage.

Bille, M. & Simonsen, K. (2021). Atmospheric practices: on affecting and being affected. *Space and Culture*, *24*(2), 295-309.

Böhme, G. (1993). Atmosphere as the fundamental concept of a new aesthetics. *Thesis Eleven*, *36*, 113-126.

Brook, P. (1968). *The Empty Space*. New York: Touchstone.

Busch, B. (2020). Discourse, emotions and embodiment. In A. De Fina & A. Georgakopoulou (Eds.), *The Cambridge Handbook of Discourse Studies* (pp. 327-349). Cambridge: Cambridge University Press.

Christensen, M. (2017). The empirical-phenomenological research framework: Reflecting on its use. *Journal of Nursing Education and Practice*, *7*(12), 81-88.

Coulter, J. (1986). Affect and social context: Emotion definition as a social task. In R. Harré (Ed.), *The Social Construction of Emotions* (pp. 120-134). Oxford: Blackwell.

Correia, A., Kozak, M., Gnoth, J. & Fyall, A. (Eds.) (2017). *Co-Creation and Well-Being in Tourism*. Cham: Springer.

De Matteis, F., Bille, M., Griffero, T. & Jelić, A. (2019). Phenomenographies: describing the plurality of atmospheric worlds. *Ambiances*, 5, 1-22.

Demmerling, Ch. & Landweer, H. (2007). *Philosophie der Gefühle. Von Achtung bis Zorn*. Weimar: Metzler.

Diaconu, M. (2012). *Sinnesraum Stadt. Eine multisensorische Anthropologie*. Vienna: Lit.

Dwyer, L., Chen, N. C. & Lee, J. J. (2019). The role of place attachment in tourism research. *Journal of Travel & Tourism Marketing*, 36(5), 645–652.

Edensor, T. (2001). Performing tourism, staging tourism (re)producing tourist space and practice. *Tourist Studies*, 1(1), 59–81.

Edensor, T. (2012). Illuminated atmospheres: anticipating and reproducing the flow of affective experience in Blackpool. *Environment and Planning D: Society and Space*, 30, 1103–1122.

Edensor, T. (2015). Producing atmospheres at the match: fan cultures, commercialisation and mood management in English football. *Emotion, Space and Society*, 15, 82-89.

Everingham, Ph., Obrador, P., & Tucker, H. (2021). Trajectories of embodiment in Tourist Studies. *Tourist Studies*, 21(1), 70-83.

Fuchs, T. (2013). Zur Phänomenologie der Stimmungen. In F. Reents & B. Meyer-Sickendiek (Eds.), *Stimmung und Methode* (pp. 17-31). Tübingen: Mohr Siebeck.

Gaudin, O. & Le Calvé, M. (2019). Across Berlin's atmospheres: Fragmentary ethnography of an on-going urban metamorphosis. *Ambiances*.

Ghidouche, K. A-Y. & Ghidouche, F. (2019). Community-based ecotourism for preventing overtourism and tourismophobia. *Worldwide Hospitality and Tourism Themes*, 11(5), 516-531.

Gifford, R. (Ed.) (2016). *Research Methods for Environmental Psychology*. Malden: Wiley Blackwell.

Goulding, Ch. (2023). 'Atmosphere' – the what? The where? And the how? *Annals of Tourism Research*, 101, 1-19.

Griffero, T. (2019). In a neo-phenomenological mood: Stimmungen or Atmospheres? *Studi di Estetica*, *47*(2), 121-151.

Gugutzer, R. (2013). Hermann Schmitz: der Gefühlsraum. In K. Senge & Schützeichel (Eds.), *Hauptwerke der Emotionssoziologie* (pp. 304-310). Wiesbaden: Springer.

Gugutzer, R. (2019). Beyond Husserl and Schütz, Hermann Schmitz and Neo-phenomenological Sociology. *Journal for the Theory of Social Behaviour*, *50*, 184-202.

Hasse, J. (2012). *Atmosphären der Stadt. Aufgespürte Räume*. Berlin: Jovis.

Heidegger, M. (1962). *Being and Time*. Oxford: Blackwell.

Husserl, E. (1970). *The Crisis of European Sciences and Transcendental Phenomenology*. Northwestern, Evanston: University Press.

Husserl, E. (1989). *Ideas Pertaining to a Pure Phenomenology and a Phenomenological Philosophy. Second Book: Studies in the Phenomenology of Constitution*. Dordrecht: Kluwer.

Jordan, E. J., Lesar, L. & Spencer, D. M. (2021). Clarifying the interrelations of residents' perceived tourism-related stress, stressors, and impacts. *Journal of Travel Research*, *60*(1), 208-219.

Julmi, C. (2016). *A Theory of Affective Communication* (Diskussionsbeiträge der Fakultät für Wirtschaftswissenschaft). Hagen: Fern Universität Hagen.

Kim, S. & Kang, Y. (2020). Why do residents in an overtourism destination develop anti-tourist attitudes? An exploration of residents' experience through the lens of the community-based tourism. *Asia Pacific Journal of Tourism Research*, *25*(8), 858-876.

Kleres, J. & Albrecht, Y. (Eds.) (2015). *Die Ambivalenz der Gefühle. Über die verbindende und widersprüchliche Sozialität von Emotionen*. Wiesbaden: Springer.

Kolehmainen, M. & Mäkinen, K. (2021). Affective labour of creating atmospheres. *European Journal of Cultural Studies*, *24*(2), 448–463.

Lewicka, M. (2011). Place attachment: how far have we come in the last 40 years? *Journal of Environmental Psychology*, *31*, 207-230.

Mackin, G. (2022). The aesthetic Habermas communicative power and judgment. *Political Theory*, *50*(5), 780–808.

Michels, Ch. (2015). Researching affective atmospheres. *Geographica Helvetica*, *70*, 255-263.

Paiva, D. (2023). The paradox of atmosphere: tourism, heritage, and urban livability. *Annals of Tourism Research*, *101*, 1-10.

Phi, G. T. (2019). Collaborative tourism-making: an interdisciplinary review of co-creation and a future research agenda. *Tourism Recreation Research*, *44*(3), 284-299.

Pink, S (2015). *Doing Sensory Ethnography*. London: Sage.

Prince, S. (2018). Dwelling in the tourist landscape: embodiment and everyday life among the craft-artists of Bornholm. *Tourist Studies*, *18*(1), 63–82.

Ramkissoon, H., Smith, L. D. G., & Weiler, W. (2013). Testing the dimensionality of place attachment and its relationships with place satisfaction and pro-environmental behaviours: a structural equation modelling approach. *Tourism Management*, *36*, 552-566.

Rauh, A. (2012). *Die besondere Atmosphäre. Aesthetische Feldforschungen*. Bielefeld: Transcript.

Richter, P. G. & Goller, K. (2008). Raumsymbolik. In P. G. Richter (Ed.), *Architekturpsychologie: Eine Einführung* (pp. 141-173). Lengerich: Pabst Science.

Roggema, R. (2017). Research by Design: Proposition for a Methodological Approach. *Urban Science*, *1*(1), 2.

Runkel, S. (2016). Zur Genealogie des Atmosphären-Begriffs. Eine kritische Würdigung der Ansätze von Hermann Schmitz und Gernot Böhme. In U. Wünsch (Ed.), *Atmosphären des Populären II. Perspektiven, Projekte, Protokolle, Performances, Personen, Posen- Beiträge zur Erkundung medienästhetischer Phänomene* (pp. 3-22). Berlin: Uni-Edition.

Saltık, I. A. & Turgut, U. (2021). The role of community based tourism in avoiding overtourism. In A. Hassan & A. Sharma (Eds.), *Overtourism, Technology Solutions and Decimated Destinations* (pp. 117-131). Singapore: Springer.

Sharply, R. (2022). *Routledge Handbook of the Tourist Experience*. Abingdon: Routledge.

Schmitz, H. (1990). *Der unerschöpfliche Gegenstand. Grundzüge der Philosophie*. Bonn: Bouvier.

Schmitz, H. (2005). *Situationen und Konstellationen*. Baden Baden: Karl Alber.

Schmitz, H. (2007). *Der Leib, der Raum und die Gefühle*. Bielefeld: Sirius.

Schmitz, H. (2011). *Der Leib*. Berlin: De Gruyter.

Schmitz, H. (2012). Atmosphärische Räume. In R. Goetz & S. Graupner (Eds.), *Atmosphäre(n) II. Interdisziplinäre Annäherungen an einen unscharfen Begriff* (pp. 17-30). München: Kopaed.

Schmitz, H. (2019). *New Phenomenology: A Brief Introduction*. Milano: Mimesis International.

Schütz, A. (1967). *The Phenomenology of the Social World*. Evanston: Northwestern University Press.

Simonsen, K. (2012). In Quest of a New Humanism: Embodiment, Experience and Phenomenology as Critical Geography. *Progress in Human Geography*, *37*(1), 10–26.

Slaby, J. (2008). *Gefühl und Weltbezug. Die menschliche Affektivität im Kontext einer neo-existentialistischen Konzeption von Personalität*. Paderborn: Mentis.

Smith, J. A., Flowers, P. & Larkin, M. (2009). *Interpretative Phenomenological Analysis: Theory, Method and Research*. London: Sage.

Sumartojo, S. & Pink, S. (2019). *Atmospheres and the Experiential World. Theory and Methods*. Abingdon: Routledge.

Thibaud, J.-P. (2001). La méthode des parcours commentés. In M. Grosjean & J.-P. Thibaud (Eds.), *L'Espace Urbain en Methods* (pp. 79-99). Marseilles: Èdition Parenthèses.

Vannini, P. (Ed.) (2015). *Non-Representational Methodologies: Re-envisioning Research*. Abingdon: Routledge.

Volgger, M. & Pfister, D. (Eds.) (2019). *Atmospheric Turn in Culture and Tourism. Place, Design and Process Impacts on Customer Behaviour, Marketing and Branding*. Bingley: Emerald.

Zahavi, D. (2018). *Phenomenology: The Basics*. London: Routledge.

Chapter 3 - The overtourism phenomenon in different destination categories

Fabian Weber & Florian Eggli

Introduction

Even though capacity problems in tourism are not a new phenomenon, the debate on overtourism has gained importance with an increase in overcrowded tourist destinations. Overtourism can be defined as a "situation in which the impact of tourism, at certain times and in certain locations, exceeds physical, ecological, social, economic, psychological, and/or political capacity thresholds" (Peeters et al, 2018, p. 22). So, by definition, it can occur anywhere. However, triggered by the problems in several – mostly urban – tourist hotspots in Europe, the term "overtourism" is mainly used in an urban context. At the same time, there are other destinations that face overtourism challenges.

So far, little is known about the commonalities and characteristics of different types of destinations that have to cope with overtourism. Against this background, this chapter will address the question: what are the similarities and differences between different destination categories when it comes to root causes, impacts and solution approaches in relation to overtourism? Many results presented in this chapter are based on a study in which the authors were involved. This study was commissioned by the European Innovation Council and SMEs Executive Agency (EISMEA) and analysed the phenomenon of overtourism across Europe and in various destination types. Some of the results presented are published in the report Unbalanced tourism growth at destination level. Root causes, impacts, existing solutions and good practices (Strasdas et al., 2022). The goal of the study was to analyse the phenomenon of overtourism in Europe and to identify existing solutions at the destination level.

A central component of the report is a case study analysis looking at the identification, analysis and development of strategies aiming to mitigate or prevent overtourism. We have analysed the results of this study with a focus on similarities and differences in different destination categories that are confronted with overtourism. The findings are complemented with insights from previous studies of the authors analysing case studies worldwide such as Weber et al. (2017), Weber et al. (2019) or Eggli et al. (in: Pietzcker & Vaih-Baur, 2020, p. 173). Before we start with the methodology and the results of the analysis, a preliminary remark on terminology: even though official authorities often prefer to speak of unbalanced tourism development, overtourism is used as a synonym in this chapter.

Methodology

How did we set up the analysis? Besides an extensive literature review, a comparative case study approach was followed. Factors causing imbalances in tourism destinations were addressed by analysing the drivers and impacts of overtourism. Furthermore, best practice solutions to mitigate and prevent the impacts of overtourism were examined. A total of 15 European cases were analysed, three for each of the following five destination types: urban, rural, mountain, coastal, island. The methodological approach we followed can be divided into the following five steps (Strasdas et al., 2022):

Step 1: desk research to identify potential best practice cases

In a first step destinations facing overtourism were identified and categorised. Extensive desk research was carried out to gain a comprehensive list of possible case studies. A long-list of potential case studies for the different geographical areas was developed based on findings from existing studies such as by the UNWTO et al. (2018), Dodds and Butler (2019), Weber et al. (2019), Peeters et al. (2018) as well as journal publications, white papers and media reports.

Step 2: selection of case studies

A comprehensive set of criteria for the selection of the cases to be analysed was developed. The most important criteria were the existence of successful solution approaches as well as a balanced representation of the five destination types and geographical distribution within Europe. In addition, important aspects considered were data availability, the diversity of root causes and impacts and the informative value of the cases. Based on the selection criteria defined, three cases per destination type (urban, rural, mountain, coastal, island) were selected. As some destinations were already prominently covered in various overtourism studies, we focussed on cases that are equally interesting and allow for new knowledge creation in the overtourism literature. Table 1 shows the selection of the cases for the analysis.

When analysing unbalanced tourism growth, scope and perspective really matter. Therefore, for example, we looked at Palma de Mallorca as a coastal destination separately, while simultaneously dealing with the island Mallorca as a whole.

Step 3: development of a framework for the analysis

For the analysis a case study framework was developed. The framework in which this resulted contains quantitative as well as qualitative criteria. In the analysis we employed the framework as a structure for the cross-comparison of all case studies as well as an interview guideline for the researchers working on each of the cases. The framework includes general categories that are of research interest as well as specific case study items for each category and guiding questions. It covers the following areas of interest:

Destination Category	Destination Case
Urban	Florence, Italy
	Lucerne, Switzerland
	Vienna, Austria
Coastal	Lübeck Bay, Germany
	Geirangerfjord, Norway
	Palma de Mallorca, Spain
Island	Mallorca, Spain
	Iceland, Iceland
	Malta, Malta
Rural	Burren and Cliffs of Moher, Ireland
	Regional Nature Park Monts d'Ardèche, France
	Plitvice Lake, Croatia
Mountain	Bled, Slovenia
	Dolomites, Val Pusteria, Italy
	Rigi, Switzerland

Table 1 *Selection of cases for the analysis (source: Strasdas et al., 2022)*

1. General information about the destination (country, region, tourist area size, population, inhabitants, etc.)

2. Tourism figures/development (share of GDP, employment, development of arrivals and overnights, etc.)

3. Tourism management in the destination (organisation of tourism, stakeholders, responsibilities, DMO, etc.)

4. Description of overtourism phenomenon (root causes, impacts, stakeholder affected, etc.)

5. Solution approaches (measures and strategies, digital solutions, challenges, transferability, etc.)

6. Monitoring (indicators, challenges, success factors, etc.)

7. Management of the pandemic (changes in tourism development, changes in management, etc.)

8. Outlook (expected future changes, uncertainties, recommendations)

9. Additional comments

Step 4: data collection and cross-comparison of the cases

The methodological design for the case studies is based predominantly on the compilation of secondary data from published academic and industry reports and on interviews with representatives and other tourism stakeholders of the destinations. . The interviews contributed to the completion of the case study analysis and validated part of the information compiled from secondary sources. The case studies were compiled using a template, providing a basic structure for each case and allowing us to compare the results and to derive similarities and differences.

Step 5: validation in workshops

Five destination workshops and one concluding EU-level workshop were organised to promote peer learning, exchange and networking among tourism actors, governments, academics and local stakeholders. The destination workshops aimed to connect tourism stakeholders from destinations to foster peer-to-peer learning on the problems of, and solutions to, unbalanced tourism growth. Participants were invited to present solution approaches to unsustainable tourism growth and its environmental and socio-economic impacts on the territories. Moreover, the results from the case study analyses were presented, discussed and supplemented with the experiences from the different destinations.

European destinations under pressure

In this section, the results of the analysis are presented. What did we find? Interestingly, the literature review on rural, urban, mountain, island, and coastal destinations under pressure from overtourism shows that nearly all European regions are represented with some cases. It is only the eastern region of Europe where the topic seems to be less relevant (except for in selected cities). The cases analysed are all destinations where tourism growth in recent years has led to unbalanced and/or overtourism developments. Nevertheless, the stage and development of overtourism turns out to be vastly different amongst the cases. From the literature review as well as the analysis of the case studies some general drivers, impacts and solution approaches can be identified.

Drivers of overtourism on destinations

Based on the analysis of the case studies and the workshop discussions several common mega-trends and drivers can be identified. At the same time, it is important to note that unbalanced tourism is a process that evolves uniquely at each destination. One of the key drivers is international tourism growth. Other relevant developments enhancing overtourism are the increased affordability and accessibility of travel (HOTREC, 2018), the raise of privately rented appartements (Jordan, Pastras & Psarros, 2018) and the seasonality and dependency on certain types of tourism in some destinations (Weber et al., 2017). Social media can be a driver leading to overtourism at specific sites too. Also destination governance is a decisive factor for the emergence of overtourism (Strasdas et al., 2022).

Impacts of overtourism on destinations

In terms of impacts, the most visible effects of overtourism are various types of congestion, such as the concentrated number of visitors or vehicles in a limited geographic space, including beaches, parking facilities, queues in front of museums or ports (Strasdas et al., 2022). Overcrowding in public spaces (Koens, Postma & Papp, 2018) is probably one of the most obvious indicators of overtourism. Nevertheless, the non-visible impacts of unbalanced tourism are more diffuse and include socio-economic and socio-cultural impacts such as touristification, a lower quality of life for local residents, damage to historical sites and monuments, environmental impact including waste, noise, air quality and water quality issues, degraded tourist experience as well as increased real estate prices and rising costs of living (HOTREC 2018; Jordan et al., 2018; Weber et al., 2017; McKinsey & Company and World Travel & Tourism Council, 2017).

The issue of increasing housing prices is frequently discussed since this affects local residents (via out-pricing) as well as (seasonal) employees in the sector who are not able to find affordable accommodation. Yet, in many cases, the perception of overtourism differs depending on the perspective of the stakeholders. Moreover, stakeholders note that overtourism is often season dependent (Strasdas et al., 2022). But where do formal strategies stop and informal strategies begin? There is indeed no clear-cut demarcation between them. For analytical purposes, however, it is useful to make a clear distinction between both concepts (Walter, 2013). Formal strategies emerge from formal institutions, while informal strategies come from informal institutions.

Formal institutions have been referred to as being primarily "based on explicitly defined rules and norms, on rights and duties to enable and to limit social interactions, to achieve certain goals and to structure the distribution of power" (Meyer, 2006, p. 17). Informal institutions, on the other hand, involve codes of conduct, norms of behaviour and conventions (North, 1990). The concept of informality has been used to understand some specific territorial formations. McFarlane and Waibel (2012) state that informality is often understood as being "territorialised within (…) the legal, political, economic, social and environmental margins of the city" (p. 18). Informality has also been captured as a mode of organisation. Whereas the formal is associated with characteristics such as predictability, rationality and regularity, the informal deals with spontaneous, tacit, and affective elements. Informality could also be referred to in terms of processes, as a particular form of interaction or as "a process characteristic of policy making at the local level" (Walter, 2013, p. 72). The concept of informality has also been used to understand and capture specific forms of knowledge, namely "modes of knowing the city (e.g. formal and informal knowledges and practices)" (McFarlane & Waibel, 2012, p. 17).

Solution approaches for overtourism in destinations

Several studies propose general solution approaches for overtourism destinations (HOTREC, 2018; Jordan et al., 2018; UNWTO et al., 2018; Koens et al., 2018; McKinsey & Company and World Travel & Tourism Council, 2017; Weber et al., 2017). The solution approaches applied by the different destinations analysed in the case study analysis can be structured and described as follows (Strasdas et al., 2022):

Laws, regulations, and policies. Most destinations implement variants of legally binding rules and regulations to address unbalanced tourism development. These include, for example, imposing limits to the construction of new hotels or the numbers of cruise passengers, the regulation of privately rented accommodation as well as pollution control measures for cruise ships. Less restrictive policies may create incentives to use public transport instead of cars, for instance.

Stakeholder cooperation. This solution approach includes different interest groups, tourism companies and even the visitors themselves. Often, it is implemented as a precondition to developing appropriate solutions to unbalanced tourism. Participation and consultation of residents in policymaking (e.g. via surveys) and means to financially compensate residents (e.g. by means of benefit-sharing) are identified as success factors.

New and expanded tourism infrastructure, such as additional parking lots or increased waste collection capacities in the high season, are obvious means to accommodate higher visitor numbers in an orderly manner. New infrastructure, new tourism offers or enhanced information campaigns are also used to disperse tourists to other parts of a destination. 'De-concentration' and the redirection of visitor streams do not only help to alleviate the burden on areas with 'must-see'-attractions, but also enable other areas to participate economically.

Digital solutions, particularly the use of big data from mobile technologies and centralised tourism data observatories, seem to be key aspects of successful management of unbalanced tourism as they enable data-driven decision-making. Detailed information provides a common ground for stakeholders of diverging interests and power levels to consider appropriate solutions from their own perspectives. Real-time and up-to-date information provision (crowd monitoring at destinations etc.) and the use of services and amenities are often highlighted as solution approaches.

The systematic monitoring of unbalanced tourism with a key set of indicators still needs to be developed in most destinations that were analysed. So far, overtourism mostly remains a subjective phenomenon at some destinations. Systematic information collection and analysis relevant to a destination is key to managing unbalanced tourism. This information needs to be made accessible to all stakeholders, including residents of the destinations. The importance of impact measurement has also been confirmed because of the fact that impacts may vary even within smaller regions (e.g. between municipalities).

It has to be considered that most approaches also have their downsides. For example, Eggli (2021) points out that whereas the spreading of tourists enables a better levelling of visitor numbers at peak times, it also causes some negative effects. Former pauses during calmer days and during off-peak seasons, which were needed to recover and recuperate from tourism, are vanishing. And less visited areas, used by people as retreats from the tourism buzz, become increasingly frequented and thus are losing their qualities (Eggli, 2001).

Different destination categories

Overall, many commonalities can be observed amongst cities, coasts, islands, rural areas and mountain areas. However, how destinations experience unbalanced tourism significantly varies and partly relates to the type of place. Below we present some characteristics of different destination types. These results are based on the findings of Strasdas et al. (2022) and subsequently enriched with examples from additional studies. As there are some commonalities between coastal and island destinations at the one hand and rural and mountain destinations at the other, the results for these destination categories are presented together.

(1) Overtourism in urban destinations

Urban destinations have been in the focus of the recent overtourism debate. There are many well-documented cases, especially in the European context. In cities, there are several basic aspects of tourism that distinguish them from touristic activities in other types of destinations:

• In cities a multitude of tourist attractions is typically concentrated in a relatively small area.

• These attractions are diverse and thus attract different types of tourists.

• Most urban facilities have not been built primarily for tourists, which leads to a mutual interaction between different types of urban users (tourists, residents, workers, commuters, etc.).

• Different types of economic activities take place in cities and tourism is only one of these activities.

• Cities are significant regional centres and as such they have a well-developed infrastructure, not only when it comes to transportation, but also with regard to services (e.g. restaurants, cafes, bars or shops) and accommodation (hotels, pensions or hostels) (Dumbrovská & Fialová, 2014).

More and more European cities are becoming popular as destinations for holidays and short weekend breaks. In fact, the cases analysed all showed quite high growth rates in tourist arrivals for the period 2009-2019: Florence (+26%), Lucerne (+39%) and Vienna (+81%). Tourism intensity is particularly high in the small city of Lucerne with 20 overnights per inhabitant, followed by Florence (16) and by Vienna (10).

Drivers for overtourism in urban destinations

Relevant drivers for overtourism in many urban destinations are increased destination accessibility and the expansion of privately rentable accommodation However, the root causes can be very specific depending on the destination and the predominant types of tourism.

General drivers
High accessibility
Low-cost carrier expansions
Expansion of privately rented accommodations
Case specific drivers
Bus tours / coaches (Lucerne)
Cruise tourism (Florence, Vienna)
Seasonal attractions / events (Florence, Vienna)

Impacts of overtourism in urban destinations

In the case of Lucerne (Eggli et al., 2019) and Vienna (Lalicic, 2019), overtourism issues are often concentrated on specific areas of interest and become visible only at certain attractions. In a lot of the urban destinations, a slowly progressing touristification is observed, which leads to an increase in prices and living costs. Overcrowded attractions and public spaces often lead to a reduced quality of life for the residents and sometimes even to a reduced visitor experience. Ecological impacts are much less represented in the urban context, although waste and littering issues do occur.

Socio-economic impacts
Increased real estate prices and cost of living
Touristification

Changes in neighbourhood structures
Reduced visitor experience quality
Reduced quality of life for locals / exodus of local residents in historic centres
Ecological impacts
Waste management issues

Solution approaches for overtourism in urban destinations

For the urban context, various strategies have already been identified that can be applied to manage the impacts of overtourism (UNWTO, 2019). One advantage of urban destinations is that there is usually a municipal government that has a general interest in smart tourism management. A challenge in turn lies in the situation that cities have to take into account the needs of many different stakeholders. Regulations (especially rules regarding short-term rentals) are quite common in the urban context. Furthermore, in cities, there are usually more alternative tourism attractions and infrastructural facilities available than in rural destinations. This is useful, because it enables the implementation of physical dispersion strategies. In addition, the case studies showed some interesting digital solution approaches.

Solution approaches
• Various controls and limits embedded in laws, regulations and policies (e.g. extending opening hours and monitoring and regulating short-term rentals)
• Soft approaches such as marketing strategies to balance out seasonal bottlenecks and address new visitor segments

• Digital solution approaches:
    – Florence: FeelFlorence App with real time monitoring ('pop up info')
    – Lucerne: Digital visitor card, and iParking App for coach busses
    – Vienna: Pilot of the Ivie App digital bus management system and digital concierge for city explorers

Example 1 The city of Florence has launched a strategic territorial cooperation project, containing an interactive website and the FeelFlorence app providing real time data. All participating 41 municipalities are able to update contents and

news. The data gathered enables the destination management organisation to better respond to users' needs, implement crowd monitoring and provide visitors with alternative suggestions and tips, a calendar and a personalised travel diary. The city has also been experimenting with mobile phone and CCTV data. However, the urban workshop of the project demonstrated that several challenges exist when working for instance with mobile phone data. The datasets need to be purchased from the providers and subsequently also the software and platforms necessary to analyse the data. This is associated with high costs, while very specific know-how is required to evaluate the data in a meaningful way (Viviani, 2022).

Example 2 The city of Lucerne has launched a process to develop a *Vision for Tourism Lucerne 2030* in order to counter the growing discontent in parts of the population. The project phases were embedded in a comprehensive participation process including various stakeholder groups, a population survey and several workshops. Based on the initial analysis and the survey and workshop results, the new vision has set the following new focal points: (1) Promotion of quality and sustainability, (2) Improvement of transport infrastructure, (3). Involvement of the population and (4). Management of visitor flows. In particular, the population survey proved to be helpful for a better understanding of the pain points. The vision has created a basis for a common understanding of a balanced future tourism development in Lucerne. It remains to be seen whether this consensus still exists when it comes to the implementation of the vision, (Stadt Luzern, 2021).

(2) Overtourism in coastal and island destinations

Even though there are of course very different coastal and island destinations, they often have similar characteristics such as high vulnerability (due to limited geographic space and resources), natural attractions and biophysical fragility (especially beaches, dunes and places of biodiversity value), water-based activities (such as swimming, sunbathing, snorkelling, diving and water sports) and – since recent the last two decades – dependency on cruise tourism. Furthermore, island tourism destinations are typically isolated from the mainland and may have limited infrastructure, such as few transportation options and few medical facilities. The limited space poses also a challenge with respect to further tourism growth. The coastal and island destinations analysed showed strong and continued tourism growth in the last decade. Most destinations, but especially the popular and classic beach destinations (Palma de Mallorca, Bay of Lübeck), experience high visitor concentration during the summer months. Growth rates of tourist arrivals in the period 2009-2019 were particularly high in Mallorca (36%), Malta (107%) and Iceland (308%). When comparing tourism intensity (overnights per inhabitant) with tourism density (overnights per km2 of admin. tourism area), large differences can be observed. Tourism intensity varied between 24 (Iceland), 57 (Mallorca) and 94 (Malta), while tourism density showed even more variation, ranging from 82 (Iceland) and 1,503 (Malta) to even 13,980 (Mallorca).

Drivers for overtourism in coastal and island destinations

Besides the general tourism drivers, the growth of cruise tourism is particularly relevant for many coastal and island destinations. Nature is often a key attraction and beach holidays are still popular, especially in the summer season. In addition, social media and film tourism are important drivers at some island destinations. But there are also very specific drivers such as educational tourism and language courses that are very popular in Malta.

General drivers
Cruise tourism
High accessibility and low-cost carrier expansions
Popularity of beach and nature tourism
Expansion of privately rented accommodations / Airbnb
Increased social media representation ("must-see" iconic destinations)
Case specific drivers
Cruise tourism (Palma de Mallorca, Geirangerfjord)
Film tourism ('Frozen-effect' in Geirangerfjord, Malta)
Education and foreign investments (Malta)
Increased residential tourism (second homes) (Mallorca)
Social media and effect of films as well as iconic attractions (Iceland)
Cultural attractions (Malta, Mallorca)

Impacts of overtourism in coastal and island destinations

In coastal and island destinations, the impact of unbalanced tourism growth is evident in both the socio-economic and environmental spheres. The case studies all showed the fragility of these destinations, particularly where nature is a key attraction and where beaches, fragile dunes and places of biodiversity values are at risk. When it comes to the environment, air pollution due to cruise tourism, waste and water issues are the most common risk factors. Since the ecosystems are often sensitive, even minor damages can lead to long-lasting consequences. Other impacts include rising prices, touristification or overcrowded beaches leading to reduced visitor experience. The lack of appropriate infrastructure and investments to manage the phenomena often pose challenges to small island destinations as Benetatos, Evagelou, Stergiou and Manousou show in the case of Santorini (Greece) Weber et al., 2019). Finally, common consequences of unbalanced tourism in coastal and island destinations are insufficient capacities and expansion possibilities.

Socio-economic impacts
Pressure on infrastructure, congestion, overcrowding
Increased real estate prices, cost of living
Touristification
Reduced visitor experience quality
Reduced quality of life for locals, noise pollution
Ecological impacts
Waste management issues (all)
Decreased air and water quality due to intensive cruise tourism (Mallorca)
Noise pollution (Mallorca and Malta)
Water use (Mallorca and Malta)
Unsuitable recreation in nature (Iceland and Mallorca)

Solution approaches for overtourism in coastal and island destinations

In addition to general solution approaches like regulations or dispersion strategies also innovative marketing strategies to balance out seasonal bottlenecks and address new visitor segments as well as soft approaches addressing the visitors and engaging them to behave responsibly are found in island and coastal destinations. In island destinations, management solutions can be set in a very specific scope that is suitable for and adapted to a 'closed' destination. Islands have an advantage when it comes to monitoring arrivals from outside, while the movement and management of crowds is similar to other destination types.

Solution approaches
Laws, regulations and policies, for example: • only zero-emission ships allowed Fjords from 2026 onwards (Geirangerfjord) • definition of max. 8 beds per hectare (Palma de Mallorca) • Intervention Plan for Tourism; Sustainable Tourism tax (Mallorca)
Dispersion strategies: soft approaches such as marketing strategies to balance out seasonal bottlenecks and address new visitor segments
Soft approaches directly addressing visitors (e.g., Iceland Pledge)

Monitoring frameworks: • Malta: Tourism Observatory (planned)   • Iceland: Tourism Balance Axis (in development)   • Mallorca: Sustainable Tourism Observatory of Mallorca (by the UNWTO)
Digital solution approaches: • Beach Ticker App - Bay of Lübeck measuring visitor numbers at parking lots and at certain beach sections   • Welcome Palma App with a real-time heat map showing most congested zones, chat-bot recommending alternative sights   • ALTER ECO (Interreg) Carrying Capacity-Tool (e.g. Venice, Dubrovnik and Genua)

Example 1 To address the challenges of traffic congestion and overcrowded parking facilities, the Bay of Lübeck in Germany developed a Beach Ticker App that assembles data about visitor density at beaches and related parking lots to help visitors determine where space remains. The tool has been improved to provide beach safety information. Within one year, page views increased from a little less than 400,000 to about 4.2 million. For the future it is planned to expand the system geographically, to gain and include more useful data (e.g. level of occupancy of popular attractions) and to combine information in order to do predictions (Rosinski & Stellmacher, 2022).

Example 2 The island of Mallorca is a good example that shows the importance of data in visitor management. The island-based Sustainable Tourism Observatory is part of the UNWTO International Network of Sustainable Tourism Observatories (INSTO) and tracks more than 700 key performance indicators. The goals of the observatory are to monitor changes, to make challenges visible, to raise awareness about sustainable tourism and to better coordinate development strategies and policies. The observatory allows to work with real time data and to make the economic, social and environmental impact of tourism in the destination visible and accessible for all interested stakeholders (Strasdas et al., 2022).

Example 3 The German island of Juist, which is known for its goal of becoming climate-neutral by 2030, has long been gearing up for sustainable development. Several measures have been implemented here. Worth mentioning is the Guest Parliament, which was already founded in 2014. It aims to involve the guests as relevant stakeholders in the development of the destination. The guest parliament consists of 10 members, meets three times a year (for three days), has an advisory function and can make suggestions (but no decisions) (Weber et al., 2017).

(3) Overtourism in rural and mountain destinations

Rural and mountain destinations have many things in common, since most mountain destinations are also rural destinations. Characteristics that can be found in many mountain and rural destinations are a high fragility (both biophysical and socio-cultural), high tourism dependency, a high amount of day visitors and a lack of organisational structures. Besides, a sudden appearance of large crowds at a few attraction points can take place in these areas, while 'new' destinations are particularly challenged (so-called 'instagrammable' spots). Finally, many rural and mountain destinations had to cope with increasing pressure during the COVID-19 pandemic. While many classic excursion mountain destinations are used to seasonal peaks and have a lot of experience managing crowds, a lot of other rural destinations lack the capacity for a sudden increase in tourist numbers.

A large number of rural destinations have numerous municipalities within their geographic or political spatial boundaries (e.g. Dolomites and Mount Rigi) representing complex structures that demand extra coordination. At the same time, rural destinations sometimes do not have a destination management organisation. In some mountain destinations tourism management is dominated by a few single stakeholders such as the mountain railway company. Another challenge is the lack of data that can be used to manage visitor numbers in a sensible way. There is a high uncertainty for instance regarding day visitors or the number of visitors staying in private accommodations. For both rural and mountain destinations, it is often difficult to get accurate data. Official statistical data often do not correspond to the geographical boundaries of the tourism destination.

Drivers for overtourism in rural and mountain destinations

Besides the general factors that drive tourism in rural and mountain areas, for many of these destinations nature is a key attraction and driver. Weather dependency if often high, since many guests are day trippers who decide on excursions at short notice. Interestingly, the pandemic led to an increase in tourism and recreational activities in many mountain and rural destinations, mostly driven by domestic tourism. Furthermore, there are several examples where social media activities led to a sudden increase in tourist numbers, often overwhelming smaller destinations. At some places, such as Ohrid (Macedonia), activities towards rural tourism development in surrounding rural areas are initiated as alternative forms of tourism resulting in increased pressure on these previously untouched areas (Weber et al., 2019).

General drivers
Nature as a key attraction
Growth of tourism and new emerging markets
High accessibility and low-cost carrier expansions

Expansion of privately rented accommodations / Airbnb
Increased social media representation ('must-see' iconic destinations)
Case specific drivers
Pandemic situation (e.g. Dolomites and Mount Rigi)
Film or series (e.g. popular Italian TV Series *Un passo dal cielo* at Lake Braies)
Social media (e.g. iconic Lake Bled)
General shift in tourism markets (e.g. growth in international (Asian) tourism markets in Central Switzerland)

Impacts of overtourism in rural and mountain destinations

Since nature is a key attraction in most mountain areas, these destinations are often fragile and sensitive to disruptions. The most common consequences observed are ecological ones such as traffic problems, waste issues or challenges regarding landscape, biodiversity and wildlife. The pressure on infrastructure and overcrowding sometimes lead to discontented residents. In addition, despite the tourism masses the regional revenue and value added by tourism is often rather low. Both rural and mountain destinations often struggle with the contradiction of capturing economic benefits while offering idyllic rural landscapes (especially in protected areas).

Socio-economic impacts
Pressure on infrastructure, congestion, overcrowding
Reduced visitor experience quality
Low value added (in relation to number of visitors)
Undesirable visitor behaviour
Reduced quality of life for locals
Ecological impacts
Traffic (congestion, parking capacities, air pollution)
Waste management issues
Landscape, biodiversity and wildlife
Water use

Solution approaches for overtourism in rural and mountain destinations

The rural areas analysed demonstrate how regions depend on tourism flows and that the sudden appearance of large crowds at a few attraction points is not easy to manage. Rural and mountain destinations tend to be better suitable for approaches aiming at stricter regulations and controls (particularly within nature and heritage parks) as well as digital solutions to disperse visitor flows. In many rural and mountain destinations transport management is a major challenge. In the cases analysed, most visitors arrive on their own or in rented cars, contributing to traffic jams and exceeding the carrying capacities of parking facilities. In Bled, the lack of suitable road and parking infrastructure is an important challenge that is being addressed by different infrastructure projects to relieve the streets around the town and the lake. Similarly in the Dolomites the arrival mode by private car presents challenges. It leads to a high amount of pressure on the local road infrastructure capacities, which are often overstretched during peak summer days and weeks with negative consequences for tourists (e.g. waiting time) and for the local community (e.g. traffic jams and limited access for ambulances in medical emergencies). The measures addressing such issues range from the introduction of shuttle buses and advanced reservation systems for car parking to closing off roads during the high season to address the traffic situation in the valleys.

Solution approaches
Restrictions for conservatory purposes (e.g. Burren and Cliffs of Moher and Dolomites).
Dispersion strategies: soft approaches such as marketing strategies to balance out seasonal bottlenecks, address new visitor segments or better distribute visitors to less iconic locations
Off-season promotion of attractions (e.g. Bled and Lake Plitivce)
Infrastructure development: investments in public infrastructures (transport, parking lots, waste management, visitor facilities).
Participative process in tourism planning and management (e.g. Rigi Roundtable)
Code of conduct for visitors (e.g. 'Dolomeyes' in the Dolomites)
Education of both locals and visitors to the particularities and conservation needs of the sites (e.g. Burren and Cliffs of Moher).
Digital approaches • App with trekking routes to encourage visitors to explore less visited parts of the mountains (Monts d'Ardèche)

• Online Guide Training Programme under development, digital booking systems and site monitoring systems are becoming key to visitor management strategies to influence consumer behaviour (Burren and Cliffs of Moher)
Further approaches (Burren and Cliffs of Moher): • Dynamic prices with reduced prices out of peak hours • Package bookings and joint tickets to other fee-paying attractions • Mandatory overnight offering in packages • No license for day tour operators is given unless they engage in the two previously cited measures • Increased opening hours • Capping of number of visitors by setting capacity • Marketing to influence customer behaviour for longer stays, purchasing local and supporting the local economy

Example 1 Where a region can be clearly delineated, it is easier to implement monitoring and tracking systems. Monts d'Ardèche Regional Natural Parc follows a promising approach. The nature park officials developed a monitoring system including data gathering via locally placed sensors and statistics gathered by key tourism businesses (hotels, museums, the Park's House) as well as by the Ardèche department via the 'Flux Vision Tourisme' tool to measure visitor flows. Among other things, the app makes it possible to encourage visitors to explore new less visited areas of the nature park.

Example 2 Plitvice Lakes National Park in Croatia developed an application that allows a better visitor management. Tickets can now be bought online in advance and there are defined time slots for the entrance. A dynamic pricing system (with different prices depending on the season and time of the day) makes it easier to manage peaks. With the measures implemented, the officials from the national park aim to achieve better visitor dispersion, more visits to less known locations, lower system loads in high season and higher visitor satisfaction (Turkalj, 2022).

Example 3 Increasing numbers of guests and tourism expansion plans led to tensions and differing views on the tourism development of the Mount Rigi. A 'round table' was set up with representatives from business, politics and associations. In several workshops, a joint sustainability charter on the future development of the Rigi was drawn up, which also sets out principles on participation procedures. In a follow-up step, a system of sustainability indicators was developed and various implementation projects were launched in cooperation with different stakeholder groups (Pietzcker & Vaih-Baur, 2020).

Conclusions

The cases we analysed across Europe in this chapter illustrate how tourism in destinations can develop in an unbalanced way. The cases highlight certain similarities on a general level, but simultaneously show many differences when it comes to the specific challenges and solution approaches.

Even though each destination is unique and faces specific challenges, there are, depending on the type of destination, certain commonalities. For example, the expansion of privately rentable accommodation is more important in urban areas than in rural locations, where day tourism or pandemic-related shifts in tourist flows seem to be more relevant. When it comes to impacts, rising prices, reduced quality of life for locals and touristification are particularly significant in urban settings. Coastal destinations (notably those that are confronted with cruise tourism) often suffer from air pollution and waste issues as well as low added value from tourism. In rural and mountain destinations, on the other hand, it is mainly the ecological impacts on landscape, biodiversity, the pressure on infrastructure and congestion that are responsible for causing imbalanced tourism settings. Due to the evolution of social media use, some sites have become hotspots without key management organizations having a rapid response.

Accordingly, the solution approaches destinations employ vary as well. They differ in purpose, content and meaning. For example, both at the urban level and in some rural and coastal destinations, there are interesting experiments with digital solutions, e.g. by using data from apps or mobile phones to track and better manage visitor flows. Such approaches can be promising, but also involve challenges with regard to costs, resources, know-how and data protection. Island destinations tend to have easier ways of imposing restrictions and monitoring developments. This is also true for protected areas that usually have a formal management structure and can rely on stricter conservation laws, such as the possibility to impose capacity limits for heavily visited sites. The monitoring of unbalanced tourism exists in several destination types, but is generally not well advanced yet.

Finally, there are promising approaches in all destination types to limit and better distribute visitor flows seasonally and spatially. The variety of solution approaches shows that no one single solution is suitable for all destinations. After all, geographic and socio-economic conditions tend to vary heavily. Furthermore, stakeholder values, beliefs and attitudes differ, while they are key aspects of successful management of overtourism. Whether a solution approach is appropriate must be decided by local stakeholders. In any case, the solutions to manage unbalanced tourism need to be multidimensional as tourism is a complex and dynamic sector.

Although this chapter has given a more profound insight into the phenomenon of unbalanced tourism growth, there are also some limitations to consider. First of all, the challenges and conditions are very specific to each destination. Comparability and transferability of solution approaches is limited. In addition, in the end there is no clear demarcation of destination types. This can be illustrated, for example, by the case of Palma de Mallorca, which is an urban destination on a coast on an island. Many mountain and some island destinations are also rural destinations. And there are other differentiations (e.g. city size, dominant drivers and dominant impacts) that might be more useful when deriving common challenges or looking for multipliable solution approaches. Furthermore, the pandemic and the associated setback of tourism have made it harder to evaluate the impact of strategies and measures implemented a few years ago. While the pandemic has increased pressure from visitor flows in some places, the decline in tourism has also provided relief in many places. However, with the worldwide recovery of tourism, the debate about overtourism has flared up again with similar impacts. Hopefully, the proposed and already implemented solutions will be able to mitigate the problems of overtourism in the future.

Literature

Dodds, R. & R.W. Butler (Eds.) (2019). *Overtourism: Issues, Realities and Solutions*. Berlin: De Gruyter Oldenbourg.

Dumbrovská, V. & D. Fialová (2014). Tourist intensity in capital cities in Central Europe: comparative analysis of tourism in Prague, Vienna and Budapest. *Czech Journal of Tourism*, 3(1), 5-26.

Eggli, F., Huck, L., Weber, F. & J. Stettler (2019). 14 Case study Lucerne, Switzerland. In UNWTO & Centre of Expertise Leisure, Tourism & Hospitality (Eds.). *'Overtourism?' Understanding and Managing Urban Tourism Growth beyond Perceptions* (volume 2) (pp. 61-63). Madrid: UNWTO.

Eggli, F., Stettler, J., Huck, L. & Weber, F. (2020). Overtourism am Beispiel von Luzern und der Rigi. In Pietzcker, D. & Chr. Vaih-Baur (Eds.). *Ökonomische und soziologische Tourismustrends* (pp. 173-191). Wiesbaden; Springer/Gabler.

Eggli F. (2021). *Living with Tourism in Lucerne: How People Inhabit a Tourist Place* (dissertation). Lausanne: University of Lausanne.

HOTREC (2018). *Putting Sustainable Tourism on Top of the EU Policy Agenda for the Benefits of Society* (position paper on overtourism). Brussels: HOTREC.

Jordan, P., Pastras, P. & Psarros, M. (2018). *Managing Tourism Growth in Europe: The ECM Toolbox: Toposophy*. Dijon: CityDNA (formerly known as European Cities Marketing).

Koens, K., Postma, A. & B. Papp (2018). Is overtourism overused? Understanding the impact of tourism in a city context. *Sustainability*, 10(12).

McKinsey & Company & World Travel & Tourism Council (2017). *Coping with Success: Managing Overcrowding in Tourism Destinations*. London: WTTC.

Peeters, P., Gössling, S., Klus, J., Milano, C., Novelli, M., Dijkmans, C., Eugelaar, E., Hartman, S., Helsinga, J., Isaac, R., Mitas, O., Moretti, S., Nawun, J., Papp, B. & A. Postma (2018). *Research for TRAN Committee: Overtourism: Impact and Possible Policy Responses*. Brussels: European Parliament.

Pietzcker, D. & Vaih-Baur, Chr. (Eds) (2020). *Ökonomische und soziologische Tourismustrends*. Wiesbaden; Springer/Gabler.

Rosinski, A. & Stellmacher, P. (2022). *Coastal Destinations Workshop: challenges and solutions in the Bay of Lübeck*. Presentation (unpublished).

Strasdas, W., Lund-Durlacher, D., Wolf-Gorny, L., Schuh, B., Badouix, M., Gaugitsch, R., Gorny, H., Münch, A., Weber, F., Priskin, J. & M. Wyss (2022). *Unbalanced Tourism Growth at Destination Level: Root Causes, Impacts, Existing Solutions and Good Practices* (commissioned by European Innovation Council and SMEs Executive Agency EISMEA). Brussels: European Commission.

Turkalj, M. (2022). *Plitvice Lakes National Park: how we solve problem with overtourism, what happened during pandemic and what are our future plans?* Presentation (unpublished).

UNWTO & Centre of Expertise Leisure, Tourism & Hospitality (2018). *'Overtourism?' Understanding and Managing Urban Tourism Growth beyond Perceptions* (executive summary). Madrid: UNWTO.

UNWTO & Centre of Expertise Leisure, Tourism & Hospitality (2019). *'Overtourism?' Understanding and Managing Urban Tourism Growth beyond Perceptions* (volume 2). Madrid: UNWTO.

Viviani, C. (2022). *Urban Destinations Workshop: challenges and solutions in Florence: the FeelFlorence experience*. Presentation (unpublished).

Weber, F., Stettler, J., Priskin, J., Rosenberg-Taufer, B., Ponnapureddy, S., Fux, S., Camp, M.-A. & Barth, M. (2017). *Tourism Destinations under Pressure: Challenges and Innovative Solutions*. Lucerne: Lucerne University of Applied Sciences and Arts.

Weber, F., Eggli, F., Stettler, J., Crameri, U. & Barth, M. (2019). *Measuring Overtourism: Indicators for Overtourism: Challenges and Opportunities*. Lucerne: Lucerne University of Applied Sciences and Arts.

Chapter 4 - The struggle to manage tourism re-growth in post-pandemic Amsterdam

Lola Kuenen, Robert Fletcher, Tom Jakobs, Martijn Duineveld & Ko Koens

Introduction

Amsterdam is one of many cities that have struggled with the issues of overtourism over the past decade. These issues encompass nuisances, overcrowding, escalating housing prices and an economic dependency on tourism, among others. In the years leading up to the COVID-19 pandemic, city administrators were aware of these challenges and implemented a variety of measures, such as imposing restrictions on tourism rentals and launching campaigns to address problematic behaviour by tourists. Then COVID-19-related travel restrictions brought tourism in Amsterdam to a sudden halt. The scale of the pandemic and its ongoing uncertainty have caused serious economic damage to the city. Given that over 80% of Amsterdam's visitors originate from foreign countries, the suspension of international travel has disproportionally affected the city in comparison to other Dutch destinations (City of Amsterdam, 2020). It has been estimated that Amsterdam incurred losses of at least 8 billion euros from the tourism sector in 2020, in contrast to a total revenue of 18.6 billion euros in 2019 (RTL Z, 2021). However, with the global dissemination of vaccination programs and the gradual easing of travel restrictions, tourism is once again experiencing an upswing in Amsterdam, just as in other popular tourist cities.

As was the case after the 2008 global financial crisis, tourism development is seen as an important strategy for Amsterdam's economic recovery (Blanco-Romero et al., 2019). It is apparent, however, that without concerted intervention to prevent problems of overtourism, these problems will return together with the tourists. This chapter explores the strategies currently being proposed or implemented by stakeholders within Amsterdam's tourism sector after COVID-19 with a view to forestalling the resurgence of overtourism and its discontents in the post-pandemic era. Our analysis demonstrates that trajectories initiated prior to the pandemic are now being augmented and are getting higher priority. Additionally, new strategies aimed at further curbing tourism growth are also being put into effect, with a noteworthy example being an ordinance ostensibly limiting Amsterda's tourism to 20 million visitors annually. Furthermore, decentralization of tourism governance has resulted in a more diffuse distribution of responsibility for sustainable tourism development among the City of Amsterdam, the private sector and city residents than before.

Overtourism and its discontents

Overtourism is defined by the United Nations World Tourism Organization (UNWTO) as "the impact of tourism on a destination, or parts thereof, that excessively influences perceived quality of life of citizens and/or quality of visitors experiences in a negative way" (UNWTO, 2018, p. 4). In the years leading up to the pandemic, attention to overtourism in both popular and scholarly media grew rapidly in relation to popular destinations worldwide (see e.g., Koens et al., 2019; Milano et al., 2019). However, all of this changed with the onset of the global COVID-19 crisis in 2020, as virtually the entire globe went into simultaneous lockdown, resulting in stringent travel restrictions to nearly every tourism destination worldwide.

Consequently, preoccupation with overtourism was swiftly replaced by complaints about 'undertourism', a previously marginal focus of discussion, as destinations now struggled to deal with the economic consequences of the sudden loss of tourism revenue on which they had become dependent. This led some to suggest that overtourism was no longer a concern, and even to deride those who had previously critiqued and resisted it for 'getting what they wished for' and then experiencing the consequences of this outcome (Hall, Scott & Gössling, 2020). On the other hand, many within and beyond the tourism industry advocated using the crisis to transform tourism and prevent the resurgence of overtourism once the pandemic would end. However, it did not take long for a counter-narrative to emerge that instead advocated for a rapid economic recovery and renewed growth in tourism (Butcher, 2021; Higgins-Desbiolles, 2022). This echoed the predominant response to the 2008 economic crisis when tourism growth was actively encouraged as a means to re-stimulate local economies (Koens et al., 2019; Milano et al., 2019). In this chapter, we explore how this debate is unfolding as Amsterdam prepares for the return of increasing tourism numbers after the pandemic.

Materials and methods

Data for this analysis is based on two different periods of field research conducted by this chapter's first and third author, respectively. Research was undertaken both before and after the onset of the COVID pandemic. To assess perspectives concerning tourism development among Amsterdam municipal administrators pre-COVID, between June and August 2018, seventeen in-depth interviews were conducted with civil servants from different departments within the municipality of Amsterdam and the wider metropolitan region. Additionally, participant observation was carried out at a tourism workshop comprising fifteen civil servants, with the focus on producing concrete actions to address current and future tourism growth. To contextualise the primary empirical materials, we also used the LexisNexis database to identify and analyse newspaper articles published on the topic of tourism in Amsterdam between 1993 and 2018 in local and national outlets. Furthermore, we studied relevant policy documents produced by the municipality as well as the electoral programs of a selection of the largest political parties in Amsterdam that have included tourism within their planning.

Using this pre-COVID research as a baseline, further research was conducted between July and September 2021, with a follow-up in October 2022. This entailed two interrelated qualitative methods of data collection. Firstly, desk research was employed to analyse (non-)governmental documents and policy papers concerning the issue of overtourism in Amsterdam. The second method entailed interviewing different stakeholders of Amsterdam's tourism sector, many of whom were part of the initial research period. In total, thirteen interviews were conducted, with durations ranging from 30 to 60 minutes, and an average of 40 minutes. The results mention the job titles of the interviewees in some parts but not all. As all interviewees were also residents of Amsterdam, they sometimes spoke from a professional perspective and sometimes from a more personal one.

In the following section, we outline the results of the comparative analysis developed in this way. We start by describing the pre-COVID policy climate.

The tourism boom and its discontents, pre-COVID

City marketing policies in Amsterdam can be traced back to the 1990s, aiming "to boost the local economy by attracting tourists and foreign investment in luxury hotel chains and other tourism-related services" (Pinkster & Boterman, 2017, p. 458; cf. Gerritsma & Vork, 2017). In 2004, the 'I Amsterdam' marketing campaign was launched, led by the municipal councillor for economic affairs at the time, in close collaboration with urban and regional companies. The campaign was legitimised by the idea that the 'position of Amsterdam in the world is under pressure and that this could have serious economic consequences. Because competition between cities in Europe is becoming stronger, cities across the continent are more effectively emphasizing their strong features to attract visitors, companies, and new residents than ever before' (Berenschot, 2004, p. 14).

To ensure the continued growth of tourism, both right- and left-wing parties advocated for less regulation to enable tourism expansion (Van Kampen, 2014). These actions were not without success. Not only was tourism one of the few industries in Amsterdam that grew continuously after the 2008 economic crisis, but as of 2018, the city became the fifth most visited city in Europe. Both the campaign and deregulation measures contributed to the arrival of nearly 20 million visitors in 2019 (City of Amsterdam, 2020). In the same post-crisis period, the number of hotel rooms increased by 30%, with the tourism industry growing to provide more than 61.000 jobs (Haanen, 2018).

Until 2014, the tourism boom and the prevailing optimism concerning it were rarely criticised (Milikowski, 2018). What dominated was a clear impetus to push tourism growth (Koens et al., 2018). 'Everyone in the world should have seen

Amsterdam in their life once', a well-known politician tweeted in 2014 (D66 Amsterdam, 2014). In the two years after this statement, however, public attitudes towards tourism shifted dramatically. The 3rd of May 2014 is seen as a key turning point in this shift when a combination of events (multiple activities, good weather, roadworks) made the Dam Square in the centre of the city largely inaccessible, leading to a massive outcry in the local newspaper the following day (Van Raamsdonk, 2019).

A few years later, tourism was formally recognised as a problem in the media and by the then-mayor of Amsterdam, among others. This recognition provoked most political parties to instead advocate for more regulation and limitations on tourism expansion (Milikowski & Naafs, 2017). Overcrowding was now perceived as a significant issue, especially in the historical city centre being linked to issues such as pollution, nuisance, decreased tourist experiences and frustrated residents (City of Amsterdam, 2016; Municipality of Amsterdam, 2016a; Pinkster & Boterman, 2017). It was therefore not surprising that a fierce social and political dispute in the city arose.

A balanced city

As a result of this growing discontent with tourism, the municipality of Amsterdam set up a small team of civil servants under the direct authority of the city council in 2017, with the aim to propose a series of measures to ensure the city's liveability (City of Amsterdam, 2017). This team developed a plan called *Stad in Balans* (City in Balance), intending to address the negative impacts of tourism growth by stimulating quality and diversity in retail and facilities, reducing nuisance to local residents and creating more space on streets in busy areas, among other measures (City of Amsterdam, 2017). The focus was on the negative impacts of tourism growth, and not on stopping tourism growth itself. Experimental solutions were also designed and implemented to tackle the problem in collaboration with stakeholders in the wider Amsterdam Metropolitan Region, such as the distribution of tourists to currently less touristy areas in and even beyond Amsterdam itself (Couzy, 2016; Koens et al., 2018).

The Stad in Balans-campaign was based in the economic department of the municipality of Amsterdam where the emphasis has historically been on stimulating economic growth. The campaign did not diverge from this, as it aimed to balance tourism with other demands in the city rather than trying to reduce tourism. A civil servant who switched from spatial planning to the economics department told us that in the spatial planning department he was accustomed to looking 'with a broader view', while in the economics department "the focus is especially on employment opportunities. And economic vitality. [...] I am very much surrounded by colleagues who are foremost talking about employment opportunities." As none of the policies of the Stad in Balans-strategy aimed to put a halt to tourism growth, soon people started to condemn this ameliorative approach, concluding that "only a major crisis can inhibit tourism" (Couzy, 2018, n.p.). The municipal elections of 2018 showed that an increasing number of politicians on all sides of the political spectrum agreed that the city suffered from rapid population growth, increasing tourism and too much foreign property ownership and investment leading to unaffordable housing and gentrification. The city of Amsterdam, it was said, had become tantamount to a theme park (Milikowski, 2018).

The legitimacy of discontent

By this time, hundreds of local and national newspapers, TV programs, and surveys had reported on the discontent among Amsterdam residents concerning the presence of tourism masses and related problems in the city centre. Yet many interviewees who advocated tourism as a catalyst of economic progress believed that such people did not represent the majority of people but were a minority who had got into the habit of complaining, or even whining, about tourism development. Rather than using this input to develop alternative options, the complaints were framed as holding back progress in the city. According to the advocates of tourism prescribing a generic policy that might frustrate the city's further development would be based on only a small group of people experiencing overtourism. Interviewees further noted that these voices were partly from newcomers to the city who should have known that Amsterdam is a touristy city. For those people who had lived in the city for a longer period of time, one interviewee suggested that "if you really, really, really don't like it, you can sell your house, go enjoy living in Oost-Groningen" [a region in the Northeast of the Netherlands that is considered to be remote and quiet].

The post-pandemic shift

Since the outbreak of COVID-19, by contrast, a widespread consensus has developed that the city does not want to return to the pre-pandemic situation. Instead, a more balanced visitor economy is desired that benefits the residents while still welcoming visitors, as they are part of the city's international ambiance. Here, we will elaborate on the dynamics of the post-pandemic shift in the eyes of the interviewees. According to them, the nuisance caused by tourists can be roughly divided into three categories: crowdedness, littering and noise disturbance. All of these problems are seen to negatively impact the city's liveability. The area most often commented on by interviewees is the Red Light District. They argued that this area contributed to Amsterdam's reputation of being free and welcoming to all but in a negative way, by attracting the 'wrong' tourists. A municipal official explained that the issue is that in such a small geographical space, there is "prostitution, cheap accommodation, coffeeshops, touristic stores such as erotic shops, and cheap, tourist-focused bars and food corners. A toxic combination." Also, the ambiance of the city, "with weed leaves at every street corner and on all sorts of packaging, makes it seem like you are walking in some sort of drugs city." Furthermore, it was said that the misbehaviour of some tourists in this area, such as shouting, stimulated others to misbehave as well because of people's herd mentality. All this, combined, "creates a certain demand, which is difficult to control".

Attracting the 'right' tourists

The municipality therefore now aims to repel those tourists "who only visit Amsterdam to drink and to smoke weed, who only stay at the Red Light District, who sleep in their car or who throw up in the streets" (City of Amsterdam, 2020). One tool the Amsterdam mayor and city council have considered is the so-called 'i-criterium' (which would allow only people registered as living in the municipality of Amsterdam to enter a coffeeshop), possibly in combination with a ban on smoking weed in public space. Interviewees generally did not think positively about the i-criterium, arguing that it is unwelcoming, difficult to explain to tourists, promoting street trade and resource-intensive – if not impossible – to enforce and control. In fact, the mayor decided not to implement the i-criterium after the city council informed her that they would not support this decision (ANP, 2022).

Another proposed tool to mitigate tourist nuisance is the spreading of coffeeshops, via more intensive spatial planning, possibly in combination with decreasing the total number of coffeeshops. Finally, interviewees have indicated that the (further) legalization of weed in the United States and Europe could help in deterring the 'wrong' tourists, as "people need a different reason to travel to Amsterdam, because they already have those coffeeshops at home". Instead of 'party and drugs'-tourists, the City of Amsterdam wants to attract 'valuable', or respectful, visitors "who come to enjoy our beautiful city, to shop and go to restaurants and such, without bothering the residents" (City of Amsterdam, 2020). Valuable visitors are said to contribute to the city in economic, social, and environmental aspects. The term 'valuable tourist' is not to be confused with the notion of the 'quality tourist', who carries the connotation of someone with a big wallet and an appetite for luxury. On the contrary, it was argued that, for instance, backpackers are just as welcome as wealthy visitors, as long as they behave respectfully in the city and towards the Amsterdam residents.

Amsterdam's destination marketing organisation continues to implement several campaigns to reframe the city's image and emphasize its cultural value. One specific group of valuable visitors being targeted is business people engaged in congress and business travel. An interviewee from amsterdam&partners (the city's destination marketing organisation) indicated that for a renewed Amsterdam to attract congress visitors, it also needs to showcase culture, culinary and nightlife opportunities. As these visitors usually "stay for a few days, go to a concert, go out for dinner and visit a museum if they have an extra day off, they are respectful visitors that we increasingly want to attract and for which we have to put in the work". The city aims to attract organisations hosting congresses, preferably on a long-term basis, by presenting itself as an attractive location.

Distributing the problem

Although Amsterdam's charming, 17th-century ring of canals is unique in its beauty, the historical city centre's spatial planning also poses some problems related to crowdedness in the public space. Yet the significance of this issue is contested by some interviewees, suggesting that Amsterdam is not as crowded as London or Paris or as crowded as the city used to be in the 1950s. It was also said that extreme events of overcrowding are exaggerated in how often they occur, contributing to its negative perception. Yet, the general agreement among interviewees was that Amsterdam struggles with its public space, with examples offered such as narrow roads and limited space for cycle parking. One tool to tackle this is to try to spread tourists by promoting sites outside of the city, such as Volendam, Zandvoort (re-designated 'Amsterdam Beach') and Muiderslot (now called 'Amsterdam Castle'). The general opinion was that such spreading is only effective in the case of repeat visits, so for people coming to Amsterdam for the second, third or fourth time. People visiting Amsterdam for the first time and staying for two or three days, by contrast, still want to see the touristic highlights, which are mainly located in the city centre, such the Red Light District, the Anne Frank House and the Museum Square.

Because certain shops and services move out of the city centre when the rents become too high, the spreading of tourist experiences is also partially a spontaneous process. However, this mainly affects residents and not tourists. As one interview notes: "Residents go to other parts of the city because of the nice restaurants and stores there; they do not come to the city centre anymore, but tourists do not know about those facilities, so they stay in the city centre." Hence, the municipality aims to improve communication about such facilities for tourists. One tool for this is the 'inspiration-activation campaign', which focuses on highlighting certain attractions and drawing certain groups of people to them. Especially holiday tourists are targeted here, as congress visitors more often already stay outside of the city centre (around the RAI, a large conference centre in the south of the city). This method of spreading tourists across the city region could give the city multiple centres, rather than just the historical city centre, creating a more comfortable, enjoyable city for all those who move around there.

Not another cheese shop

Spreading does not necessarily tackle the issue of increasing a monoculture of shops and facilities in the city, however. The pandemic has emphasized the city's dependence on tourists, especially in the inner city. Although the vulnerability of such a visitor economy was already recognized in the Stad in Balans-strategy, when tourists were suddenly absent, a sense of urgency to address this issue arose. A major public intervention at this level was the halt to touristic shops (City of Amsterdam, 2021). For instance, shops selling souvenirs, Nutella waffles and 'ready to fly'-packaged cheese outplaced resident-focused stores due to rising rental prices. Government intervention was necessary to put a halt to the growing number of such shops, as "money does not bring out the best in people" and to support social entrepreneurship instead. This led to a cat-and-mouse game between the government and creative entrepreneurs working to avoid the 'touristic shop'-label, as there is little clear distinction between tourist and non-tourist shops. However, a municipal official claimed that entrepreneurs should take responsibility for the impact that they have on the long-term future, not only for the city's sake as well as for the fortune of their own business.

The Airbnb dilemma

Besides the hotel sector the tourist rental sector plays a significant role in the availability of accommodations in Amsterdam. The original idea behind Airbnb and similar platforms is quite romantic, as explained by interviewees: it was about a home swap between two parties, visiting each other's place for a holiday. These interviewees also claimed that if Airbnb were still a small-scale platform for such swaps, it would not be an issue. However, in the span of ten to fifteen years, a lot has changed: commercial investors have become involved and people see it as their right to rent out their homes. This has led to several problems. When raising these issues, a main argument was: "A house is for living in." Tourist rentals are seen to drive up housing prices and remove properties from the housing market. Because people could make money with their homes, the option to rent out (part of) a house for some time actually became a selling point. According to a municipal officer: "Advertisements on Funda [a home sale site] said 'This house has a nice room for the use of a B&B' which drove up the asking price."

Furthermore, property investors could buy houses to then rent out them at outrageous prices, supposedly supported by the Dutch government, according to an interviewee from the former city council saying: "Policy in 2015 recommended the Dutch housing market to foreign investors by letting go of the rental regulation so that rental prices could further be increased. Hence, the current housing crisis touches upon Airbnb and tourist rentals, but it is a lot more complex than just that." A hotel owner argued that COVID-19 proved the effect of Airbnb on rental prices, because when properties remained unoccupied by tourists, the demand went down, and so did the prices. A common view was that the commercialisation of homes drives up purchase/rental prices and forces out many Amsterdam residents, such as young people who grew up in the city but now cannot afford to live there anymore. Furthermore, there is a social impact of tourist rentals as the community feeling is disturbed. Hence, interviewees agreed that Airbnb must be constrained in order to counter the ongoing process of gentrification.

Limits to growth?

Some problems related to overtourism, such as crowdedness, nuisance and a tourist-oriented monoculture, could be curbed by controlling the number of tourists coming to Amsterdam in the first place. A more drastic proposal to manage this number is to limit transportation opportunities to and from the city. In this respect, the national airport (Schiphol) has been a topic of extensive discussion. Budget flights as cheap as €30 for a round trip are said to strongly – and negatively –

influence both the number and type of tourists visiting the city. Furthermore, multiple interviewees argued that the current price of air travel does not adequately account for its severe environmental impacts. The first and most commonly proposed strategy to address this is to increase the price of plane tickets by implementing a flight tax. Secondly, interviewees suggested that the number of flights arriving at and departing from Schiphol Airport could be reduced by influencing slot coordination (i.e., the management of airport capacity). Thirdly, opening up Lelystad Airport[1] to the public could help distribute the pressure away from the region around Schiphol Airport, although opinions on this matter varied and were carefully nuanced, as one interviewee mentioned it was a sensitive topic in the city council. However, interviewees pointed out that the responsibility and opportunity to make such changes in air transport lie with the national government rather than the municipality. In fact, slot coordination actually falls under European law, but the Dutch government is working on increasing its control over this. Nonetheless, interviewees stressed the necessity of the City of Amsterdam to lobbying for a flight tax and a halt to the growth of Schiphol Airport.

In addition to encouraging an increase in plane ticket prices, the municipality could also raise the tourist tax. In 2019, the tourist tax was already increased to 7% for all providers in the city (City of Amsterdam, 2019a). In 2020, on top of that a € 3 fee per night was added (City of Amsterdam, n.d.). Economists have argued that the hotel stop, implemented before the global pandemic, significantly increased accommodation prices, as demand kept growing while supply stagnated. Therefore, a higher tourist tax would be justified to allow the city to benefit from the profits made by the hotel sector (Van Dijk & Badir, 2019). However, a potential downside of making the city more expensive for tourists is that it could also become less inclusive. Additionally, the idea of a day tripper tax is being discussed to charge tourists who use the city's public facilities but do not stay overnight in Amsterdam. Some of the difficulties in this discussion include how to define a day tripper or tourist and how to avoid disadvantaging residents, for example by implementing a tax on museum tickets.

Finally, a significant event in 2021 has been the introduction of the ordinance 'Tourism in Balance' that sets a limit of 20 million yearly tourists in Amsterdam, with a threshold of 18 million. This number encompasses both tourists who stay overnight and day trippers (City of Amsterdam, 2019b). The ordinance obligates the municipality to take action when the threshold is reached to prevent exceeding the upper limit. Some interviewees expressed dissatisfaction with this ordinance. They did not support the idea of setting a maximum on the number of tourists, arguing it is highly unwelcoming and, above all, unachievable: "Are you going to close the gates?", one of the interviewees wondered rhetorically. For example, a hotel owner was sceptical about its practical implementation: "Our first reaction

---

[1] Airport in Flevoland (The Netherlands), about sixty kilometres away from Amsterdam. The airport is mainly being used for training purposes. No commercial flights are departing from or arriving at Lelystad Airport.

was: sure, the election campaigns have started. There were 30.000 people supporting this initiative, and it has been re-written a number of times to make it at least a little doable on a juridical level. Do we have to take that seriously?"

Conversely, other interviewees expressed their support for this measure, asserting that imposing a quantitative limit on tourism should help alleviate both the direct and indirect negative impacts of tourism, rather than solely focusing on attracting 'valuable' visitors. They argued that the implementation of this ordinance was a unique event in Amsterdam, demonstrating that drastic measures need to be – and are being – taken. They also criticized the other measures already undertaken to address tourism growth: "The growth in tourist numbers from 20 to 22 million, you cannot deal with through spreading. Maybe it helps a little, but it is not a sufficient solution" In short: although there are still many questions about the practical enforcement of the 'Tourism in Balance'-ordinance, it certainly does indicate a shift in the Amsterdam discourse on tourism regrowth.

Conclusions

Although the pandemic has ended, it is too early to accurately assess its precise effects. However, in this chapter we have identified some interesting trends in the changing approach to tourism policy in Amsterdam since the outbreak in March 2020. The findings illustrate that measures are indeed being implemented to mitigate the tourism sector's negative impacts, but that these tend not to directly address its continuous growth. For instance, the dispersion of tourists aims to alleviate pressure on the city centre. But it does not challenge the underlying status quo of continuously attracting more tourists. Similarly, diversifying the supply of goods and services, attracting 'valuable' visitors and encouraging social entrepreneurship do not confront the dominant economic drive that characterizes the tourism sector and the associated prevalence of consumerism. Consequently, our results make clear that the city government is constrained from enacting more radical changes in tourism policy due to prevailing economic interests.

However, some actions have been taken, such as moves towards the de-commodification of housing in Amsterdam and efforts to reduce consumerism within the city more broadly. This implies that monetary interests have become somewhat diminished in priority compared to those of city residents. Additionally, it is asserted that revenues from the accommodation sector benefit the city more collectively now due to heightening of the tourist tax as well as the proposed day tripper tax. Proposals for a renewed spatial planning approach for the city centre acknowledge that many issues related to tourism are interconnected, necessitating a comprehensive, overarching strategy to deal with them all simultaneously. This applies similarly to the efforts to reframe the city's image. Moreover, the Tourism in Balance-ordinance does indeed directly challenge the tourism sector's pursuit of continual growth both qualitatively and quantitatively, provided that the practical aspects of implementation can be resolved before the threshold is breached.

While these strategies may not completely reverse the prevailing pro-growth orientation of current policies in Amsterdam, they do signify a new step towards directly confronting the overall expansion of tourism in the city. As a matter of fact, this shift was not prominently evident prior to the pandemic.

Literature

ANP (2022). *Geen meerderheid voor i-criterium coffeeshops Amsterdam* [Online]. Available at: https://www.binnenlandsbestuur.nl/juridisch/halsema-respecteert-standpunt-raad

Berenschot (2004). *The Making of the city marketing of Amsterdam* [Online]. Available at: https://www.eurib.net/wp-content/uploads/2009/04/The-making-of-the-city-marketing-of-Amsterdam.pdf

Blanco-Romero, A., Blázquez-Salom, M., Morell, M. & Fletcher, R. (2019). Not tourism-phobia but urban-philia: understanding stakeholders' perceptions of urban touristification. *Boletín de la Asociación de Geógrafos Españoles, 83*, 1-30.

Butcher, J. (2021). Covid-19, tourism and the advocacy of degrowth. *Tourism Recreation Research*, 1-10.

CBS (2020). *Aantal toeristen in logiesaccommodaties naar 46 miljoen in 2019* [Online]. Available at: https://www.cbs.nl/nl-nl/nieuws/2020/10/aantal-toeristen-in-logiesaccommodaties-naar-46-miljoen-in-2019

City of Amsterdam (2016). *Stad in Balans Voortgangsrapportage* [Online]. Available at: https://www.amsterdam.nl/bestuur-organisatie/volg-beleid/stad-in-balans/publicaties-programma-stad-balans/

City of Amsterdam (2017). *Uitvoeringsprogramma Stad in Balans 2017-2018* [Online]. Available at: https://openresearch.amsterdam/nl/page/35477/evaluatie-experimenten-stad-in-balans

City of Amsterdam. (2019a). *Stad in Balans 2018-2022: naar een nieuw evenwicht tussen leefbaarheid en gastvrijheid* [Online]. Available at: https://www.analyzus.nl/uploads/1/0/7/0/10709603/stad_in_balans_amsterdam.pdf

City of Amsterdam (2019b). *Verordening van de gemeenteraad van de gemeente Amsterdam houdende regels omtrent toerisme (Verordening op toerisme in balans Amsterdam)* [Online]. Available at: https://lokaleregelgeving.overheid.nl/CVDR660686/1

City of Amsterdam (2020). *Toerisme MRA 2019-2020* [Online]. Available at: https://openresearch.amsterdam/nl/page/68398/rapport-toerisme-mra---2019-2020

City of Amsterdam (2021). *Winkels binnenstad meer gericht op bewoners* [Online]. Available at: https://www.amsterdam.nl/nieuws/nieuwsoverzicht/winkels-binnenstad-bewoners/

City of Amsterdam (n.y.). *Toeristenbelasting voor hotels* [Online]. Available at: https://www.amsterdam.nl/veelgevraagd/toeristenbelasting-2c7c2#

Couzy, M. (2018). *Alleen grote crisis remt het toerisme nog* [Online]. Available at: https://www.parool.nl/amsterdam/alleen-grote-crisis-remt-het-toerisme~a-4572607/

D66Amsterdam (2014). *D66Amsterdam* [Online]. Available at: https://twitter.com/d66amsterdam/

Dodds, R., & Butler, R. (2019). The phenomena of overtourism: a review. *International Journal of Tourism Cities*, 5(4), 519-528.

Gerritsma, R. (2019). Overcrowded Amsterdam: striving for a balance between trade, tolerance and tourism. In C. Milano, J. M. Cheer & M. Novelli (Eds.), *Overtourism: Excesses, Discontents and Measures in Travel and Tourism* (pp. 125-147). Wallingford: CABI.

Gerritsma, R. & Vork, J. (2017). Amsterdam residents and their attitude towards tourists and tourism. *Coactivity: Philosophy, Communication/Santalka: Filosofija, Komunikacija*, 25(1), 85-98.

Hall, C. M., Scott, D. & Gössling, S. (2020). Pandemics, transformations and tourism: be careful what you wish for. *Tourism geographies*, 22(3), 577-598.

Hannam, K. & Knox, D. (2005). Discourse analysis in tourism research a critical perspective. *Tourism Recreation Research*, 30(2), 23-30.

Higgins-Desbiolles, F. (2020). The "war over tourism": challenges to sustainable tourism in the tourism academy after COVID-19. *Journal of Sustainable Tourism*, 29(4), 551-569.

Koens, K., Postma, A. & Papp, B. (2018). Is overtourism overused? Understanding the impact of tourism in a city context. *Sustainability*, 10(12), 4384.

Koens, K., Postma, A. & Papp, B. (2020). Management strategies for overtourism. In H. Pechlaner, E. Innerhofer & G. Erschbamer (Eds.), *Overtourism: Tourism Management and Solutions*. London: Routledge.

Milano, C., Cheer, J. M. & Novelli, M. (2019). Overtourism: an evolving phenomenon. In C. Milano, J. M. Cheer & M. Novelli (Eds.), *Overtourism: Excesses, Discontents and Measures in Travel and Tourism* (pp. 1-17). Wallingford: CABI.

Milikowski, F. (2018). *Van wie is de stad: de strijd om Amsterdam*. Amsterdam: Atlas Contact.

Milikowski, F. & Naafs, S. (2017). *Oprollen die rotkoffertjes* [Online]. Available at: https://www.groene.nl/artikel/oprollen-die-rotkoffertjes

Pinkster, F. M. & Boterman, W. R. (2017). When the spell is broken: gentrification, urban tourism and privileged discontent in the Amsterdam canal district. *Cultural Geographies*, *24*(3), 457–472.

RTL Z (2021). Wegblijven toeristen kostte Amsterdam vorig jaar 8 miljard euro. *RTL Nieuws.* [Online]. Available at: https://www.rtlnieuws.nl/economie/artikel/5219958/toerisme-2020-nederland-abn-amro-amsterdam-harde-klap

UNWTO (World Tourism Organization) (2018). *'Overtourism?' Understanding and Managing Urban Tourism Growth beyond Perceptions* (executive summary). Madrid: World Tourism Organization (UNWTO).

Van Dijk, J. & Badir, M. (2019). Toerismebelasting is veel te laag. *Het Parool.* [Online]. Available at: https://www.parool.nl/columns-opinie/toerismebelasting-is-veel-te-laag~b5bb877d

Van Kampen, A. (2014). *Toerisme redt de stad, maar crisis is nog niet voorbij* [Online]. Available at: https://www.nrc.nl/nieuws/2014/01/31/toerisme-redt-de-stad-maar-crisis-is-nog-niet-voo-1340433-a500999

Van Raamsdonk, R. (2019). *Amsterdam is te druk en te vol. Of is dat te simpel?* [Online]. Available at: https://touristico.nl/alles/amsterdam-is-te-druk

Chapter 5 - Tourist city Prague on the way to cultural sustainability

Miroslav Roncak

Introduction

In this chapter we explore the case of Prague as an example of a city coping with overtourism. Prague is the capital of the Czech Republic and the largest city in the country, inhabited by 1.3 million people. In 1992, the historic centre of Prague was named UNESCO World Heritage. In 2000, the European Union designated Prague as a „European Capital of Culture" (European Commission, n.d.). According to Euromonitor International (2017) Prague was in 2017 the fifth most visited city in Europe, following London, Paris, Rome and Istanbul. The Prague key attractions are located on the Royal Way. This originally former coronation route is 2.4 kilometres long and connects the major sights in Prague on both sides of the river Vltava (Dumbrovska, 2017). It includes the Municipal House, the Old Town Square, the Old Town City Hall, the Klementium, the Charles Bridge, Prague Castle and St. Vitus Cathedral.

Tourism development in Prague

Prague has experienced a tourist boom in recent decades. Every year, records were broken when it comes to the number of guests and overnight stays in collective tourist accommodation facilities. While in 2012 5.7 million tourists stayed overnight in Prague, spending a total of 14.4 million nights in collective tourist accommodation facilities, in 2019 8 million tourists and 18.5 million overnight stays were counted (Czech Statistical Office, 2022). The share of foreign visitors in the total number of visitors to Prague represented more than 84%. There were several reasons for this growth. First of all, Prague's rich history, stunning architecture and a vibrant culture have made it a highly desirable tourist destination. Second, the rise of the sharing economy, online booking platforms and social media has facilitated easy travel planning, which increased the visibility of Prague as a popular destination. Third, the availability of low-cost airlines and improved transportation infrastructure have made Prague more accessible to tourists from various regions. Finally, effective marketing campaigns and positive word-of-mouth recommendations have contributed to the growth in tourism interest in Prague (Roncak, 2019).

Unfortunately, Prague was not prepared for such an increase in the number of tourists. Local authorities did not take enough measures to prevent the negative impact of tourism. A clear vision on long-term sustainable tourism development was missing. The unwillingness of the government to interfere with the market has led to an uncontrolled development of tourism in Prague`s historic centre. The City of Prague largely focused on marketing and forgot to take measures to manage the development of the destination (Roncak, 2019). There were no clear rules and regulations in the local tourism business. Additionally, the city suffers from environmental degradation. Overtourism in Prague has increased foot traffic, waste generation and pollution from transportation. This has created tensions on Prague's infrastructure and natural environment (Deichmann, 2002). Also local resources have come under pressure. Overtourism has resulted in overcrowding in Prague (Simson, 1999), an increased demand for utilities and scarcity of resources. This has had a negative impact on the quality of life for local residents (Deichmann, 2002). In terms of tourist penetration, Prague is one of the most overcrowded tourist destinations in Europe: the density of tourists per square kilometre and the level of tourist intensity exceeds that of Vienna and Berlin and is twice the size of that in Budapest (Dumbrovska, 2013). In particular, the Royal Way, which connects the major sights in Prague on both sides of the river Vltava, including Charles Bridge, suffers from overtourism.

The influx of tourists has led to rising housing prices, making it difficult for residents to afford homes, and in some cases, contributing to the displacement of locals from city centres. In 2018, 80% of the real estate units offered through the Airbnb platform could not be categorised as 'sharing economy', but were just part of normal entrepreneurial activity (Kljucnikov et al., 2018). Many Airbnb hosts, however, do not declare their income. According to estimates by the Czech government, the state loses 460 million Czech crowns (approximately 20 million USD) annually in taxes related to these concealed rents. The use of Airbnb by tourists in Prague has changed the nature of the Old City and has reduced the quality of life of residents. For instance, the use of residential buildings for short-term tourist accommodation had disrupted relations within neighbourhoods while it has at some places created excessive noise levels, as many visitors do not respect quiet hours in the night. Finally, cultural erosion is an issue in Prague. According to Dumbrovska (2017) in Prague the Royal way and the entire Old City and Leser Town lost their original values of residential area. The areas have been transformed into a 'tourism ghetto'. In particular, overtourism has led to the commodification of culture, touristification, and loss of authenticity, commercialization and the displacement of traditional businesses by those catering solely to tourists (cf. Hoffman & Musil, 1999).

Like in other countries across the world, the Czech Republic experienced a negative impact of the COVID-19 pandemic on daily life, the economy and tourism (Roncak, Scholz & Linderova, 2021). The pandemic has greatly changed the positive development of tourism in the Czech Republic. In 2020, tourism in in this country became one of the industries most affected by the coronavirus pandemic. Its share in the gross domestic product fell from 2.76% to 1.48%, representing CZK 84.3 billion in financial terms. Employment in the sector decreased by 7.3%

year on year (Czech Statistical Office, 2022). Also in Prague the COVID-19 pandemic had a severe and unprecedented impact on the tourism industry. In 2020, there has been a deep drop in the number of visitors to Prague: year-on-year, there was a decline of almost 5.9 million guests (72.9%) and 13.6 million overnight stays (73.5%). During 2021, when border crossing barriers were eased, there was a gradual slight recovery in tourism. The number of visitors to the Czech capital increased by 7.9% year-on-year to around 2.3 million. The number of overnight stays rose by 7.2% to 5.3 million. Compared to 2019, however, this amounts to 70.7% fewer guests and 71.6% fewer overnight stays (Czech Statistical Office, 2021). During 2022 5,976,267 guests arrived in collective tourist accommodation facilities in Prague. Guests from abroad accounted for 75% of the total. The remaining quarter were guests from other regions of the Czech Republic. A total of 13,370,616 overnight stays took place in Prague from January to December 2022, with foreign guests accounting for 10,775,889 (80.6%) of them. Compared to 2021, collective tourist accommodation establishments in Prague reported 8.11 million more overnight stays (154.3%) in 2022. In comparison to the successful year 2019, Prague lagged behind in 2022 with 25.7% of guests and 27.6% of overnight stays (Czech Statistical Office, 2023).

A new strategy of tourism development

Paradoxically, it was the COVID-19 pandemic that allowed a walk through Prague without crowds of tourists. The pandemic took away the key revenues for the local tourism sector, but also provided the opportunity to cultivate a new phase of tourism in Prague. As a result of the negative impact of the pandemic and given the new sustainable recovery, in 2020 Prague could approve of a new tourism strategy that should change tourism development in the city. The aim of the strategy was to achieve sustainable tourism development with an emphasis on the cultural heritage and the quality life of the Prague residents. Interests of the local residents, public spaces and destination should be taken care of more. Thus, the objective is to maintain a high quality of life in the capital city. The implementation plan had 67 project cards in five main areas: contributing to sustainability, addressing the negative impacts of tourism, improving access to culture and heritage, balancing tourism in the city centre and cultivating public spaces (Prague City Tourism, 2020).

Prague's new strategy for sustainable tourism development consists of the following key components:

Stakeholder collaboration The strategy emphasises collaboration between key stakeholders, including local residents, tourism organisations, government authorities and businesses with a view to ensuring a holistic approach to sustainable tourism development.

Destination management The strategy focuses on effective destination management by implementing measures such as visitor management systems, zoning regulations and monitoring mechanisms to balance the needs of tourists and residents while preserving the city's cultural and natural heritage.

Diversification of tourism offerings Prague aims to diversify its tourism offerings beyond the traditional popular attractions by means of promoting lesser-known areas, cultural experiences and sustainable outdoor activities. In this way, tourist flows can be distributed more evenly throughout the city.

Infrastructure and carrying capacity The strategy recognises the importance of investing in improvements in the local infrastructure, including transportation networks, waste management systems and public amenities. These measures can enhance overall visitor experience and support the city's carrying capacity.

Education and awareness The strategy includes initiatives to educate tourists, residents and tourism stakeholders about responsible and sustainable tourism practices, thus fostering a sense of responsibility and understanding among all participants in the tourism industry.

Monitoring and evaluation Prague's strategy emphasises the importance of ongoing monitoring and evaluation to assess the effectiveness of sustainable tourism initiatives, identify potential issues and make necessary adjustments to achieve the desired outcomes for local tourism development (Prague City Tourism, 2020).

First steps to implement the new sustainable strategy

In line with the new tourism strategy, Prague is trying to foster the development of more sustainable tourism. The following steps have been taken so far:

(1) Cultural sustainability

Prague has a new philosophy: cultural sustainability. The focus of the city is to present itself referring to the city's authenticity, local communities as well as the people and their stories and creativity. Prague has recognised the importance of cultural sustainability as a vital aspect of its overall sustainable tourism strategy. The city is trying to implement various measures to preserve and promote its rich cultural heritage while ensuring that tourism development aligns with the interests of local communities. Below we discuss some key elements of Prague's cultural sustainability strategy:

Heritage conservation and restoration Prague places great emphasis on the conservation and restoration of its cultural heritage. Historic buildings, landmarks and sites are protected and maintained to preserve the authenticity and historical value of the city. Strict regulations are in place to ensure that any restoration or renovation work is carried out in accordance with preservation guidelines.

Community involvement and empowerment Engaging local communities in tourism decision-making processes is seen as a crucial aspect of Prague's cultural sustainability strategy. Local residents are encouraged to actively participate in discussions, consultations and planning issues related to tourism development. Their insights and perspectives are valued, while efforts are made to ensure that their cultural interests and concerns are also taken care of.

Cultural education and awareness Prague recognises the importance of educating both tourists and locals about the city's cultural heritage. Educational initiatives, such as guided tours, exhibitions and workshops are organised to promote more understanding and appreciation of Prague's history, art, architecture and traditions. This helps to create a more informed and culturally sensitive visitor base.

Promotion of local arts and crafts Supporting and promoting local arts and crafts is a key element of Prague's cultural sustainability strategy. The city encourages the production and sale of authentic, locally-made crafts, such as traditional handicrafts, artwork and souvenirs. This helps sustain local cultural practices, provides economic opportunities for artisans and reduces the reliance on mass-produced and imported goods.

Festivals and cultural events Prague actively promotes and organises cultural festivals and events that celebrate its heritage. These place-based events showcase local traditions, music, dance and culinary specialties, offering visitors an authentic cultural experience while contributing to the preservation and promotion of Prague's unique identity.

Sustainable tourism practices Prague integrates cultural sustainability into broader sustainable tourism practices. This includes responsible tourism guidelines, such as encouraging respectful behaviour toward cultural sites, supporting local businesses and minimizing the environmental impact of tourism activities. By adopting sustainable practices, Prague aims to ensure the long-term preservation of its cultural heritage.

Tourism management and carrying capacity Prague's cultural sustainability strategy involves effective destination management and monitoring of tourist flows to prevent overcrowding and ensure a positive experience for both visitors and residents. Carrying capacity studies are conducted to determine the appropriate limits for visitor numbers in sensitive cultural areas in Prague, thus preventing overtourism and protecting the integrity of cultural sites.

By implementing these strategies, Prague aims to foster cultural sustainability, maintain the authenticity of its cultural heritage and ensure that tourism development respects and benefits local communities. These efforts should contribute to a more responsible and sustainable tourism industry that balances and reconciles the needs of visitors with the preservation of Prague's unique cultural identity (Prague.eu, 2023a).

(2) Campaign "Enjoy & Respect"

Prague has long been struggling with the negative impacts of incoming tourism, from short-term accommodation in apartments to disturbance of the night's rest to problems associated with various means of transport for tourists (e.g. e-scooters), which are definitely not suitable for the historic centre (Roncak, 2019). That is why Prague launched an awareness campaign called „Enjoy & Respect". The aim of this campaign was to inform and educate visiting tourists in a civil way that there are clear rules to follow, especially with regard to residents, in the historic centre. Banners of "Enjoy & Respect" still can be seen at Prague`s airport and in the city centre. The campaign includes a website "Enjoy & Respect" with ten recommendations for staying in the capital and promoting the idea of slow tourism. The ten points cover, for example, respecting Prague`s environment, its monuments and residents and the recommendation to use only licensed guides, visit Prague in low season, buy local products or use eco-friendly form of transport (Prague.eu, 2023b).

(3) Program "Visitis"

Prague puts great emphasis on data collection and analysis. As a base for a new dynamic tourism management system "Visitis", which is supposed to be launch at the end of 2023, Prague has decided to take an internationally unique approach to destination management and conducted extensive research on key source markets. The humanities part of the research provided specific narratives that connect the key markets with Prague and thus aim to get more insights into the deeper motivation of foreign tourists. The social science part of the research explored in detail the typology of tourists and their behaviour. Prague will use the findings of this research to strategically target more affluent tourists (Prague City Tourism, 2023). Prague City Tourism (PCT) will use the results of the humanities part of the research in digital marketing campaigns and in the development of a new destination website. The contents of this website will be individually tailored to visitors depending on the country they come from. The results of the research will also be taken into account in the development of new PCT products and services, such as tourist routes and local souvenirs. This system should help to bring about a better balance in tourism development in Prague (Prague City Tourism, 2023).

(4) Campaign "At Home in Prague"

The Covid-19 pandemic has taken away the key revenues for the Prague tourist sector, but has also provided the opportunity to turn Prague into a city that is attractive to Czech families (Roncak & Hobza, 2022). In 2020, Prague launched a campaign called "At Home in Prague" that focused on domestic tourists and on special tourist vouchers. The amount allocated in the tourist voucher project was 121 million CZK, which was spent by means of so-called 'carriers'. Anyone who stayed in Prague overnight received a 400 CZK carrier; these carriers were provided up to a maximum of four nights (ICOT.cz, 2020a). The vouchers were accepted in more than sixty Prague cultural and tourist sites, primarily in local contributory organisations, e.g. the zoo, the botanical garden, the Planetarium and the Prague Gallery and Museum. The purpose of the voucher system was to support Prague hotels, cultural institutions and monuments, restaurants and Prague guides.

According to Prague City Tourism, the campaign "At Home in Prague" attracted more than 70,000 tourists (ICOT.cz, 2020b). The economic benefit of the campaign in 2020 can be quantified based on the average amount per visitor spent (2,737 CZK), totalling more than 202 million CZK. The number of domestic tourists increased by 16% (Prague City Tourism, 2021a). Given the success of the campaign, the Prague City Hall in cooperation with Prague City Tourism repeated the campaign under the same conditions in 2021. In the second year of the campaign "At Home in Prague" more than 76,000 visitors were attracted to Prague during the summer, the majority from the Czech Republic. This led to an increase of domestic guest numbers by 45,4% compared to July and August 2019. The campaign helped Prague to become an attractive destination for domestic clients (Prague City Tourism, 2021b). In 2021, Prague was visited by 2,4 million visitors; 40% of them were domestic tourists. Obviously, the campaign played a role: it successfully motivated Czechs to come to Prague (Prague City Tourism, 2022).

There are several other new initiatives. The City of Prague approved that profits from tourism will go back into city development and the promotion of sustainable tourism. Furthermore, the new section "Sustainable Prague" on the website www.prague.eu offers a lot of practical tips for visitors how to behave sustainably in Prague, for example where to find sustainable accommodation, how to support local community or visit hidden gems of Prague (Prague.eu, 2023a). The City of Prague also introduced the Prague Visitor Pass and launched a nostalgic tram to maximise the quality of visitors' experience. Next, the Prague municipality has implemented procedures and regulations to address the impact of Airbnb and other short-term rental platforms on the city. These measures are taken with a view to managing the growth of Airbnb rentals, protecting the housing market and ensuring the sustainable development of tourism.

Finally, Prague tries to reduce the use of plastic. For example, if you attend one of the events on the Prague embankments or at the Holesovice Exhibition Centre, you will get a returnable cup when buying a drink. In its communication of sustainable tourism Prague has made great progress. Quite a number of aspects of sustainability and social responsibility are communicated, including environmental care, the protection of cultural heritage, the promotion of undiscovered neighbourhoods and putting emphasis on environmentally friendly transport and accommodation facilities that are socially responsible.

This focus on sustainable tourism has generated positive results. According to a survey among selected tourism stakeholders from the public and private sectors in 2022), 70% of these actors, after the approval of the new sustainable tourism strategy, could record positive changes towards sustainable tourism (Roncak,

2022). Positive aspects mentioned in the survey are among other things a focus on target groups that have a less negative impact on the quality of life of the city-dwellers, a greater effort to implement sustainable solutions and the creation of new sustainable tourism products.

Challenges in achieving sustainable tourism

Although Prague has successfully made first steps to implement sustainable tourism practices, there are still several challenges Prague has to deal with:

- lack of sustainable products and missing certification

- optimising tourism numbers and changing tourist behaviour

- balancing stakeholders' interests and communication problems

Below these issues will be discussed in more detail.

Lack of sustainable products and missing certification

Although Prague has improved its GDS sustainability score (from 39% in 2019 to 51% in 2022), it lags behind in comparison with top destinations and neighbouring competitors like Berlin and Vienna. In particular, Prague has large gaps in the sustainability and social responsibility of DMOs and suppliers. For instance, in 2022 the Czech capital received a score of 45% for the DMO's sustainability and social responsibility, while Gothenburg boasts 97% and Copenhagen 91%. The situation is similar for suppliers. There, Prague's rating is even lower (29%) compared to Gothenburg (87%) and Copenhagen (84%). Prague performs relatively well in the social sector. The implementation of the UN goals is as high as 80%. However, the rating in this area is significantly affected by the corruption acceptance index, which is 54% in Prague (Global Destination Sustainability Movement, 2023).

The number of sustainable certified hotels in Prague is still very low. The value of 16% of certified rooms presented for Prague in the GDS Index 2022 is represented mainly by the multinational chains' own programmes. Key initiatives include Accor's Planet 21, Holiday Inn's Green Engage and Hilton's ISO 14001 and Hilton Lightstay. Hotel Adria, located in the historic centre and with tradition dating back to 1912, presents itself as a Green Hotel. In the past, the hotel has received numerous awards such as the "EU Ecolabel Communication Award", "Wayaj" and "Green Manager". The prestigious "Green Key" certification is held just by the Hermitage Hotel Prague. Hotel Adalbert is a recipient of the "Eco-friendly Service" and "The Flower" awards. A number of other hotels boast sustainability certifications, such as the Mosaic House, Hotel Botanique, Hotel Plaza, the Metropolitan Old Town Hotel, Hotel Occidental and Hotel Jurys Inn. As these certifications have to be defended and renewed, it is hard to specify the exact number of hotel facilities with internationally recognised sustainability certifications. Prague can take an example from top socially responsible destinations such as Copenhagen or Gothenburg, where 54% and 68% of the local hotel rooms respectively are certified (Global Destination Sustainability Movement, 2023).

Optimising tourism numbers and changing tourist behaviour

Although Prague is planning to launch the new dynamic tourism management system Visitis, Deutsche Welle still identified the capital of the Czech Republic among the most crowded cities that "boast fantastic architecture and culture but attract so many tourists that locals are suffering" (Forbes, 2023). The key challenge for Prague in the coming years will be to balance the number of tourists and encourage tourists to adopt more responsible behaviour, such as respecting the needs of local residents. After a break caused by Covid-19, for the local residents short-time rentals and night's rest disturbances are still the biggest problems connected with tourism. Although research shortly after the pandemic indicated a change in travellers behaviour towards more sustainable travel (Booking.com, 2021), party tourism is returning to Prague. The centre of Prague was already under enormous pressure from tourism before the pandemic. Especially in the evening, at night and in the morning certain places (Dlouhá and adjacent streets, Karoliny Světlé, Karlova Street) were turning into party zones. Pub crawls as well as the rollout of accommodation platforms like Airbnb caused troubles for the local population. To manage problems concerning the night disturbances caused by tourists the City of Prague introduced a night mayor-position. But this position ended with the start of the pandemic (Metro.cz, 2023).

Balancing stakeholders' interests and communication problems

Like in any other destination, in Prague there are various stakeholders with different interests related to tourism. These stakeholders include local residents, tourists, businesses, local authorities and cultural heritage organisations. While tourism brings economic benefits, it can also create challenges and conflicts of interest among these stakeholders. Here are some specific problems concerning the different stakeholders and tourism interests in Prague:

(1) *Local residents*

a. Housing affordability: the influx of tourists has led to an increased demand for short-term rentals, which can drive up housing prices and reduce the availability of affordable housing for local residents.

b. Overtourism and crowding: overcrowding in popular tourist areas can disrupt the daily lives of residents, create noise and inconvenience, and lead to a sense of overcrowding and loss of community.

c. Cultural erosion: the commodification of culture and the dominance of tourist-oriented businesses can impact the authenticity of local neighbourhoods and result in the displacement of traditional businesses.

(2) Tourists

a. Crowded attractions: popular tourist attractions in Prague can become overcrowded, leading to long queues, limited access to attractions and a reduction of enjoyment for tourists.

b. Authenticity and cultural experience: some tourists may be concerned about the preservation of Prague's cultural heritage and the authenticity of their travel experiences, particularly if they perceive that tourism development is negatively impacting local traditions and landmarks.

c. Safety and security: tourists expect a safe and secure environment when visiting Prague, while issues related to crime, scams or safety concerns can affect their travel experience and perception of the destination.

(3) Businesses

a. Seasonality and financial stability: seasonal fluctuations in tourism demand can pose challenges for businesses, particularly smaller establishments, as they may struggle to maintain consistent revenue throughout the year.

b. Regulatory compliance: compliance with regulations, such as licensing requirements, zoning restrictions and taxation, can be a challenge for businesses operating in the tourism sector.

c. Competition and market saturation: the growth of the tourism industry in Prague has led to increased competition among local businesses, particularly in popular tourist areas, which can make it challenging for smaller businesses in the city to thrive.

(4) Local authorities

a. Balancing tourism growth and sustainability: local authorities in Prague face the challenge of managing the growth of tourism while ensuring sustainable development, preserving cultural heritage and protecting the quality of life for residents.

b. Infrastructure and transportation: meeting the infrastructure demands of a growing tourism industry, including transportation networks, waste management and public amenities, requires careful planning and investment.

c. Regulatory framework: establishing and enforcing regulations that strike a balance between supporting tourism development and mitigating negative impacts is a complex task for government authorities.

(5) Cultural heritage organisations

a. Preservation and conservation: cultural heritage organisations have a vested interest in preserving and conserving Prague's cultural heritage, and they may raise concerns if they perceive that tourism development is compromising the integrity or authenticity of cultural sites.

b. Access and visitor management: ensuring controlled and sustainable visitor access to cultural sites and managing visitor flows is a challenge to protect sensitive areas while allowing visitors to experience and appreciate Prague's cultural heritage (Prague.eu, 2023a).

The coordination of different views on tourism development is highly needed. Aligning the interests and expectations of various stakeholders, including residents, businesses, and tourists in Prague, may pose a challenge in implementing sustainable tourism practices. The author's research revealed obvious deficiencies in the coordination and communication of sustainable tourism towards various groups of tourism stakeholders in Prague (Roncak, 2022). Among the most crucial problems are communication problems and conflicts between the public and private sector, between the private sector and residents and between residents and tourists. According to representatives of Prague, the conflicts may be caused mainly by information and structural conflicts. Local authorities believe that stakeholders rely on incorrect information, which is why they do not know the real situation or are unable to assess it properly. An almost equally important reason may be a structural conflict, such as the fact that owners of real estate cannot limit the economic purpose of their buildings. In turn, residents face problems like troubles with the short-term rental of flats, high rents and the depopulation of buildings in the district.

A number of strategic documents of the City of Prague deal with sustainability and social responsibility. The overarching document is the "Strategic Plan", which presents Prague`s vision for the future (Strategicky plan, 2016). Other important documents include, for example the "Smart Prague Concept", the "Prague Climate Action Plan 2030" or "Circular Prague 2030". The Smart Prague Concept focusses on six key areas: mobility of the future, smart buildings and energy, waste-free city, attractive tourism, people and urban environment and data (Smart Prague Concept, 2018). However, for further development, it is essential that the individual documents complement each other and are applicable in practice. In other words: tourism must be a solid and integral part of the city's development. At the moment, a complex view is missing. In practice, idealism and pragmatism still have to be balanced. A more coordinated approach and mutual communication is required to meet the needs of the different parts of the city and the various tourism stakeholders. Implementation is key. To be sure, this issue is relevant in tourism planning in all places. According to international research, almost 50% of all strategic plans fails to be implemented in practice (Lai, 2006).

Conclusions

In this chapter we showed how Prague has made steps towards a more balanced tourism. Prague's new strategy for sustainable tourism development demonstrates a proactive approach with a view to addressing the challenges of overtourism and promoting responsible tourism practices by putting emphasis on stakeholder collaboration, destination management, infrastructure improvements and education. Prague aims to achieve a balance between tourism growth and the well-being of its residents, environment and cultural heritage. The city-dwellers generally support this focus on a more balanced tourism policy. According to a survey conducted by Czech Tourism in the summer of 2022, residents think that the positive impact of tourism (32%) still outweighs the negative impacts (16%). They also tend to support tourism development (33%) and prefer it above the option to limit tourism development (11%) (CzechTourism, 2023). At the same time, challenges such as stakeholder alignment, changing tourist behaviour and effective monitoring and enforcement need to be addressed to ensure the successful implementation of the strategy and the long-term sustainability of tourism in Prague. Addressing these problems requires stakeholder collaboration, effective communication and a balance between the economic benefits of tourism and the preservation of Prague's cultural and social sustainability. It is crucial for the city's authorities to engage with stakeholders, conduct comprehensive planning and implement sustainable tourism strategies that take into account the diverse interests and concerns of all the parties involved.

Literature

Booking.com (2021). *Sustainability travel report 2021*. Available at: https://www.sustainability.booking.com/industryinsights/2021-sustainability-report

Czech Statistical Office (2022). *Praha: prijezdovy cestovni ruch 2012–2021*. Available at: https://www.czso.cz/csu/xa/praha-prijezdovy-cestovni-ruch-2012-2021

Czech Statistical Office (2023). *Navstevnost hromadnych ubytovacich zarizeni hl. m. Prahy v roce 2022*. Available at: https://www.czso.cz/csu/xa/navstevnost-hromadnych-ubytovacich-zarizeni-hl-m-prahy-v-roce-2022

CzechTourism (2023). *Iritace rezidentu – prezentace vysledku*. Available at: https://tourdata.cz/data/tracking-domaciho-a-prijezdoveho-cr/iritace-rezidentu-prezentace-vysledku/

Deichmann, J. I. (2002). International tourism and the sensitivities of central Prague's residents. *Journal of Tourism Studies*, *13*(2), 41–52.

Dumbrovska, V. (2013). *Vyvoj postaveni Prahy: destinace cestovniho ruchu ve stredoevropskem prostoru* (unpublished bachelor's thesis). Prague: Charles University.

Dumbrovska, V. (2017). Urban tourism development in Prague: from tourist Mecca to tourist Ghetto. In N. Bellini & C. Pasquinelli (Eds.), *Tourism in the*

City: Towards an Integrative Agenda on Urban Tourism. Basel: Springer, 275-283.

Euromonitor International (2017). *WTM London 2017 edition. Top 100 City Destinations Ranking.* Available at: https://www.euromonitor.com/top-100-city-destinations-ranking-wtm-london-2017-edition/re%20port

European Commission (n.d.). *European Capitals of Culture.* Available at: https://ec.europa.eu/programmes/creative-europe/actions/capitals-culture_en

Forbes (2023). *Summer in Europe? Anti-tourists and over-touristed destinations.* Available at: https://www.forbes.com/sites/ceciliarodriguez/2023/05/28/summer-in-europe-anti-tourists-and-over-touristed-destinations-unveiled-by-experts/

Global Destination Sustainability Movement (2023). *GDS Index.* Available at: https://www.gds.earth/2022-results/

Hlaváček, P. (2016). *Strategicky plan hl. mesta Prahy.* Available at: https://iprpraha.cz/uploads/assets/dokumenty/ssp/SP/STRATE-GICKY_PLAN_HLAVNIHO_MESTA_PRAHY_AKTUALIZACE_2016.pdf

Hoffman, L. M. & J. Musil (1999). Culture meets commerce: tourism in post-communist Prague. In D. Judd & S. Fainstein (Eds.), *The Tourist City.* New Haven, CT: Yale University Press, 179–197.

ICOT.cz. (2020a). *Metropole spusti kampan buďte v Praze jako doma.* Available at: https://www.icot.cz/metropole-spusti-kampan-budte-v-praze-jako-doma/

ICOT.cz. (2020b). *Kampan V Praze jako doma bude prodlouzena.* Available at: https://www.icot.cz/kampan-v-praze-jako-doma-bude-prodlouzena/

Kljucnikov, A., Krajcik, V. & Z. Vincurova (2018). International sharing economy: the case of Airbnb in the Czech Republic. *Economics & Sociology, 11*(2), 126–137.

Lai, K., Li, Y., & X. Feng (2006). Gap between tourism planning and implementation: a case of China. *Tourism Management,* 27(6), 1171-1180.

Metro.cz (2022). *Nocni mejdany v centru jsou po covidove pauze zpet.* Available at: https://www.metro.cz/nocni-mejdany-v-centru-jsou-po-covidove-pauze-zpet-fwb-/praha.aspx?c=A220509_132807_metro-praha_peskk

Prague City Tourism (2020). *Koncepce prijezdového cestovního ruchu hl. mesta Prahy.* Available at: https://www.praguecitytourism.cz/file/edee/2020/11/koncepce-2020.pdf

Prague City Tourism (2021a). *More and more tourists are coming to Prague.* Available at: https://www.praguecitytourism.cz/en/media/press-releases/more-and-more-domestic-tourists-are-coming-to-prague-18291/

Prague City Tourism (2021b). *Prague kicks off the summer season with the At Home in Prague campaign.* Available at: https://www.praguecitytourism.cz/en/media/press-releases/prague-kicks-off-the-summer-tourist-season-with-the-at-home-in-prague-v-praze-jako-doma-campaign-17980/

Prague City Tourism (2022). *Prague City Tourism is launching its summer season with the At Home in Prague campaign.* Available at: https://www.praguecitytourism.cz/en/media/press-releases/prague-city-tourism-is-launching-its-summer-campaigns.-in-addition-to-international-travellers-these-will-also-appeal-to-domestic-visitors-to-prague-with-motiva-19027/

Prague City Tourism (2023). *Italové zjistí, je patronem Karlova mostu je sicilský chlapec a Korejci si myslí, ze Jan Zizka je zena. Prague City Tourism vyuziva vysledky humanitniho a spolecenskovedniho vyzkumu pro osloveni kultivovanych turistu.* Available at: https://www.praguecitytourism.cz/cs/media/tisk/italove-zjisti-ze-patronem-karlova-mostu-je-sicilsky-chlapec-a-korejci-si-mysli-ze-jan-zizka-je-zena.-prague-city-tourism-vyuziva-vysledky-humanitniho-a-spolece-19500

Prague.eu (2023a). *The official tourist website for Prague: sustainable Prague.* Available at: https://www.prague.eu/en/sustainable-prague

Prague.eu (2023b). *The official tourist website for Prague: enjoy respect Prague.* Available at: https://www.prague.eu/en/articles/enjoy-respect-prague-19277

Roncak, M. (2019). Prague and the impact of low-cost airlines. In R. Dodds & R.W. Butler (Eds.), *Overtourism: Issues, Realities and Solutions.* Boston: De Gruyter, 152-168.

Roncak, M., Scholz, P. & I. Linderova (2021). Safety concerns and travel behavior of Generation Z: case study from the Czech Republic. *Sustainability*, *13*(23), 13439.

Roncak, M. & V. Hobza (2022). The impact of the COVID-19 pandemic on the tourism industry in the Czech Republic. *e-Review of Tourism Research*, *19*(2), 261–279.

Roncak, M. (2022). *Survey: Prague – Tourism Friendly City*. Olomouc: Palacký University Olomouc.

Simpson, F. (1999). Tourist impact in the historic centre of Prague: resident and visitor perceptions of the historic built environment. *The Geographical Journal*, 165(2), 173–183.

Smart Prague concept. (2018). *Koncepce Smart Prague do roku 2030*. Available at: https://smartprague.eu/files/koncepce_smartprague.pdf

Chapter 6 - Columbus' egg or Trojan horse? Assessing the value of Cittaslow-membership to avoid local overtourism

Gert-Jan Hospers & Sebastian Amrhein

Introduction

One of the causes of overtourism is the herd behavior of tourists who are tempted by images they already know. For instance, many foreign tourists would never visit the Dutch water village of Giethoorn – beautiful as it is – on their own accord. That they do anyway is due to manipulation from the tourism industry through marketing, guidebooks and social media like Facebook, Twitter and Instagram. Mainstream tourists strive for the same picture taken by millions of tourists before them (Hospers, 2019). In turn, local entrepreneurs try to capitalise on visitors' expectations with tours, events and souvenirs. Take Giethoorn: because the canals in the village are photogenic (these days we might say 'instagrammable'), most tourists get into boats, resulting in huge crowds in the village centre. The result is a variant of the well-known 'Matthew-effect' that reinforces itself over time: tourist destinations that are already busy become even busier (Merton, 1968). Giethoorn is popular because it is popular.

Obviously, to avoid overtourism, a place can decide to stop promoting itself. Another option is 'de-marketing', i.e. explicitly discouraging potential visitors to come (Kotler & Levy, 1971). Paradoxically, however, this can actually be a reason for people to visit the place – after all, something one is not supposed to do arouses interest. In practice, therefore, we see some destinations engaging in 'selective de-marketing': target groups are segmented, excluding some (e.g. mass tourists) and inviting others (such as eco-tourists) to come (cf. Kotler & Levy, 1971). In marketing terms, places that are members of the Cittaslow-network – more on this later – engage in such selective de-marketing: through their positioning, they signal that they are no destinations for mass tourism, but places where 'slow' tourists will feel at home. In so doing, these destinations actually practice 'niche marketing': the choice of a specific target group makes them special and stand out amidst 'colourless' destinations. In principle, this could lead to 'overtourism of slow tourists' in a place. Is that what we intend?

In this chapter, we address the question of whether selective de-marketing is an appropriate means for towns to prevent overtourism. We do so by looking at the Cittaslow-network, an association of small cities focussing on the quality of life.

Is becoming a Cittaslow-member a genius idea ('Columbus' egg') or does a town (unsuspectingly) craft its own misfortune with it ('Trojan horse')? After describing the Cittaslow-philosophy, we explore this question from a theoretical point of view. Following this, we deal with three mini-case studies from practice and discuss the results. The chapter ends with conclusions.

Cittaslow as a 'glocal' movement

Cittaslow is an Italian invention that emerged in the well-known wine region of Chianti. Together with some colleagues, Paolo Saturnini, mayor of the town of Greve, founded the Cittaslow-network in 1999. The aim of the mayors was to apply the principles of Slow Food (a movement that since 1986 has asked for more appreciation of high quality food anchored in the local context) to the development of towns and villages. About a quarter of a century later, Cittaslow has developed into a global network of nearly 300 municipalities that promotes itself as an assocation of local communities 'where life is good' (Cittaslow, 2023). The members of the network – mostly small towns, villages or rural communities – strive for sustainable development by promoting a slower way of life, which is aptly symbolised by a logo showing a snail. Instead of blindly following trends like globalisation and economic growth, members of the Cittaslow-network declare to have an eye for local specificities, conscious living, sustainability and diversity. They emphasise the importance of their unique identity and the particular culture of the place in an increasingly homogenous world. According to the members, it is precisely the local roots that make places specific, distinctive and attractive.

The emphasis on local authenticity does not mean that Cittaslow-members are anti-global, conservative and backward looking. While it is true that the movement is sometimes seen as a form of 'mobilisation against globalisation' (Semmens & Freeman, 2012), it is better to frame it as a kind of 'indirect activism' (Pink, 2009). According to Servon and Pink (2015), Cittaslow is even a 'glocal movement' that combines the best of the global and the local. In this respect, the concept fits well into the current era, in which globalisation is progressing more slowly than previously due to successive crises (e.g. pandemics and rising energy prices) and structural developments (e.g. climate change). Thus regarded, Cittaslow is a highly modern concept. Radstrom (2011) already put it in plain and simple terms: "The slow in Cittaslow concerns the idea of taking the time for quality. However, residents of Cittaslow do not necessarily have a slower pace of life" (p. 95). But then, what does 'taking the time for quality' mean? Cittaslow Germany, which currently has 21 members, sums it up by referring to the networks' manifest on its website: "Cittaslow is a town inhabited by people curious about time found again, rich in places, theatres, shops, cafés, restaurants, places full of spirit, original landscapes, fascinating craftsmanship, where people still acknowledge the slow, enjoy the change of seasons, the authenticity of products and the spontaneity of customs, respect taste and health" (Cittaslow Deutschland, 2023, translation from German by GJH & SA).

In order to be included in the Cittaslow-network, municipalities must meet several requirements. To start with, the population of the place must not exceed the limit of 50,000. Furthermore, the locality in question must sign the Cittaslow Manifesto and pay a small annual registration fee. More importantly, however, is the obligation for the community to subscribe to the Cittaslow-philosophy. This consists of 72 requirements divided into the following seven categories, which can be seen as 'membership criteria' for Cittaslow (Bernat & Flaga, 2022):

(1) *Energy and environment* (e.g. sustainable water and waste policies, sufficient attention to energy conservation and consideration of biodiversity);

(2) *Infrastructure* (in particular the provision of sufficient space for pedestrians and cyclists as well as investment in sustainable logistics and eco-mobility);

(3) *Quality of urban life* (including appropriate consideration of public space, gardens/parks and green spaces where residents and visitors can recreate);

(4) *Agriculture, crafts and tourism* (with special attention to organic and artisanal products, local public catering services and the organisation of local events);

(5) *Hospitality, training and awareness* (including a welcoming culture, providing information and education as well as visibility of the Cittaslow-logo to residents and visitors);

(6) *Social cohesion* (for example, anti-discrimination and inclusion policies, with particular attention to people of migrant background, children and people with disabilities);

(7) *Partnerships* (for example, working with other actors at home and abroad – with a focus on developing countries – who are active in areas in the Cittaslow-domain).

For a town or village to be included in the Cittaslow-community, it must meet at least half of the above requirements whereby members are free to pay more attention to some categories than others (Bernat & Flaga, 2022). However, some criteria from the list are mandatory, such as a sustainable sanitation policy, a protection scheme for local crafts or the use of the network's logo on websites and in public spaces. Every five years an evaluation takes place where the Cittaslow Coordinating Committee checks whether the participating localities still meet the membership criteria.

Linking the Cittaslow-concept to (over)tourism: theory

Cittaslow does not only focus on one aspect of town or village development, such as the environment or cultural heritage. Based on the idea of 'taking the time for quality', it has a broader, more holistic view of a place. This means that the Cittaslow-concept encompasses numerous issues on the local level, from climate adaptation to a good work-life balance for residents. In addition, the tourism development of a place is considered in the concept. In the academic literature, a connection is immediately made to the topic of sustainable tourism. For instance, Ekinci (2014) considers the Cittaslow-criteria as a practical guide for towns and villages that aim to focus on sustainable tourism. According to him, global tourism would even get a huge sustainability boost if we simply encouraged places to join the Cittaslow-network (ibid.). Fallon (2021) also sees clear parallels between the discourse on sustainable tourism and the network when she writes: "The stated agenda for Cittaslow towns has much in common with the United Nations World Tourism Organization (UNWTO) 2017 One Planet Sustainable Tourism Programme, which is a set of guidelines that aims to drive sustainable change by 2030" (p. 278).

Also Presenza et al. (2015) regard Cittaslow-membership as a sensible method for local tourism governance. In their view, the concept can be helpful to safeguard the balance between a place's attractivity for tourists and its livability for residents. In their theoretical exploration of the linkages between Cittaslow and tourism, the authors identify two major advantages of the concept. On the one hand, the criteria set by the network are useful starting points for places that want to focus on quality tourism and develop 'good governance' in this field. The list of Cittaslow-criteria more or less 'forces' local stakeholders to have an eye on all relevant aspects that play a role in high-quality tourism development, be it hospitality, eco-mobility, local cultural heritage or arrangements for people with disabilities. This reduces the risk that the place slips into too much tourism, overcrowding and commercialisation. On the other hand, Cittaslow-membership gives towns and villages – that often lack the personal and financial resources that are available to bigger cities – access to knowledge, expertise and contacts that are useful to develop a long-term strategy on local tourism. Presenza et al. (2015) therefore conclude without reservations: "Cittaslow gives to the local government planning and managing tools helpful to govern the destination in a more sustainable manner" (p. 86).

Park and Kim (2016) point out another benefit of Cittaslow-membership, which is the involvement of the local community in tourism matters. If all goes well (and this is certainly not the case for all participating municipalities in the Cittaslow-network, as we shall see), a certified municipality involves its residents from the beginning and takes their ideas, concerns and wishes into account in order to arrive at good tourism policies. Any complaints from residents about nuisance from tourists will come to light immediately. In other words: there is no need for citizens to go to the streets to protest. According to Park and Kim, Cittaslow-membership can even enhance local community's empowerment for touristic purposes. They base this argument on field research in Goolwa (South-Australia). Their conclusion speaks volumes: "The results reveal that not only did Cittaslow-accreditation and its accompanying practices encourage local community participation in decision-making processes, but also revitalised the locality of Goolwa through promoting local specialities and products, in particular food and wine" (Park & Kim, 2016, p. 351).

Practice: three mini-cases from the Cittaslow-network

To analyse the extent to which the Cittaslow-philosophy is applied in practice and possibly be used to avoid the fear for overtourism, three mini-case studies follow. In selecting them, we have ensured that they differ in terms of geographical and cultural context, as well as in terms of the length of Cittaslow-membership and the focus chosen by the locality. As we are interested in a general impression rather than an in-depth study, we base our analysis on existing research, supplemented by looking at how places profile themselves on the web. Our desk research is thus a 'quick scan'; for a full picture, research on spot and interviews with locals would be required. One by one, we look at the Cittaslow-members Abbiategrasso (Italy), Vize (Turkey) and Berching (Germany).

Abbiategrasso (Lombardy, Italy)

The Italian town of Abbiategrasso has been a member of the Cittaslow-network since 2000, making it one of the 'pioneers'. Abbiategrasso is a town with about 32,500 inhabitants in the Lombardy region. Located some 25 kilometres southwest of Milan, it looks back on a rich history that is reflected in the castle, churches and villas in the old town centre. Abbiategrasso is surrounded by the green-blue expanses of the Po Valley (such as the Parco del Ticino) and is known for its farmhouses with a centuries-old agricultural tradition of grain and rice cultivation and the production of Gorgonzola cheese.

The results of the research by Hoeschele (2010) and Rushenova Salieva (2016) as well as our own desk research (2023) paint a largely consistent picture of the municipality: with the designation as Cittaslow, Abbiategrasso highlights its already existing features and wants to promote its local produce, among others for tourists. Already in 2000, it was not difficult for the locality to meet the Cittaslow-criteria. From the beginning, Abbiategrasso has focused on further raising awareness of Slow Food, for example by designating locations to sell local food and drinks in the town centre, and providing promotional materials to participating shops and also by drawing international attention to its local specialities to diversify the sales markets. Local producers, such as Marco Gelmini, a Gorgonzola cheese-maker, apparently appreciate this intention. Gelmini stated in an interview with *The Independent* in 2010, "It's very important for us, because we have a niche product that needs to be promoted outside the country and the European Union, to win market share while safeguarding the product's artisanal nature" (The Independent, 2010). To generate income for the community as well as to finance further development projects, tourists have also been an important target group since the beginning. In the same article, the then mayor's deputy Valter Bertani noted, "Being a slow city can help us develop tourism" (ibid.).

To be sure, this interview took place in 2010. What has happened around Cittaslow in Abbiategrasso since then? Research by Rushenova Salieva (2016) and our own investigation indicates that the label is primarily being used for marketing purposes, but not in a systematic way. When Abbiategrasso refers to its Cittaslow-membership, there is usually a focus on 'slow food'. While some projects have been launched over the years in public space (e.g. guidelines for shops to offer their products outdoors or the promotion of cycling as a means of transport), there is no sign of Cittaslow being employed as a systemic compass for the town's development in which the residents have a say by means of participation. It rather depends on the local political officials on whether or not they think it is important to use the network during their term of office, as Rushenova Salieva (2016) notes. Due to the relative openness of Cittaslow in terms of its application, this creates the risk that local decision-makers will adapt the concept to their personal preferences. A case in point is the organisation of Cittaslow-events in Abbiategrasso: they have taken place irregularly, sometimes with many years in between.

Vize (Marmara, Turkey)

Vize is a Turkish town with a population of slightly more than 12,000 inhabitants. It is located about an hour and a half's drive from Istanbul in the Marmara region, not far from the border with Bulgaria. The town advertises its history, which it says dates back to about 4,000 BC when it used to be a significant town. Also in the Byzantine Empire and the Ottoman period Vize was an important place. Evidence of its past includes the small Hagia Sophia Church (which was converted into a mosque), a castle, an amphitheatre and a bathhouse. The surrounding area of Vize is characterised by waterfalls, caves and fertile land. In Turkey, Vize is known for its many lime trees and honey that is produced by hand.

Traditionally, agriculture provided many employment opportunities in Vize. When this sector shrank at the beginning of the 21st century, more and more residents went to work in the two neighbouring towns of Cerkezkoy and Corlu, where the textile industry has traditionally been an important employer. In 2010, the regional development agency pointed the municipality of Vize to Cittaslow as an interesting way to revitalise the local economy (Hatipoglu, 2015). The mayor at the time was looking for ways to stop the exodus of young people from the municipality and to create entrepreneurial opportunities for women. After introducing measures that focused on some important Cittaslow-criteria, Vize received the longed-for membership in the international network in 2012.

The town has mainly focused on the development of 'slow tourism'. Since the beginning of its membership, Vize has been working on the implementation of the Cittaslow-philosophy, for which mainly municipal politicians acted as catalysts. Attracting tourists has been an important element from the beginning. Examples of projects that have been carried out are the restoration of cultural heritage, the establishment of courses for training in old craft practices, the organisation of gastronomic festivals and tourism marketing. Vize takes advantage of its border location, for example, by bringing Turkish and Bulgarian cooks together and letting them exchange traditional recipes. Thus, tourists are encourages to have a look beyond the border. There are also financial reasons for this: many projects are funded by the EU's cross-border partnership programme.

Hatipoglu (2015) concludes that the population is satisfied with the changes that Cittaslow has brought about in Vize. The number of tourists has increased, but is limited and does not affect the local identity and culture. According to Güleç and Şahinalp (2022), this still seems to be the case today – in contrast to some other Turkish places where Cittaslow-membership actually hurts the 'genius loci' (spirit of the place) through the influx of tourists. For instance, the authors note, "In other cities such as Vize and Yalvaç that attract relatively few tourists and possess a historical-cultural identity, the traditional food and beverage culture has not been affected adversely" (Güleç & Şahinalp, 2022, p. 16). However, their research also revealed that communication with the local population about the principles and the aims of Cittaslow remains a challenge. Many residents in Turkish Cittaslow-membership towns and villages are not aware of the concept or simply see it as a tool to give the local tourism sector a boost.

Berching (Bavaria, Germany)

In the Altmühltal Nature Park (Bavaria) lies Berching, one of the oldest towns in the region. The municipality, about 60 km from Nuremberg, has about 9,000 inhabitants and within its borders counts not only a core town but also many small villages. A local landmark is the Berching town wall from the 15th century. The centre with its old houses, squares and streets evokes a medieval atmosphere. Berching contains three parks and lies on the Main-Danube Canal. The surrounding area is close to nature, while centuries-old cultural traditions are kept alive. The area is popular with tourists from Germany and abroad, especially because of the good opportunities for cycling (e.g. the Altmühltal Cycling Route), hiking, relaxing and family holidays. However, it is not a destination for mass tourism.

The desire to maintain and strengthen these local qualities through an overarching concept was an important reason for the municipality to apply to Cittaslow and join the network (Sept, 2021). In 2013, the municipality was awarded the Cittaslow-membership, of which it remains proud, as shown by the wide coverage of the predicate on the municipal website (www.berching.de). The Cittaslow-snail also appears on several posters and signs in the townscape of Berching, e.g. to remind pedestrians of the value of 'slow living'. Some local catering establishments have adopted Slow Food, including a hotel, the local monastery and an inn that explicitly focuses on 'slow brewing'.

Another tangible result of the Cittaslow-membership in Berching is the development of so-called 'Slow Spots' in 2017. These are rest areas in and around the town that are located away from busy roads and paths. At these spots, residents and visitors are to find themselves in the 'here and now', be inspired and mentally recharge. The Slow Spots initiative stems directly from the Cittaslow-accreditation, as Sept (2021) found out during her interviews in Berching. She also detected that the Cittaslow-predicate motivated the municipality to refrain from carrying out a set of planning measures. For example, local politicians have decided, with reference to Cittaslow, that certain plots of land in Berching may not be built on. In addition, the municipality claims that the conferences organised annually by the network have led to inspiration and learning effects (Sept, 2021). In other words: Cittaslow offers Berching the opportunity to gain new ideas.

When it comes to tourism, Berching takes advantage of Cittaslow. Berching's tourism website refers to it as follows: "Cittaslow - not slow, just less hectic. The chosen motto of the Cittaslow-movement reflects many things that have been important to the people of Berching for centuries" (Berching, 2023). This philosophy is reflected in the local tourism offer, which is divided into the categories of 'culture and identity', 'regional identity', 'living history', 'hospitality' and 'characteristic cultural landscape'. Interestingly, this positioning with 'less hectic' seems to pay off in the tourist sector. For example, under the headline 'Off the beaten track', a bike holiday company offering package tours in the Altmühltal (with lodging for the travellers in Berching), the town is promoted as: "Away from the hustle and bustle of the big cycle paths, you will find a gem of peace and tranquility in Berching" (Donau Touristik, 2023, p. 51).

Confronting theory with practice

The three mini-case studies paint a mixed picture of the value of Cittaslow to avoid local overtourism. On the one hand, the Cittaslow-label allows members to highlight local priorities. With the tangible logo of the snail, abstract issues such as sustainability, quality of life and slow tourism are made concrete and visible to residents and visitors. Although Cittaslow has not guided long-term local policy in any of the cases mentioned, it has played a role in policy-making (tourism in Vize), refraining from them (no building on a plot in Berching) or confirming existing practices (Abbiategrasso). Moreover, Cittaslow still seems to have close ties to the movement from which the network emerged, namely Slow Food: in all three mini-case studies, attention for slow food plays a role in putting the Cittaslow-philosophy into practice, for example to inspire entrepreneurs to do so (Abbiategrasso) or to attract tourists (Vize). Finally, the view of Berching is interesting: by sharing experiences with other members, there is a learning effect for the town and it does not need to reinvent the wheel itself.

On the other hand, we can also see how much the application of the Cittaslow-philosophy depends on the enthusiasm of individual local authorities. When these decision-makers are no longer in office, attention to the brand can also dwindle or priorities are adjusted, as the example of Abbiategrasso shows. This also points directly to the importance of structurally anchoring Cittaslow in the municipal organisation, which seems not to be the case in any of the three communities we discussed. It is also striking that despite the potential holistic nature of the Cittaslow-concept and the possibilities it offers for participatory decision-making and involvement of the local community, the resulting actions are rather fragmented and top-down. This comprises for instance the irregular organisation of festivals (Abbiategrasso), the application for euregional funding to bring together chefs from across the border to exchange recipes (Vize) and the creation of 'slow spots' in the municipality where people can relax and that may help to relieve the pressure in the town centre (Berching). The places we looked at are thus missing out on opportunities that the literature on Cittaslow points to.

The Vize and Berching cases also highlight what the literature on de-marketing and Cittaslow warns against (Radstrom, 2011; Güleç & Şahinalp, 2022): Cittaslow-accreditation with its associated logo enables a place to distinguish itself from surrounding areas. This distinctive profile may attract new visitor groups and thus lead to more rather than less tourism. In the cases of Vize and Berching, the inhabitants do not seem to mind (yet). In other Cittaslow-member cities, however, there are concerns that the increasing arrival of tourists might have negative impacts on the quality of life of the inhabitants, as Hoeschele (2010), Semmens and Freeman (2012) or Hatipoglu (2015) point out. Hence, awarding a town the Cittaslow-certificate can have the opposite effect, resulting in increasing tourism demand. Although no signs for this can be found so far in our three mini-cases, the marketing activities of the places do not indicate that this risk is taken seriously, let alone that they are prepared for coping with overtourism.

Cittaslow provides its members opportunities to learn from experiences elsewhere at low cost: after all, they can fall back on an international network with a lot of knowledge, expertise and contacts (Presenza et al., 2015). Learning is great, but at the same time Cittaslow-members usually have to raise their own financial resources to realise their ambitions. Often, however, the places are too small and budget-wise unable to achieve all their goals within the seven categories (e.g. energy or infrastructure) that Cittaslow International demands. It is also not self-evident that all local parties are enthusiastic about the label. Business owners, for example, might fear that the snail logo could create a negative image: as if the locality does not want to move forward and take a step back into the past!

These are all points that show how important it is for Cittaslow-members to engage the local community in the whole process, from the phase of application for the accreditation to its implementation. If a town or village is to take full advantage of the benefits of Cittaslow-membership for a balanced form of tourism development and local empowerment, then involving residents from the start is essential (Park & Kim, 2016). This is precisely where the shoe often wrings in practice. In none of the cases examined, it could be established that residents have an important voice in Cittaslow. If there is any contact between the initiators and the local population at all, it is usually limited to communication about what the Cittaslow-concept is. In short: localities that are or want to become 'Cittaslow' should realise that making use of the accreditation is not a 'one-(wo)man' show, but a play with many acts and actors on the stage.

Conclusions

In this chapter, we raised the question of whether it makes sense for a town or village to be part of the international Cittaslow-network to avoid the risk of overtourism. Is Cittaslow-membership a Columbus' egg or rather a Trojan horse? Let us start by saying that the answer is not straightforward and strongly depends on the different prerequisites of the members – it is a highly place-specific issue, requiring thorough research on the spot. In line with the philosophy of Cittaslow to put emphasis on the desires and needs of the local population, we should add to this that such an on-site analysis should notably involve residents as those stakeholders who are directly affected by tourism. Therefore, the findings of the mini-cases in this chapter are only a first step in answering the question of whether Cittaslow can be a useful instrument against overtourism.

With this caveat in mind, we argue that Cittaslow-membership might be a Columbus' egg for towns or villages preventing overtourism. However, this requires that local decision-makers take the concept seriously, focus on the well-being and needs of the local population and are aware of the risk that it – due to its distinctive profile – might lead to more rather than less tourism. If these conditions are met, we see Cittaslow as a promising concept. Moreover, the mini-case studies show that the approach offers opportunities to reduce the risks of overcrowding. For example, setting up 'slow spots' outside the town centre (example Berching) or promoting cross-border culinary tourism (example Vize) can help to 'spread' tourists. But possibly there is already a self-correcting effect among the target group. Because if there is one thing 'slow tourists' dislike, it is crowds and nuisance – they will automatically start looking for quiet places, thus avoiding overtourism. The question is, of course, whether one wants it to get that far at all.

Literature

Berching (2023), *Berching ist eine Cittaslow-Stadt* [Online]. Available at: www.berching.de

Bernat, S. & Flaga, M. (2022). Cittaslow as an alternative path to town development and revitalization in peripheral areas: the example of Lublin province. *Sustainability, 14*, 14160.

Cittaslow Deutschland (2023). *Cittaslow: das internationale* Netzwerk [Online]. Available at: https://www.cittaslow.de/

Donau Touristik (2023). *Trauni's Radferien International: Europa's schönste Radwege entdecken*. Linz/Donau: Donau Touristik.

Ekinci, M. (2014). The Cittaslow philosophy in the context of sustainable tourism development: the case of Turkey. *Tourism Management, 41*, 178-189.

Güleç, M. & Şahinalp, M.S. (2022). Slow city inhabitants' attitudes toward the Cittaslow status. *Coğrafya Dergisi/Journal of Geography, 45*, 15-32.

Hallon, J. (2021). Feelin' Groovy: exploring slow(ness) in tourism experience. In R. Scharpley (Ed.), *Routledge Handbook of Tourist Experience* (pp. 274-285). London: Routledge.

Hatipoglu, B. (2015). "Cittaslow": quality of life and visitor experiences. *Tourism Planning & Development, 12*(1), 20-36.

Hoeschele, W. (2010). Measuring abundance: the case of Cittaslow's attempts to support better quality of life. *International Journal of Green Economics, 4*(1), 63-81.

Hospers, G.J. (2019). Overtourism in European cities: from challenges to coping strategies. *CESifo Forum, 20*(3), 20-24.

Kotler, Ph. & Levy, S. (1971). Demarketing, yes, demarketing. *Harvard Business Review, 49*, 74-80.

Merton, R.K. (1968). The Matthew Effect in science. *Science, 159*(3810), 56-63.

Park, E. & Kim, S. (2016). The potential of Cittaslow for sustainable tourism development: enhancing local community's empowerment. *Tourism Planning & Development, 13*(3), 351-369.

Pink, S. (2009). Urban social movements and small places: slow cities as sites of activism. *City, 13*(4), 451-465.

Presenza, A., Abbate, T. & Micera, R. (2015). The Cittaslow Movement: opportunities and challenges for the governance of tourism destinations. *Tourism Planning & Development, 12*(4), 479-488.

Radstrom, S. (2011). A place-sustaining framework for local urban identity: an introduction and history of Cittaslow. *Italian Journal of Planning Practice, 1*(1), 90-113.

Rushenova Salieva, G. (2016). *Cittaslow: fluctuating between improvement and commodification of 'quality of life'. Two case studies: Abbiategrasso and Seferihisar*. Milan: Politecnico di Milano.

Semmens, J. & Freeman, C. (2012). The value of Cittaslow as an approach to local sustainable development: a New Zealand perspective. *International Planning Studies, 17*(4), 353-375.

Sept, A. (2021) 'Slowing down' in small and medium-sized towns: Cittaslow in Germany and Italy from a social innovation perspective. *Regional Studies, Regional Science. 8*(1), 259-268.

Servon, L. & Pink, S. (2015). Cittaslow: going glocal in Spain. *Journal of Urban Affairs, 37*(3), 327-340.

The Independent (2010). *Abbiategrasso, a 'slow' town in Milan's backyard. The Independent*, 2. October 2010 [Online]. Available at: https://www.independent.co.uk/travel/news-and-advice/abbiategrasso-a-slow-town-in-milan-s-backyard-2095927.html

Chapter 7 - Exploring tourism workers' perspective on transformational job policies: the case of Barcelona

Moritz Langer

Introduction

At the beginning of the COVID-19 pandemic, there was a general hope in society as well as in academia that the pandemic hiatus could serve as an impulse for some kind of rethinking of our relationship with the environment. The forced halt due to the pandemic highlighted the need to abandon the destructive path that Western societies in particular had embarked upon in their pursuit of increasing economic growth and prosperity. As so often in human history, massive crises had provided the occasion for transformative change (Brouder, 2020). So maybe the hope for a turnaround was not groundless. Perhaps it was the time now to initiate the much-needed socio-ecological transformation that would bring our economy back within planetary boundaries?

With reference to tourism, it can nevertheless be observed now that the anticipated turn towards sustainability in our society has mostly not taken place. In many places, tourism-specific indicators are already at pre-pandemic levels and a path-dependent response to the crisis is evident. The pandemic highlighted the dependencies and lack of alternatives to tourism that prevail in many destinations. Hence the question arises how to break up these dependencies and the associated locked-in growth path of the sector. The degrowth discourse is a growth-critical theory that has generated more and more attention in recent years, due to the impossibility of continuing the current tourism model.

Degrowth in tourism can be defined as a deliberate transition in tourist destinations and their local economies to stop the overexploitation of resources as well as their overproduction respectively overconsumption. The aim is to bring the tourism system back into the given planetary boundaries through responsible and fulfilling, slow and low-carbon travel (Andriotis, 2018). Leading degrowth researchers (Hickel et al., 2022) called for a new research agenda particularly seeking to identify and address growth dependencies on a sector-by-sector basis. Durand et al. (2023) at this point recognise strikingly little research on what planning for degrowth would actually look like. Only through engaging with the question on how to break up path dependencies rooted in neoliberal growth oriented economies, it will be able to proceed towards a sustainable degrowth transition.

The aim of this chapter is to add value to the tourism degrowth debate by elucidating the often neglected perspective of tourism workers regarding their situation on the labour market and the resulting demands and proposals for change. For this purpose, through a focus group with nine tourism workers from Barcelona, the current situation is analysed and furthermore discussed. The aim is to determine to what extent different popular policy proposals (universal basic income, working time reduction, economic democracy, job guarantee) being debated in progressive agendas, including the degrowth debate, influence the situation of workers and thus potentially pave the way for a sustainable transformation of the tourism industry.

The contribution of this chapter lies in the added value to the degrowth debate regarding the lack of research on planning instruments (Durand et al., 2023), an extension to the path creation concept in Evolutionary Economic Geography (Hassink et al., 2019) and the establishment of a necessary constructive dialogue between the workers' voices and the degrowth literature (Barca, 2017). The results outline that the workers find themselves in an exploitative system, rooted in neo-colonial capitalist practice, which reproduces a process of precarising predominantly female and migrant labour even more since the beginning of the COVID-19 pandemic. To improve the situation on the labour market, the workers endorse all of the discussed policy programs, but seemingly favour bottom up initiatives for empowerment like a strengthening of economic democracy, simply because the trust in institutions and governmental structures implementing top down policies is lacking.

Literature review

Path dependence and path creation are key concepts within Evolutionary Economic Geography (EEG), which is one of the most prominent research areas in the last ten years in the field of economic geography (Boschma & Frenken, 2011; Hassink et al., 2019; Martin & Sunley, 2006). While path dependency is defined as forms of development that are rooted in the past and have limited capacity for change (Anton Clavé & Wilson, 2017), discourses supporting a shift from the past are being explained under the term 'path creation' (Karnøe & Garud, 2012). Nielsen et al. (1995, p. 7) theorise that 'within specific limits, social forces can redesign the board on which they are moving and reformulate the rules of the game'. Garud and Karnoe (2012) add to this theorisation and characterise path creation as anthropogenic agency or event-centred interventions, which modify path-dependent trajectories and thus influence them. Path creation can occur through, inter alia, policy measures, political and social movements, collaboration and entrepreneurial innovation-led mechanisms (Martin & Sunley, 2006). The relationship between path-dependent forces and path-creating forces is delineated as continuous (Williams, 2013). Gáspár (2011) considers this interaction as "the bonds that tie the present to the past and to the future" (p. 94).

The focus within tourism research has been the analysis of potentially negative outcomes of path dependence in mature destinations with high tourism dependency to avoid future regional ruination (Brouder et al., 2017; Wilkinson et al., 2022). The concept of path creation on the other hand has been used to assess the transformative evolutionary trajectories in tourism destinations. One example is the analysis of agency driven processes towards sustainability in Whistler, a ski resort municipality in British Columbia (Canada). Gill & Williams (2011; 2014) illustrate how the involvement of the local community in the decision to establish affordable resident-restricted housing in the aftermath of the 2010 Winter Olympic and Paralympic Games pushed a transition in governance from growth-orientation to principles of sustainability.

Hassink et al. (2019) called to rethink critical research on path creation and follow up upon new research strands. EEG analysis has primarily been dealing with firm-level processes and hence also firm-level agency (Boschma & Frenken, 2011). In order to include influences outside of the institutional and organizational limits of firms, Hassink et al. (2019) argue for a broadening of the scope of study to include the system-level agency of a wider range of actors, such as policy actors and the state. This adds to a general critique of EEG neglecting the role of the social and institutional environment of economic activities (Henning et al., 2013; Pike et al., 2016), while also not incorporating potentially influential exogenous sources, such as national and supranational policies and regulations (Dawley et al., 2015; Martin & Sunley, 2006).

Due to the identified lack of conceptual and empirical research evaluating these facets, this chapter contributes to the further development of the path creation literature. By doing so, it broadens the analytical scope of path creation research beyond firms as relevant actors and discusses the potential that selected labour policies could have as path-creating factors for a sustainable future in the tourism industry. The chapter particularly and explicitly includes the perspective of the tourism industry's workers and strives to foster a necessary constructive dialogue between the workers' voices and the degrowth concept (Barca, 2017).

Degrowth policy proposals generally pay attention to three main goals (Cosme et al., 2017). The focus is on (1) reducing the environmental impact of the economy, (2) creating more justice through a redistribution process of wealth within and between nations and (3) fostering the transition towards a participatory society of care and conviviality. Degrowth policies targeting the field of work essentially aim for a de-prioritisation of wage labour, the reduction of unemployment, a redistribution of productive activities towards care and volunteer work as well as the promotion of social and ecologically meaningful jobs (Fitzpatrick et al., 2022). The four selected policy features addressed in this chapter are universal basic income, working time reductions, economic democracy and job guarantee. The choice for these aspects had been made because they are frequently outlined and cited within the degrowth literature (Hickel et al., 2022). According to Fitzpatrick et al. (2022) they belong to the ten core policy instruments of a degrowth transformation and as such can be seen as central elements to realise a degrowth vision[1]. Let us have a closer look at the selected four policy features.

A universal basic income (UBI) is generally understood as a state-led programme in which every citizen receives an unconditional income, sufficient to cover one's basic needs, on a regular basis (Birnbaum, 2016). People no longer need to work to meet their fundamental necessities because of the UBI, but everyone is still free to choose to engage in income-generating activities (Mayrhofer & Wiese, 2020). With the implementation of a UBI poverty and economic insecurity will almost be eradicated (D'Alisa et al., 2015), hence fostering more egalitarian and happier societies (Pickett & Wilkinson, 2010). The wealth redistribution induced by UBI could also lead to environmental benefits, as research shows that income inequality and environmental degradation are highly interlinked (Wiedmann et al., 2020). Additionally, it creates a pathway to more fulfilling jobs, as workers would improve their bargaining power regarding the negotiation of their working conditions, by being less dependent on paid employment (D'Alisa et al., 2015). This aspect might also contribute to higher engagement in environmentally and socially beneficial non-profit oriented work (Birnbaum, 2009).

Work time reductions (WTR) refer to measures that reduce total spent working hours at constant or higher income levels. This can result in shorter working weeks and an increase in the minimum number of holiday days per year. It can also strengthen rights towards maternity and paternity leave and rights to reduce working hours (e.g., for care-work), and earlier retirement policies (Pullinger, 2014). Increased productivity (Bourlès & Cette, 2006), a better work-life balance that enables people to participate more in welfare-enhancing activities (Albertsen et al., 2008) and a decrease in involuntary and structural unemployment through work sharing are among the key advantages of cutting down on time spent in wage labour (Schor, 2015). WTR regulations are additionally getting more attention as a useful way to decrease carbon emissions and overall environmental pressure (Fitzgerald et al., 2018; Kallis et al., 2013).

Johanisova and Wolf (2012) define economic democracy (ED) as "a system of checks and balances on economic power and support for the right of citizens to actively participate in the economy regardless of social status, race, gender, etc." (p. 564). The goal of ED policies is thus a redistribution of control over firms basically from shareholders to a larger group of stakeholders, particularly the workers (Archer, 1995). There are various types of ED, all of which aim to democratize power and control over procedures, decisions and working conditions within an organization, as well as the mission, objectives and operational course of the company (Cumbers et al., 2020). Cooperatives, social enterprises, worker-

---

[1] The other elements within the ten core policy instruments are: setting maximum income caps, declining caps on resource use and emissions, holding deliberative forums, reclaiming the commons, establishing ecovillages and setting up housing cooperatives (Fitzpatrick et al., 2022).

managed private and public businesses or worker-owned businesses are ED examples that can be observed in practice. The most frequently outlined benefits of ED are a reduction of inequality within contemporary societies (Cumbers, 2018; Johanisova & Wolf, 2012), more resilient and economically stable organisations (Mayrhofer & Wiese, 2020), higher quality of life among the workers (ESS, 2016) and a general strengthening of democracy (Timming & Summers, 2020). Furthermore, it is argued that ED might have environmental benefits as, unlike capitalist firms operating within the growth imperative, economic-democratic firms are likely to incorporate sustainability more in their decision-making processes (Gunderson, 2019).

The job guarantee (JG) is a permanent, federally funded and locally administered policy program through which the government offers voluntary employment opportunities for everybody of legal working age, regardless of his or her labour market status, race, sex, colour or creed, who is willing to work at a living wage (Tcherneva, 2018). Although the state funds the jobs and related projects, their administration is decentralized, local and democratic in order to address the needs and characteristics of the local communities (Tcherneva, 2018). JG should especially be applied in fields that are not sufficiently covered by the private sector, such as care work, social community services, environmental community development and setting-up renewable infrastructure installations (Fitzpatrick et al., 2022). Key strengths of JG are the elimination of involuntary unemployment and its function as a macroeconomic stabilization and inflation control tool (Tcherneva, 2018). It might also be an instrument to mobilise labour towards urgent social and ecological objectives (Hickel et al., 2022).

Research context

Barcelona is one of the world's leading urban tourism destinations. It is estimated that the tourism sector contributes 14% percent to the local GDP (Ayuntamiento de Barcelona, 2023b) and has a share of about nine per cent of all employment (Ayuntamiento de Barcelona, 2023a). Before the outbreak of the COVID-19 pandemic, with the city experiencing severe overtourism symptoms, the governance of urban tourism was heavily discussed (Blázquez-Salom et al., 2019; Mansilla & Hughes, 2021; Milano et al., 2019). There is growing acknowledgement that neoliberal organised and growth-driven tourism management such as in the case of Barcelona leads to precarious jobs and deteriorating working conditions (Bianchi & Man, 2021). Notwithstanding, extensive engagement with tourism employment – and the associated marginalised situation of many tourism workers regarding the involvement in decision-making – is still lacking in the field of tourism research (Cañada, 2018; Walmsley et al., 2022).

This chapter assesses the situation of tourism workers in Barcelona and explores their perspectives with regard to potentially path creating policy instruments that would fundamentally affect the whole labour market. In this respect it applies the empowerment concept understood as 'a multidimensional, context-dependent, and dynamic process that provides humans, individually or collectively, with greater agency, freedom, and capacity to improve their quality of life as a function of engagement with the phenomenon of tourism' in the analysis (Aghazamani & Hunt, 2017, p. 343). According to Scheyvens (1999) a distinction should be made between economic, psychological, social and political forms of empowerment, respectively disempowerment, referring to the lack of participation in decision making or governance, to assess the path creation potential of the presented policy instruments.

Materials and methods

So far tourism geography research has mostly neglected the views and perceptions of workers on potentially transformative national and supranational policies and regulations (Cañada, 2018). Focus groups are a particular promising methodological access to get insight in the viewpoints of workers on this issues. Through the diversity of perspectives involved in the focus group, patterns, commonalities and different social and psychological dimensions among the participants can be identified. The method therefore contributes to a comprehensive and deep understanding of the researched issue and involved processes.

In the study we carried out in Barcelona, the composition of the participants of the focus group followed the principle of purposive sampling, aiming for a group, characterised by homogeneity in terms of circumstances of employment, insofar as there are no hierarchies or power imbalances within the group, but diversity in terms of sociodemographic attributes, opinions, personal backgrounds (Patton, 2015). The focus group that forms the empirical basis of this research took place on 24.08.2022 in Barcelona. It was conducted in Spanish. Subsequently the transcript was translated by the author. Participants were nine tourism workers from different employment fields (kitchen work, cleaning, hospitality, night life, events, and retail) and employed by different companies. The group constellation reflected the predominant female and migrant workforce in the Spanish tourism sector (Cañada & Izcara, 2022), insofar as eight out of nine participants were female and six out of nine participants did not have the Spanish nationality, but had a Brazilian (2x), Colombian, Ecuadorian, Peruvian or Belgian background. The analysis of the data followed an inductive approach with an open coding process. This was supported by the usage of the qualitative data analysis software tool MAXQDA to guarantee rigour by enhancing validity, transparency and credibility.

Results of the focus group research

The following sections discusses broadly the current situation of the workers, as well as the demands and necessary changes that arise out of the context they are confronted with. In particular, we pay attention to the different forms of psychological, social, political and economic disempowerment being experienced, respectively empowerment the workers are seeking.

Situation of the tourism workers

The psychological situation experienced by the participants in the focus group is characterized by fear and uncertainty regarding the continuity of their work, which is reinforced through the COVID-19 crisis. Furthermore, the workers experience an increasing overload of work and stress at the work place, coupled with a lack of empathy and valorization towards their work from customers and employers. Finally, the participants report that the organisation of the workers has resumed after the pandemic break. They take up the fight again to claim their rights and improving the working conditions in the sector.

To confront the social forms of disempowerment experienced by the workers, they are calling for the imperative of a migrant and feminist perspective. Such a transformation is needed, they say, to deal with racism and discrimination issues with which they have to cope in their daily professional life. All participants agreed that the struggles to gain a livelihood with their respective jobs has worsened since the COVID-19 crisis. The necessary financial support during the pandemic came mainly from small self-organised collectives and the community. The state as a sponsor was largely absent.

From the preceding aspect results an enormous disappointment about political structures in their commitment to support workers during the crisis. The workers, particularly those who are in subcontracted employment relationships and who do not possess the Spanish nationality, have until now (July 2023) not achieved any financial support. Hence, there is resignation among them, that effective help should not be expected from governmental structures. This is also manifested by the non-fulfilment of political promises such as the implementation of the "Las Kellys-law" which would have meant comprehensive improvements in the working conditions of subcontracted workers[2]. Overall, there exist widespread disagreements between subcontracted workers and those in regular employment about the role of the state as well as about the major trade unions. The subcontracted workers feel left behind and have lost faith in state or trade union institutions.

---

[2] The "Las Kellys" are a group of chambermaids in Barcelona who in 2014 started chatting via social media to exchange views from the work floor. It evolved in a group denouncing precarious labour conditions. See also: https://theurbanactivist.com/idea/ meet-las-kellys-their-cause-redefines-tourism-in-barcelona/

In economic terms the externalised and subcontracted workers were most impacted by the COVID-19 crisis. Most of the focus group participants report that with the beginning of the lockdowns and the total halt of any tourism activity they have lost their jobs without any eligibility for unemployment benefits, short-time allowances or state rescue funds. Those able to continue to work sporadically give account that wages were often paid long overdue or sometimes not at all due to insolvencies of their employers. This led to the situation that a lot of workers left the sector, causing the much reported shortages of staff many destinations are experiencing now.

Demands arising from the context

The workers are calling for a better appreciation of their work from their employers. They expand this demand also towards the worker-customer relationship and emphasise that a different view on the service system is needed, in which a humanisation of the often invisible work that workers are performing is guaranteed. Furthermore, to confront the problems on the labour market in tourism, the participants in the focus group stress the necessity of ensuring basic working conditions. Above all, improving the reconciliation between job and family must be addressed. To ensure their rights, the workers highlight the imperative to continue the recently nascent organisation throughout the different workers' collectives and take their demands as a unified sector to the streets.

Regarding social advances to be made in the sector, several participants pledge for the worth of social tourism certificates to enhance the profile of sustainable travel choices for the consumers. Furthermore, the need to improve formation in the sector is identified. On the one hand this can minimise health risks and accidents, and on the other hand counterpart the emigration of human capital to other countries.

To create the necessary public pressure to move towards the far reaching changes in the tourism industry, the workers also emphasise the supporting role academia can play in this regard. Legislation changes are inevitable for the workers, according to the focus group, while the participants also highlight that the different levels of governments further have to regulate the companies. A special focus is placed on a liberation of immigration laws. Migrant workers particularly suffer from a lack of representation, inter alia because they are not allowed to vote, even though they are the basis of arguably one of the most important sectors of the whole Spanish economy.

Apart from trying to create public and hence political pressure through workers' organisations and potential alliances with the academic world, the focus group participants also formulate approaches on how to transform the economy from within. In this respect, flatter hierarchies and the organisation of companies into assemblies in particular are considered essential to be able to move towards a different economic system. A tangible and immediately implementable measure would be to stop the externalisation of the essential services of each tourism company. There is general agreement among all participants that this is the first essential step towards a more worker-friendly future in the tourism industry. The workers are optimistic that the current labour shortage in the industry offers an opportunity to strengthen their bargaining position in this regard.

Discussion of the findings

In the focus group participants were also asked to identify which of their defined forms of disempowerment and empowerment would, in their view, be addressed, improved or resolved by each of the four policy programmes presented. In addition, participants were given the opportunity to specify which issues according to them possibly would not be addressed by the policies and that therefore would require other measures.

From the workers' point of view the measure of working time reduction mainly addresses psychological factors and would improve them. The special focus of working time reduction is on the humanisation of the work situation in order to create respectable and dignified conditions at the workplace. The universal basic income primarily deals with social and political issues. From the workers' perspective, the central benefits of this measure are an immediate end to the continuous casualisation of many workers in the sector. Thus, an improvement in the balance between work and family life could take place. In all four dimensions 'economic democracy' is the participants' preferred concept. In a scenario of strengthened economic democracy, workers would aim to achieve bottom-up empowerment by structuring themselves into committees and thus overcome the predominant marginalisation of female and migrant workers. The ultimate goal of economic democracy is a new understanding of the service economy. The job guarantee programme is seen as having the potential to bring about an immediate end to externalisation and subcontracting. When compared to the other policy features, the impact of this policy measure is unambiguously in economic terms.

With regard to factors that, from the workers' view, would not be impacted by the policies presented, social factors are mentioned most frequently. Particularly the experienced racism and discrimination, which should be alleviated through systematic education offensives, are worrying the workers most.

Conclusions

Many tourism workers find themselves in an exploitative system rooted in neocolonial capitalist practice, which reproduces the precarisation of predominantly female and migrant labour. According to the participants of the focus group we spoke with in Barcelona, there has been a significant worsening of the situation within the tourism sector since the beginning of the COVID-19 pandemic. While generally all the presented policy programs are perceived as helpful in improving the situation and therefore having the potential to create new paths, the confidence in top down interventionist schemes like the universal basic income or job guarantee is lower than in bottom up empowerment through workers' organisation. A strengthened economic democracy seems to be most tangible scenario and is therefore prioritised as the most feasible and realistic option for the workers to transform their sector from within. This sheds light on a paradox inherent in the degrowth discourse. Degrowth essentially aims for bottom up empowerment, but relies predominantly on top down policy interventions as path creating forces towards a socio-ecological transformation. To harness the path creating potential of bottom up initiatives, the degrowth movement should foster dialogue with workers in precarious conditions and engage with them in organising these transformative pathways to a growth-independent future.

The results of this study illustrated the different forms of empowerment tourism workers are seeking in the four analysed policy proposals. The relevance of the findings goes beyond the degrowth debate in academic circles. It has also great value for governance and policy actors working on a socio-ecological transformation of the tourism industry. A governance approach that recognises and incorporates the perspectives of the often marginalised and oppressed voices of the workers – the essential backbone of the tourism industry – is more prone to resilience compared to purely scientific visions of destination governance and policy-making, lacking the understanding for social realities.

Following Steen (2016), who argues for attention to both context and agency in any analysis of path creation, we followed an explorative approach in this chapter. This implies that the findings are tied to the context of the tourism industry in Barcelona and to the personal experiences of the focus group participants. The limitation of this specific case is that it lacks representativeness. Further research is necessary to validate the arguments. However, the study should be understood as a first impetus for a more intensive engagement with the situation and perspective of tourism workers and their role within a degrowth scenario.

Literature

Aghazamani, Y. & Hunt, C. A. (2017). Empowerment in tourism: a review of peer-reviewed literature. *Tourism Review International, 21*(4), 333–346.

Albertsen, K., Rafnsdóttir, G. L., Grimsmo, A., Tómasson, K. & Kauppinen, K. (2008). Workhours and worklife balance. *Scandinavian Journal of Work, Environment & Health, 34*(5), 14–21.

Andriotis, K. (2018). *Degrowth in tourism: conceptual, theoretical and philosophical issues*. Wallingford: CABI.

Anton Clavé, S. & Wilson, J. (2017). The evolution of coastal tourism destinations: a path plasticity perspective on tourism urbanisation. *Journal of Sustainable Tourism, 25*(1), 96–112.

Archer, R. (1995). *Economic Democracy: the Politics of Feasible Socialism*. Oxford: Clarendon Press.

Ayuntamiento de Barcelona. (2023a). Economía, trabajo, competitividad y hacienda. *turismo*. Available at: https://ajuntament.barcelona.cat/ economiatreball/es/turismo

Ayuntamiento de Barcelona. (2023b). Economía, trabajo, competitividad y hacienda. *turismo y promoción de la ciudad*. Available at: https://ajuntament.barcelona.cat/economiatreball/es/turismo-0

Barca, S. (2017). The labor(s) of degrowth. *Capitalism Nature Socialism*, *30*(2), 207–216.

Bianchi, R. V. & Man, F. de (2021). Tourism, inclusive growth and decent work: a political economy critique. *Journal of Sustainable Tourism*, *29*(2-3), 353–371.

Birnbaum, S. (2009). Introduction: basic income, sustainability and post-productivism. *Basic Income Studies*, *4*(2).

Birnbaum, S. (2016). Basic income. *Oxford Research Encyclopedia of Politics*. [Online]. Available at: https://doi.org/10.1093/acrefore/9780190228637.013.116

Blázquez-Salom, M., Blanco-Romero, A., Vera-Rebollo, F. & Ivars-Baidal, J. (2019). Territorial tourism planning in Spain: from boosterism to tourism degrowth? *Journal of Sustainable Tourism*, *27*(12), 1764–1785.

Boschma, R. & Frenken, K. (2011). The emerging empirics of evolutionary economic geography. *Journal of Economic Geography*, *11*(2), 295–307.

Bourlès, R. & Cette, G. (2006). A comparison of structural productivity levels in the major industrialised countries. *OECD Economic Studies*, *2005*(2), 75–108.

Brouder, P. (2020). Reset redux: possible evolutionary pathways towards the transformation of tourism in a COVID-19 world. *Tourism Geographies*, *22*(3), 484–490.

Brouder, P., Clavé, S. A., Gill, A. & Ioannides, D. (2017). Why is tourism not an evolutionary science? Understanding the past, present and future of destination evolution. In P. Brouder, S. Anton Clavé & D. Ioannides (Eds.), *New Directions in Tourism Analysis: Tourism Destination Evolution*. London: Routledge.

Cañada, E. (2018). Too precarious to be inclusive? Hotel maid employment in Spain. *Tourism Geographies*, *20*(4), 653–674.

Cañada, E. & Izcara, C. (2022). Reactivació turística i transformacions del treball. Barcelona, escenari de precarietat. *Sèrie Informes en Contrast*, *21*.

Cosme, I., Santos, R. & O'Neill, D. W. (2017). Assessing the degrowth discourse: a review and analysis of academic degrowth policy proposals. *Journal of Cleaner Production*, *149*, 321–334.

Cumbers, A. (2018). A new definition of economic democracy – and what it means for inequality. *Democratic Audit Blog*.

Cumbers, A., McMaster, R., Cabaço, S. & White, M. J. (2020). Reconfiguring economic democracy: generating new forms of collective agency, individual economic freedom and public participation. *Work, Employment and Society*, *34*(4), 678–695.

D'Alisa, G., Demaria, F. & Kallis, G. (2015). *Degrowth: A Vocabulary for a New Era*. London: Routledge Taylor & Francis Group.

Dawley, S., MacKinnon, D., Cumbers, A. & Pike, A. (2015). Policy activism and regional path creation: the promotion of offshore wind in North East England and Scotland. *Cambridge Journal of Regions, Economy and Society*, *8*(2), 257–272.

Durand, C., Hofferberth, E. & Schmelzer, M. (2023). *Planning beyond Growth: The Case for Economic Democracy within Limits*. Genève: Université de Genève.

ESS (2016). *Round 8: European Social Survey Data: Data File Edition 2.2*. Norway: ESS.

Fitzgerald, J. B., Schor, J. B. & Jorgenson, A. K. (2018). Working hours and carbon dioxide emissions in the United States, 2007–2013. *Social Forces*, *96*(4), 1851–1874.

Fitzgerald, N., Parrique, T. & Cosme, I. (2022). Exploring degrowth policy proposals: A systematic mapping with thematic synthesis. *Journal of Cleaner Production*, *365*, 132764.

Garud, R. & Karnoe, P. (2012). *Path Dependence and Creation*. London: Taylor and Francis.

Gáspár, T. (2011). Path dependency and path creation in a strategic perspective. *Journal of Futures Studies*, *15*(4), 93–108.

Gill, A. & Williams, P. (2011). Rethinking resort growth: understanding evolving governance strategies in Whistler, British Columbia. *Journal of Sustainable Tourism*, *19*(4-5), 629–648.

Gill, A. & Williams, P. (2014). Mindful deviation in creating a governance path towards sustainability in resort destinations. *Tourism Geographies*, *16*(4), 546–562.

Gunderson, R. (2019). Work time reduction and economic democracy as climate change mitigation strategies: or why the climate needs a renewed labor movement. *Journal of Environmental Studies and Sciences*, *9*(1), 35–44.

Hassink, R., Isaksen, A. & Trippl, M. (2019). Towards a comprehensive understanding of new regional industrial path development. *Regional Studies*, *53*(11), 1636–1645.

Henning, M., Stam, E. & Wenting, R. (2013). Path dependence research in regional economic development: cacophony or knowledge accumulation? *Regional Studies*, *47*(8), 1348–1362.

Hickel, J., Kallis, G., Jackson, T., O'Neill, D. W., Schor, J. B., Steinberger, J. K., Victor, P. A. & Ürge-Vorsatz, D. (2022). Degrowth can work - here's how science can help. *Nature*, *612*(7940), 400–403.

Johanisova, N. & Wolf, S. (2012). Economic democracy: a path for the future? *Futures*, *44*(6), 562–570.

Kallis, G., Kalush, M., O.'Flynn, H., Rossiter, J. & Ashford, N. (2013). "Friday off": reducing working hours in Europe. *Sustainability*, *5*(4), 1545–1567.

Karnøe, P. & Garud, R. (2012). Path creation: co-creation of heterogeneous resources in the emergence of the Danish wind turbine cluster. *European Planning Studies*, *20*(5), 733–752.

Milano, C., Novelli, M. & Cheer, J. M. (2019). Overtourism and degrowth: a social movements perspective. *Journal of Sustainable Tourism*, *27*(12), 1857–1875.

Nielsen, K., Hausner, J. & Jessop, B. (1995). *Institutional Change in Post-Structuralism*. Cheltenham: Edward Elgar Publishing.

Patton, M. Q. (2015). *Qualitative Research and Evaluation Methods: Integrating Theory and Practice* (fourth edition). Thousand Oaks: SAGE Publications Inc.

Pickett, K. & Wilkinson, R. (2010). *The Spirit Level: Why Equality is Better for Everyone*. London: Penguin Books.

Pike, A., MacKinnon, D., Cumbers, A., Dawley, S. & McMaster, R. (2016). Doing evolution in economic geography. *Economic Geography*, *92*(2), 123–144.

Pullinger, M. (2014). Working time reduction policy in a sustainable economy: criteria and options for its design. *Ecological Economics*, *103*, 11–19.

Scheyvens, R. (1999). Ecotourism and the empowerment of local communities. *Tourism Management*, *20*(2), 245–249.

Schor, J. B. (2015). Work sharing. In G. D'Alisa, F. Demaria & G. Kallis (Eds.), *Degrowth: A Vocabulary for a New Era*. London: Routledge Taylor & Francis Group.

Steen, M. (2016). Reconsidering path creation in economic geography: aspects of agency, temporality and methods. *European Planning Studies*, *24*(9), 1605–1622.

Tcherneva, P. R. (2018). The job guarantee: design, jobs, and implementation, *Working Paper, No. 902*. Annandale-On-Hudson: Levy Economics Institute of Bard College (advance online publication).

Timming, A. & Summers, J. (2020). Is workplace democracy associated with wider pro-democracy affect? A structural equation model. *Economic and Industrial Democracy*, *41*(3), 709–726.

Walmsley, A., Koens, K. & Milano, C. (2022). Overtourism and employment outcomes for the tourism worker: impacts to labour markets. *Tourism Review*, *77*(1), 1–15.

Wiedmann, T., Lenzen, M., Keyßer, L. T. & Steinberger, J. K. (2020). Scientists' warning on affluence. *Nature Communications*, *11*(1), 3107.

Wilkinson, T., Coles, T. & Petersen, C. (2022). Mindful continuation? Stakeholder preferences for future tourism development during the COVID-19 crisis. *Tourism Geographies*.

Williams, A. M. (2013). Mobilities and sustainable tourism: path-creating or path-dependent relationships? *Journal of Sustainable Tourism*, *21*(4), 511–531.

Chapter 8 - Who is at Amsterdam's tourism policy making table?

Roos Gerritsma & Guido Stompff

Introduction

Policy-making always appears to lag behind the times. Initially, Amsterdam developed policies that promoted tourism. However, when Amsterdam showed signs of becoming an over-touristy city, it proved difficult to stem the tide. By now, everyone in Amsterdam has an opinion on tourism, but does everyone have an influence on the shaping of new tourism policies?

In this chapter, we will first discuss Amsterdam as a city that strives for participatory approaches within the realm of policymaking. Subsequently, we will introduce the tourism context. Then, we will share research findings drawn from desk research and interviews with stakeholders in the tourism sector. These findings reveal a lack of clear delineation regarding active involvement in the formulation of tourism policies. A rather scattered landscape unfolds that – as will be discussed at the end of this chapter – urges for a deeper understanding of (felt) in- and excluding mechanisms and alternative participatory design methods. Especially as the number of post-Covid-19 tourists is increasing in Amsterdam, tourism policies are and will keep affecting all city users, in all parts of the city.

Designing a better city together

Participation processes are more than ever a part of Amsterdam's approach to 'designing a better city together' (Christof & Majoor, 2021; Gemeente Amsterdam, 2018 & 2022a). Amsterdam is not the sole city in doing so. Comparative research among cities reveals that each local ecosystem of networks has its own characteristics: it was Löw (2013) who coined this as *Eigenlogik* (German for 'intrinsic logic'). This term refers to the specific patterns of interpretation and ways of doing things that shape the identity, state of mind and perceptions of the city's inhabitants in various ways. She discussed that this Eigenlogik of the city is also regularly reproduced through the dominant local planning practices and routines, including participation opportunities. In fact, forms of participation are strongly dependent on the intrinsic logic of a city (Christof & Majoor, 2021).

Amsterdam's Eigenlogik of pragmatic participation

Within the realm of social, health and urban planning sciences, the interest in participation is fuelled by Arnstein's seminal 'ladder of citizen participation' (1969). Her work is often referred to and quoted in the context of participation.

Arnstein's typology presents participation as a metaphorical ladder, with each ascending rung representing increasing levels of citizen agency, control and power. She includes a descriptive continuum of participatory power that moves from non-participation whereby experts decide for others (no power) via degrees of tokenism (counterfeit power) to degrees of citizen participation (actual power) whereby citizens decide for themselves.

Eigenlogik helped us to better understand what is known as the 'Amsterdam Approach': it focuses on the collaboration between citizens, civil society, the private sector, knowledge institutions, and the municipality to address social issues (Florian, 2020). "The city has steered towards more market-oriented approaches and citizen participation. […] the city's possible Eigenlogik of (overly) pragmatic co-operation and consensus-driven solutions become visible" (Christof & Majoor, 2021, p. 41). However, it is also Amsterdam where participation fatigue (e.g., Helleman et al., 2021; Welschen & Veldboer, 2019) has been observed in relation to participative urban planning. Residents feel they are not treated as serious partners, leading to participant frustration with the process and limited outcomes. Citizen participation in Amsterdam primarily concerns the first two rungs: 'manipulating' and 'co-production'. Yet, stimulating and facilitating active resident participation in policy-making and urban planning trajectories remain a focal point for the political parties in power, explicitly mentioned in their coalition agreements (Gemeente Amsterdam, 2018 & 2022).

Christof and Majoor (2021) note that Amsterdam has provided space for an empowered civil society to steer developments themselves. As we will see below, a recent example of utilising such civil power to influence policies took place within the tourism context. The latest study on participation via The Court (Rekenkamer, 2022) indicates that actively involving all stakeholders in the creation of new policies is not yet guaranteed: "We see that officials often vaguely describe what they have done about participation. This does not necessarily mean that nothing or too little has been done with Amsterdammers. […] Perhaps they do make a lot of work of participation, but have not written it down properly. But it could also be that they do not do enough to involve Amsterdammers." The Amsterdam mayor and aldermen shared the Court's analysis and will work on reviewing the so-called 'participation paragraph'.

Amsterdam's urge for redesigning its features as a tourism destination

Amsterdam has nearly nine hundred thousand inhabitants (CBS, 2023) and is renowned globally for its historical beauty and liberal lifestyle. The historic inner city with its canals is under UNESCO's protection and is one of the main tourist attractions. The tolerant atmosphere is another attraction, resulting in Amsterdam's reputation as the backpacker place to be and the 'gay capital of the world'. The city is also known for the Red-Light District and the numerous coffeeshops where cannabis can be legally purchased (Gerritsma, 2019). However, this openness has come at a cost. 'Tourist-related annoyances' topped the list of unattractive aspects of Amsterdam in 2012 (Westenberg, 2015), even before the media mentioned the 'tourist tsunami' (Volkskrant, 2017). In 2019, Amsterdam hosted over 10 million visitors who stayed for 21 million nights (Gemeente Amsterdam, 2019), representing 2.5 times the figures from the year 2000. Above all the centre of Amsterdam attracts high number of visitors. The district has been fully adapted to cater to the needs of (international) visitors: for every 1000 residents, the district offers 356 hotel beds, 69 unique Airbnb listings, 26 hotels/restaurants/bars, and 21 shops, with most establishments catering to visitors (Stompff et al., 2021).

The growing numbers of visitors started to become a nuisance to locals, albeit it depends on where the locals live (Gerritsma, 2019; Gerritsma & Vork, 2017). Those residing in the city centre often sense a loss of belonging due to the homogeneous cultural and shopping offerings, along with the presence of noisy tourists who appear to be on a "moral holiday", as the mayor put it (At5, 2021). Consequently, a growing desire and intention have emerged to attract tourists who can positively contribute to the local community, as evidenced by the report *Redesign of the visitors economy 2025* (amsterdam&partners, 2020). Noteworthy is the codesign approach that was applied by amsterdam&partners whilst making this report during the winter of 2020.

Covid-19 showed Amsterdam's dependence on tourism clearly. Therefore, the municipality requested amsterdam&partners to come up with an advisory report for a more resilient future. Amsterdam&partners is a not-for-profit organisation in the public-private sector and is actively engaging over 800 organisations. It was previously known as Amsterdam Marketing and shares knowledge that contributes to a thriving Amsterdam Metropolis. Since 2019, their focus has expanded beyond city marketing, aiming to "apply a comprehensive strategy to manage the environment around us. […] an integrated approach that centres on residents while also offering a warm welcome to visitors. Our focus is on better rather than more, quality not quantity" (amsterdam&partners, 2022). Subsequently, Amsterdam opted for a participatory approach to co-design advice, involving over 100 different stakeholders, including residents, entrepreneurs, experts, consultants, and both non-profit and for-profit organisations. Due to its urgency, this process was completed within a span of two months. The vision was subsequently presented to the local council on April 15th, 2021.

Coping mechanisms of (activist) residents and artists/entrepreneurs

Residents of Amsterdam are actively voicing their concerns not only through activism (primarily through debates and local media) but also via democratic channels. As the renowned tolerant attitude among locals towards drugs and the sex-industry is fading, the civic initiative 'Stop drugs tourism to Amsterdam' was initiated during the summer of 2020 (VVAB, 2020). The availability of drugs has attracted numerous visitors, leading to Amsterdam being dubbed the drug capital of Europe, resulting in extensive social problems (Tops & Tromp, 2019). Alongside the often-heard plea to stop selling drugs to visitors (At5, 2021), one might expect the civic initiative to easily gather the required minimum of 1200 signatures to prepare for a possible next round and aim for a referendum. However, this was not the case. Perhaps their initiative was too narrowly focused on just one aspect of tourism to Amsterdam? However, the subsequent civic initiative – 'Amsterdam heeft een keuze' (Amsterdam has a choice) – was frequently signed (Wij-Amsterdam, 2020). This even led to a regulation by the city council to cap the number of overnights stays at 20 million (Gemeenteblad, 2021).

The civic initiative is a form of citizen participation. In a civil initiative, participation takes the form of a referendum. It implies that citizens have the opportunity to put their proposal on the municipal council's agenda. Bijl's (2023) study on whether overtourism could be solved by residents showed how extraordinary successful this initiative turned out to be in a sense that getting a referendum ranked highest as an instrument for citizens to have a direct voice in a government decision (Coenen et al., 2001). The required 1,200 signatures were quickly reached. Within ten days, the popular initiative was signed 20.000 times. Interestingly, this initiative was undertaken during the early stages of the Covid-19 pandemic and was seized as an opportunity to highlight the problem of mass tourism. We believe that the sudden halt in tourism offered residents a contrasting and enriching experience, thereby revealing what constitutes a liveable city.

The initiators drafted a proposal which suggested measures like a maximum of 12 million tourists a year, a ban on renting homes to tourists and a hotel ban or permit ban on hotel expansions. Although the college of mayor and aldermen declined to adopt all of their suggestions, the city council to adopted the proposal. However, the cap of 12 million overnight stays per year was not endorsed. Instead, the city council opted for a range of 10 million to a maximum of 20 million, with a signal value of 18 million. It was defined that should the signal value be reached and liveability in neighbourhoods compromised, the college would have to draft a policy paper within six months. Astonishingly, this transpired just one year later. In December 2022, a new *Vison on the visitor's economy for Amsterdam 2035* (Gemeente Amsterdam, 2022b) was presented and adopted. It states: "In this vision, we limit growth, and outline the transformation to a sustainable visitor economy. We do this, among other things, […] by working to improving liveability, by countering nuisance and overtourism and by managing overnight stays. We focus on the multi-core city, responsible entrepreneurship and cooperation with the region." It resonates a promising transformational process; however, it contains no explicit reference to an innovative way of how to undertake a collaborative and long-standing participation approach towards 2035.

Another noteworthy initiative is the 'Reinvent Tourism' network that was able to attract quite some attention with the *Untourist Guide to Amsterdam* (Simons & Hamer, 2019). They use creative and provoking ways of developing (possible) tourism activities that are welcoming visitors and beneficial for the city and its residents in the inner city and its suburbs. Rather than just looking at what the problems are, most of their community initiatives are actively and constructively co-shaping or even co-designing alternative pathways to address Amsterdam's evolving landscape (Koens, 2021). They also organized the Reinvent Tourism

Festival for three consecutive years (2020-2022), bringing together entrepreneurs, residents, policymakers, (tourism) students and scholars (Reinvent Tourism, 2023). Pertinent policymakers and the leaders of the City in Balance - now called Visitor Management - project leaders were and still are in contact with them. One of Amsterdam's Eigenlogik characteristics is the relatively easiness to reach out towards each other and/or to meet in various debate centres, such as Pakhuis de Zwijger, where a mix of (tourism) stakeholders can be found.

Research among tourism stakeholders

At Inholland University of Applied Sciences, two research groups, i.e. New Urban Tourism and Design Thinking, worked together on 'Amsterdam as a case study' for a joined EU-funded research project, known as SMARTDEST (smart destinations). The project aimed to develop innovative solutions in response to conflicts arising from tourism mobilities in cities (SMARTDEST, 2023). One of the research questions – which also serves as our central research question for this chapter – pertained to social inclusion and exclusion within the domain of tourism policy-making: how are tourism policies constructed in Amsterdam and who has an influence on this process?

Research outline

As it concerns instilling new theory from practice, we took a grounded approach (Glaser & Strauss, 1967), whereby we used an extensive dataset. The dataset encompasses quantitative data, a media dataset and, most importantly, 27 recorded and transcribed in-depth interviews with stakeholders, including the 'powerholders' themselves. The extensive dataset enabled us to triangulate findings of the subjective interviews with more factual data. For the interviews, respondents were thoughtfully selected. A longlist of potential respondents was developed by five researchers with different expertise, resulting in 55 relevant potential respondents, including policymakers, entrepreneurs, lobbyists, activists and representatives of civil groups. After a careful evaluation, the list was narrowed down to 36 respondents, of whom 27 agreed to participate. All interviews were conducted in 2021/2022 and desk research was carried out until March 2023.

A topic list served as guidance. Also visual means were used as respondents were asked to draw a stakeholder map on tourism policy-making, as they perceived it, using a dedicated template (see Figure 1).The interviews lasted between 52 and 87 minutes, with an average duration of 68 minutes, allowing respondents to share their personal experiences and reflections.

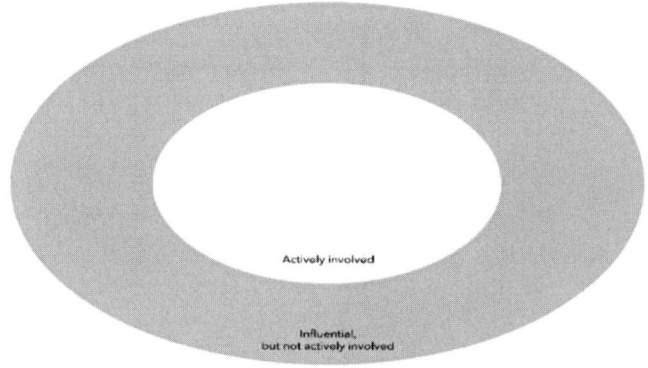

Figure 1 *Tourism stakeholders involvement template. If stakeholders are in the middle, the respondents believe they are 'at the table' of policymaking. If they are in the middle area (grey), the respondents consider those stakeholders influential. If stakeholders are on the outside, the respondents believe they should be involved, but are not.*

Interviews were conducted by six distinct researchers, encompassing varied backgrounds (sociology, tourism, design), ages (ranging from 26 to 53) and genders to reduce potential bias. All interviews were recorded, transcribed and obtained consent for utilization. In total, 13 females and 14 males were interviewed, culminating in 29 hours and 31 minutes of interview data. Each transcript was coded by two (out of the six) researchers, whereby the combination of the coders varied. If coding was unclear, or led to disagreement, they were not used. After categorizing, a systematic analysis was conducted of the data with all researchers. Interesting coded quotes were collected and clustered roughly. These clusters were discussed in several team meetings, to make sense of the data in an inductive way. First preliminary theoretical concepts emerged (sensitizing concepts) that were checked with adding more interview data and triangulating findings with a developed timeline and the extensive media database. Analysis stopped when theoretical saturations were reached and a plausible narrative could be constructed for the patterns identified, grounded in and justified by the collected data.

Findings: a scattered landscape of tourism policymaking

In this chapter, our focus is directed towards sharing the research findings that have provided insight into the degree of (dis)involvement of concerned stakeholders whilst co-designing tourism policies. A central theme in the interviews was: who are stakeholders of tourism policies and to what extend are they involved? All respondents filled in the same template (refer to Figure 1), outlining the placement of each stakeholder on the map. Their drawings are based on their experiences varying in more than twenty years or a fairly recent couple of years within the tourism policy. While some participants identified around fifteen distinct stakeholders, others mentioned only a few.

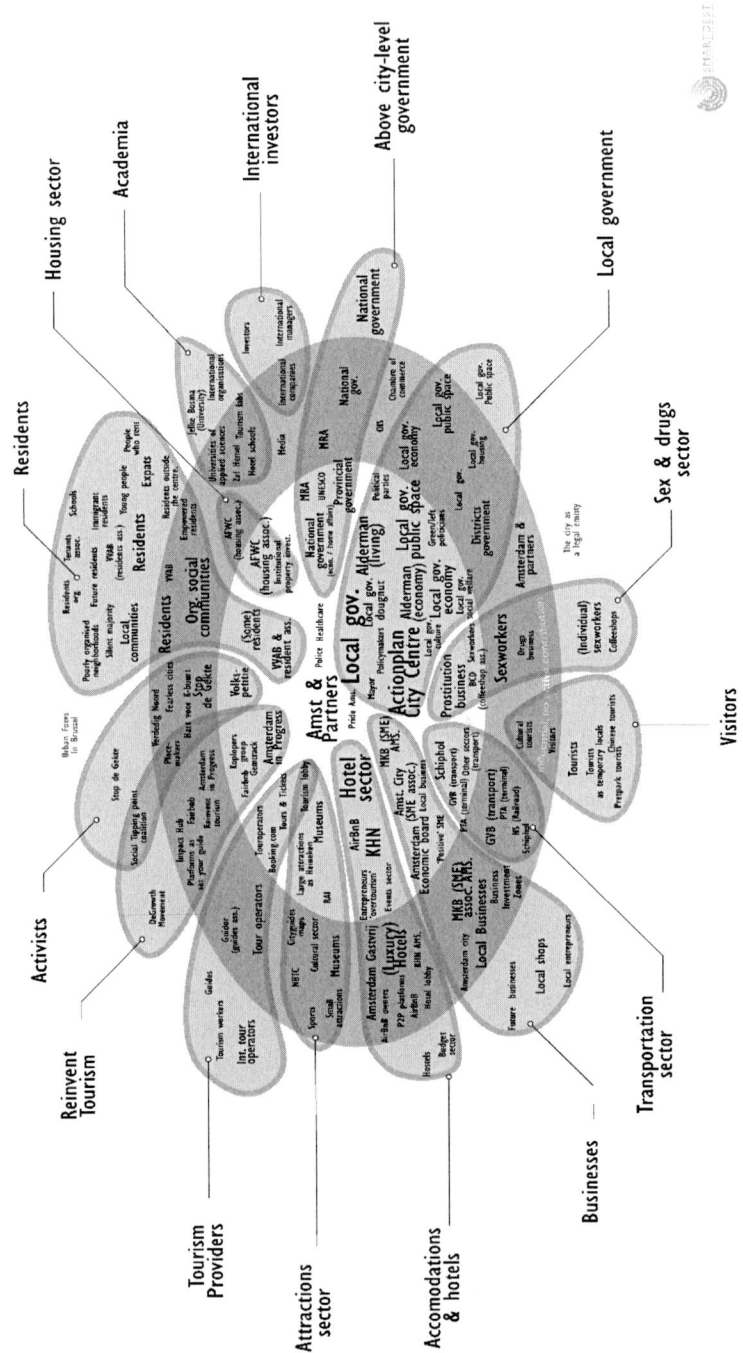

Figure 2 *Combined stakeholder map*

The map shows a comprehensive overview of all stakeholders, projecting which stakeholder is considered influential and who is not, according to the respondents. The local government, in its various forms – from the mayor to taskforces – is perceived as a particular influential stakeholder. Other influential stakeholders include the hotel sector, the association for hotels/restaurants/bars, SME associations and the sex-industry. If stakeholders are mentioned by more than one respondent, they are depicted larger. Several stakeholders are depicted more than once, as respondents had different views on the influence of those stakeholders. If the researchers could not decide to which cluster a specific stakeholder belongs, the clusters overlap. If a stakeholder cannot be clustered with other stakeholders, it is depicted outside the clusters.

A remarkable stakeholder that is considered influential is amsterdam&partners, the not-for-profit organization described before. Their perceived significance likely stems from their research capabilities, which provide data-driven insights, future projections and input for tourism development. Interestingly, the organisation is impossible to fit into any of the clusters, as its activities vary considerably, ranging from reputation management up to consulting the municipality on tourism policies. Respondents had difficulty to explain what amsterdam&partners 'is', yet most seemed to trust (the level of decision power of) the organisation.

Nobody oversees it all

Another analysis concerns the stakeholders that are not involved, but should be. Even though residents are named often, they are attributed limited influence, apart from 'some residents' or associations. Visitors are scarcely mentioned at all, which is noteworthy given that the interviews revolve around tourism. This figure also demonstrates that the perceived level of participation is at the lower rungs of Arnstein's ladder (1969). Most feel residents are left out, making remarks that hint at a degree of tokenism: "Inviting people and then telling them what the idea is, so that they can share their concerns for half an hour...after which not much is done with it? I don't think that is what participation is about" (activist). It is likely to believe that this might lead to participation fatigue. This happens when residents and organizations do not feel they have real power and influence but perceive their contribution as purely symbolic.

The combined map offers a comprehensive, but also a rather scattered view of the landscape of tourism policy making. By comparing the combined stakeholder map with individual maps, it can be observed that no respondent mentioned all clusters of stakeholders, or even got close. Regardless of their role or background, each respondent named only few of the clusters that the collective was capable to mention. The implication is that nobody genuinely oversees all. The respondents, carefully chosen for their expertise in the subject matter, lack an overview of who is/should be involved in policymaking, regardless of whether they are a seasoned policymaker, a tourism-related academic or an engaged activist. They frame the situation from their perspectives and believe they have an understanding of who is involved and who is not, but nevertheless overlook many others. This holds true for us as researchers as well: even though we meticulously mapped out stakeholders for interviews, the interviews themselves revealed individuals and groups we had entirely overlooked.

Beyond the issue of (not) mentioning stakeholders, the respondents disagree on who is influential and who is not. Some stakeholders are mentioned by distinctive respondents, but their involvement is attributed differently. A particularly interesting group in this context are residents. Most of the respondents believe that residents have no influence whatsoever, whereas a lobbyist from the hotel sector considered that "residents actually have too much influence!" And whereas some lamented that residents are not explicitly invited to the table of policymaking, an experienced policymaker claimed the opposite: "I know, because I am in that political arena: residents are genuinely and actively involved". Triangulation with other sources demonstrated that his claim is correct.

In some instances, a specific stakeholder – such as the national government – is positioned by one respondent in the centre of the map, implying high influence. In contrast, other respondents place the same stakeholder on the periphery, signifying no influence at all. This contrast in perspective is apparent.

The issue with 'who is at table' is that respondents collectively demonstrate that no individual knows who is/should be represented at the table of tourism policymaking, whilst at the same time they voiced a concern that some stakeholders are not represented adequately or are even excluded. The involved parties blame each other, perceiving another stakeholder as (excessively) influential, while simultaneously believing that others hold a decisive voice. This underscores a sense of distrust among stakeholders, stemming from a perception of limited agency and influence.

Unclear trajectories and discussed issues

What has become evident is that policy- and decision making on tourism is dispersed among many tables: "a table you say? I wonder if […] does this table even exist?" (lobbyist). The question is not just 'who is at the table', but also 'where is the table'? Tourism and its effects on the city of Amsterdam is a wicked problem, heavily interlinked with many other wicked urban challenges, such as housing, gentrification, unemployment or drug-related issues. As a result, policies related to tourism are formulated and negotiated at various distinct 'tables,' often remaining rather ambiguous for most respondents.

This is well demonstrated by comparing what respondents said about tourism policies on hotels and on short term stays (e.g. Airbnb). These policies are created and enacted by different governmental bodies: "Within Economic Affairs there is a group of people who is involved in tourism and visitor economy. And at the housing department, there are some people involved in policies on holiday rentals" (policymaker). This implies that policies for hotels and policies for short-term rentals are managed by different individuals, at different moments in time and with different aims. Policies for short-term rentals are evaluated for their impact on the (overheated) housing market, whereas policies for hotels are evaluated based on their economic potential. As a result, while the stringent legislation significantly reduced the number of Airbnb listings, the 'no more hotels, unless'-policy failed to prevent the establishment of numerous new hotels, contributing to a total of well over 7000 beds. "I think there was always such an emphasis on holiday rentals only, because the alderman for housing is not about hotels, not at all" (manager of a short-term rental platform).

Most respondents discussed policymaking and legislation at a city level only. Yet several respondents pointed out that Amsterdam is dependent on and bound by national and even international politics. In many ways, the local government hardly has influence on those policies, as those policies are developed at another legislative level and whereby other stakes are involved. "We just aren't in control, as a city [...] we do not decide about kerosene taxes, flight taxes or the like" (policymaker). These policies have direct impact on the cost of flying and thus the number of tourists arriving in Amsterdam. Additionally, there are other (inter)national agreements that exert a significant impact on tourism mobility, having larger effects than local policies can mitigate: "We have broadened the highways. We have enlarged Schiphol [Airport]. We built railway station Amsterdam South. We have created railway lines between Berlin and Amsterdam, between London and Amsterdam [...] And now we are wondering: 'where did all these people come from?'" (lobbyist).

Unfortunately, an outcome of these unclear trajectories is that stakeholders start to distrust the government: "many people lost their faith in collaborating with the government, [...] We did cocreations for I think a year or so [...] It was a very nice process, up to the moment new policies had to be made and all that we spoke about was [...] gone! There was already a new policy set [...] Ough!" (social tourism entrepreneur). Whilst being part of a more or less participatory trajectory, most stakeholders start quite positively, but at some moment in time they sense that there are implicit boundaries constraining what issues can be discussed. They get frustrated and lose attention. Policy makers tend to frame session a priori, which is poorly understood and sometimes disliked by participants. They observe that issues that are even more relevant to them, yet for reasons unknown to them are not taken into account. "Often [...] civilians feel nothing is done with their input [...] while the residents know best what their city needs" (social entrepreneur). The participants sense that 'their' topics are left out at the table, whereas for them these topics matter. Consequences are that non-discussed issues become orphaned and might lead to an unhealthy humus layer of discontent.

A different sense of time

Another issue that emerged is the differing sense of time. The respondents with experience in policymaking are aware that they have to think in terms of years before policy changes take effect and yield impact. A telling example was provided by a respondent, who explained why still new hotels are opened, years after the city council banned hotels: "We changed the strategy [on hotels] in 2015 [...]. But it takes a couple of years to develop a hotel. [...] So [...] they opened the hotel in 2018" (official). Policymaking is like navigating a super tanker: when the course has changed much later its effect can be observed, and for those who work within or closely with the municipality this is a reality they have accepted.

Less political savvy respondents implicitly voiced expectations that it takes weeks or months to implement solutions. For instance, an entrepreneur lamented how his idea developed during a workshop and presented "so simple even my children understand it" was not implemented within few weeks by the municipality, like he is used to as a businessman. He overlooks that 'the' municipality consists of many different departments and that even the best idea needs to be negotiated, budgeted and planned for. And even without concrete outcomes, participants expect near-instant responses on their input and ideas: "I even actively informed for feedback [...]. Nothing, really zero, was done with it yet. I found it very unsatisfactory" (resident).

Although respondents often criticized 'failed' collaborative and participative trajectories, they also appreciated those that went well. Notably, the development of an advisory report during the pandemic was named explicitly by several respondents: "very nicely facilitated [...]. The organizers added their own 'sauce' [...]. But even then, you do get the feeling that you have been heard, you know who is involved and you develop better networks" (social entrepreneur).

Conclusions

The most recent Amsterdam tourism policy document articulates the will and a sensed urgency for the transformation of a more sustainable future for Amsterdam as a tourism destination by 2035 (Gemeente Amsterdam, 2022). Our research question in this chapter was related to social in- and exclusion within the realm of tourism policy-making: how are tourism policies constructed in Amsterdam and who has an influence on this process?

Our research reveals the existing (dis)involvement of concerned stakeholders when it comes to policy making. This distrust is not merely a result of not involving stakeholders in the higher rungs of Arnstein's ladder. Quite contrary: the problem seems, above all, the rather scattered tourism stakeholder landscape which no one oversees as well as the different sense of time required to adapt a policy regime. Even when all participants have a positive mindset at the beginning, during the participatory processes several signs of distrust and a dislike about unclear trajectories and orphaned issues will arise as agendas seem to be set and 'nothing' is done with the input. We were unable to provide a straightforward answer to the seemingly simple question: who is at Amsterdam's policy making table? This prompts a deeper exploration of (perceived) inclusive and exclusive mechanisms, as well as drivers of participation fatigue.

New approaches for participatory design may be essential, especially considering the conspicuous rise of post-Covid-19 tourists in Amsterdam, which impacts the city's livelihood and quality of space. As the city council emphasises the importance of co-designing a city for all, new methods are required. This is particularly pertinent as the number of post-Covid 19 tourists overtly increases in Amsterdam, affecting the city's livelihood and quality of place. The city council wants to make haste for turning Amsterdam into a multi-core city, and by doing so, it hopes tourists and visitors will be tempted to visit other city districts, apart from the inner-city. City districts such as Zuid-Oost, Noord and New-West that are known for their relatively low amount of tourism offer and will rapidly be confronted with a transformation of its use of (semi) public place. Already this can be seen with the possible arrival of a new Erotic Centre in Amsterdam Noord. Even before official participatory design processes got started (due summer/fall of 2023) local stakeholders expressed their anger and despair about the intended proposal (Parool, 2023).

Policy regime changes take years and participatory processes often only last weeks or a few months before turning 'sour'. Consequently, for developing new tourism policies, such as a multi-core city, the conventional approaches for participation falter. A cuckoo clock-approach of appearing and hiding again does not work either. Participatory input needs to be organized for a period spanning years, combined with a sense of transparency and experimentation about the 'how to invite all at the table'? Amsterdam can be characterized as an innovation hub as can be witnessed for instance, by its many urban living labs and related ecosystems. The proliferation of living labs in Amsterdam is described by Steen and Van Bueren (2017) when they studied the concept of a living labs and identified and assessed 90 urban living labs in the Amsterdam Metropolitan area in 2017.

Since then, even more labs were kickstarted, addressing all kinds of topics. We experiment since 2015 with a living lab in the realm of tourism via the Urban Leisure and Tourism lab. It is located in one of those designated city-cores (Tourismlabamsterdam, 2022). It considers tourism as a possible strategy for positive change. Via place based-methods and regenerative design, researchers and students are co-designing interventions as such with the local ecosystems. One of these interventions is a Story Bench, plastered with a QR-code through which a wide variety of personal and local stories are shared in order to contribute to a deeper understanding of each other's perspectives and experiences. Visitors are encouraged to ask questions to 'strangers' around them, via the podcast and graffiti tags on the floor to start a spontaneous conversation. Slowly but surely, mutual trust and a network of engaged stakeholders is built, while pathways are developed into the municipality to discuss and advice on long term tourism polices. Although we too must acknowledge that participatory design is still in its infancy here, we are dedicated to facilitate many inclusive tables towards 2035.

Literature

Amsterdam & Partners (2020). *Redesign Amsterdam visitors economy 2025*. [Online]. Available at: https://www.iamsterdam.com/media/pdf/corporate/brochure-redesigning-the-visitor-economy-of-amsterdam.pdf

Amsterdam & Partners (2022). *Who are we, what we do*. [Online]. Available at: https://www.iamsterdam.com/en/amsterdam-and-partners/who-we-are

Arnstein, S. (1969). A ladder of citizen participation. *Journal of the American Planning Association, 35*(4), 216–224.

AT5 (2021). *Burgemeester Halsema: over verkoopverbod wiet aan buitenlanders geen moreel doel om toeristen te weren*. [Online]. Available at: https://www.at5.nl/artikelen/206620/halsema-over-verkoopverbod-wiet-aan-buitenlanders-geen-moreel-doel-om-toeristen-te-weren

Bijl, van der N. (2023). *Kan toerismeoverlast in Amsterdam opgelost worden door burgers?* [Online]. Available at: https://www.rooilijn.nl/artikelen/kan-toerismeoverlast-in-amsterdam-opgelost-worden-door-burgers/

CBS (2023). *Dashboard bevolking regionaal inwoners*. [Online]. Available at: https://www.cbs.nl/nl-nl/visualisaties/dashboard-bevolking/regionaal/inwoners

Christof, K. & Majoor, S. (2021). Amsterdam: a city of strong government and active citizens: Eigenlogik Amsterdam. In M. van der Veen & J. W. Duyvendak (Eds.), *Participate! Portrait of Cities and Citizens in Action* (pp. 40-61). Rotterdam: Nai010 Publishers.

Coenen, H. J. M., van de Peppel, R. A. & Woltjer, J. (2001). De evolutie van inspraak in de Nederlandse planning, *Beleidswetenschap, 15*(4), 313-332.

Florian, S. (2020). The "Amsterdam Approach" and the city platform connected to its urban challenges: Pakhuis de Zwijger. [Online]. Available at: https://startupsnthecity.com/amsterdam-approach-urban-challenges-pakhuis-de-zwijger/

Gemeente Amsterdam (2018). *Participatief en digitaal: coalitieakkoord 2018 – 2022*. Amsterdam: Gemeente Amsterdam.

Gemeente Amsterdam (2022a). *Coalitieakkoord 2022 – 2026: de stad maken we samen*. Amsterdam: Gemeente Amsterdam.

Gemeente Amsterdam (2022b). *Visie bezoekerseconomie Amsterdam 2035*. [Online]. Available at: https://openresearch.amsterdam/nl/page/90775/visie-bezoekerseconomie-amsterdam-2035

Gemeente Amsterdam (2023). *Aanpak binnenstad, voortgangsrapportage 2022*. [Online]. Available at: https://openresearch.amsterdam/nl/page/92974/aanpak-binnenstad---voortgangsrapportage-2022

Gemeenteblad (2021). *Verordening van de gemeenteraad van de gemeente Amsterdam houdende regels omtrent toerisme.* [Online]. Available at: https://lokaleregelgeving.overheid.nl/CVDR660686/1

Gerritsma, R. (2019). Overcrowded Amsterdam: striving for a balance between trade, tolerance and tourism. In C. Milano, J. M. Cheer & M. Novelli (Eds.), *Overtourism: Excesses, Discontents and Measures in Travel and Tourism.* Abingdon: Cabi.

Gerritsma, R. & Vork, J. (2017). Amsterdam residents and their attitude towards tourists and tourism. *Coactivity: Philosophy, Communication*, (25), 85–98.

Glaser, B. G. & Strauss, A. L. (1967). *The Discovery of Grounded Theory. Strategies for Qualitative Research.* Chicago: Aldine.

Helleman, G., Majoor, S., Peek, G. J. & van der Veen, H. (2021). *Participatiemoe(d).* [Online]. Available at: https://surfsharekit.nl/public/044cf8d5-e585-47e6-aa4a-6d5819a63f43

Koens, K. (2021). *Reframing Urban Tourism.* Amsterdam: Inholland University of Applied Sciences.

Löw, M. (2013). *Soziologie der Städte.* Frankfurt am Main: Suhrkamp Verlag.

Parool (2023). *Het erotisch centrum is een sociaal experiment dat niet hoort in een woonwijk als Zuid.* [Online]. Available at: https://www.parool.nl/columns-opinie/opinie-het-erotisch-centrum-is-een-sociaal-experiment-dat-hoort-niet-in-een-woonwijk-als-zuid~b352cd09/?referrer=https%3A%2F%2Ft.co%2F

Reinvent Tourism (2023). *Reinvent Tourism Festival #3.* [Online]. Available at: https://www.reinventtourism.com/

Rekenkamer (2022). *Wordt in de participatieparagraaf duidelijk hoe Amsterdammers konden meedenken met nieuwe plannen en beleid?* [Online]. Available at: https://publicaties.rekenkamer.amsterdam.nl/participatie/.

Simons, E. & Hamer, E. (2019). *The Untourist Guide to Amsterdam: Change with a Smile.* Amsterdam: Querido Uitgeverij.

Smartdest (2023). *What is SMARTDEST?* [Online]. Available at: https://smartdest.eu/project/

Steen, K., & Van Bueren, E. (2017). *Urban Living Labs: A living lab way of working.* Amsterdam: AMS, University of Amsterdam.

Stompff, G., Gerritsma, R., Waterreus, S. & Koens, K. (2021). *Amsterdam case study report. Smartdest H2020.* Amsterdam: Inholland University of Applied Sciences.

Tops, P. & Tromp, J. (2019). *De achterkant van Amsterdam. Een verkenning van drugsgerelateerde criminaliteit.* [Online]. Available at: https://assets.amsterdam.nl/publish/pages/918763/onderzoeksrapport_de_achterkant_van_amsterdam.pdf

Tourismlab (2022). *About us – small-scale urban living lab.* [Online]. Available at: https://www.tourismlabamsterdam.nl/en/

VVAB (2022). *Onderteken het volksinitiatief Stop drugstoerisme in Amsterdam.* [Online]. Available at: https://www.amsterdamsebinnenstad.nl/nieuws/index.html?nieuws=304

Volkskrant (2017). *Help, de stad verzuipt in bezoekers. Valt de toeristentsunami te stoppen.* [Online]. Available at: https://www.volkskrant.nl/economie/help-de-stad-verzuipt-in-bezoekers-valt-de-toeristentsunami-te-stoppen~b3f9ee46/

Welschen, S. & Veldboer, L. (2019). Sociaal werk in stadswijken waar problemen zich opstapelen. *Beleid en Maatschappij, 46*(3), 348-365.

Westenberg, M. R. M. (2015). *De beleving van drukte in de Amsterdamse binnenstad.* Amsterdam: Gemeente Amsterdam, Bureau Werelderfgoed.

Wij-Amsterdam – federatie van samenwerkende bewonersorganisatie in Amsterdam. (2020). *Grenzen aan de groei van het toerisme – volksinitiatief Amsterdam heeft een keuze.* [Online]. Available at: https://www.wij-amsterdam.eu/2020/06/11/grenzen-aan-de-groei-van-het-toerisme-volksinitiatief-amsterdam-heeft-een-keuze/

Chapter 9 - Challenges to reconciling the interests of residents with those of visitors

Andreas Kagermeier

Introduction

In recent decades, the focus of destination management organisations (DMOs) and tourism policy in general has been primarily oriented to the needs and interest of potential visitors. In light of the unease and discontent among residents of the many cities that have become highly popular with tourists and of manifold protests against the perceived negative effects of increasing tourism, the overtourism debate could signify the need for a paradigmatic change in approaches to tourism policy. Residents' needs must be accorded the same level of attention that visitors' interests have received in recent decades. Since it seems unfeasible to change the behaviour and travel patterns of tourists, scholars and policymakers must find other ways of reconciling the – often divergent – interests of visitors and residents.

Since neither individual tourists nor the tourism industry in general seem to have a particular interest in the social carrying capacity of a destination, it is up to municipal and regional destination management organisations (DMOs) to identify, consider and respect the interests of the local population as their proper constituency, just as they have been advocates for tourism interests in the past. This means that the role of DMOs will become much more complicated and extensive. However, such a development requires a comprehensive, paradigmatic change in the roles of local and regional DMOs. That said, there are no simple ways to consider the needs of residents. Accepting that economic perspectives are subordinate to residents' self-definition of their well-being is a major challenge for destination governance stakeholders and tourism research.

The aim of this chapter is to reflect on the two different rationalities of the concepts of "destination" and "living space". The intention is to analyse the options and possibilities to reconcile these two partially antagonistic approaches, reducing the conflict between residents and visitors. One of the crucial issues is to determine which approaches can be taken with a view to bringing about a balanced setting in which the interests of guests and residents of a destination are equally considered. Special emphasis is placed on the extent to which it is possible to identify and develop proactive, comprehensive approaches to better integrate residents' opinions in tourism issues.

Discourse on the carrying capacity of a destination

We still have clear memories of the media discourse that started in 2017 and came to halt when the Covid-19 lockdowns put an intermediate end to all debates and manifestations. An unease that had been simmering among residents boiled over, initially in three Mediterranean cruise-ship destinations – Barcelona, Dubrovnik and Venice (Helmes, 2016; Christ, 2017). Pre-Covid, the media had been full of reports of masses of tourists whose sheer numbers had inundated the historic icons of (mainly urban) destinations (Koens, Postma & Papp, 2018). Misbehaving party tourists encountered upset and furious local inhabitants, creating the image that those "bloody tourists" were destroying liveable urban communities. Until then, the carrying capacity of a destination had usually only been addressed in nature reserves from the perspective of vulnerable protected areas, involving a physical carrying capacity. Now it became a buzzword, with the newly coined term "social carrying capacity".

Tourism intensity (operationalised as the number of overnight stays per resident and year) was used as an indicator to compare cities and regions affected by overtourism. The tourism intensity of affected cities (cf. Fig. 1) shows that the sheer number of visitors to Dubrovnik and Venice is a striking indicator of a physical carrying capacity being exceeded, resulting in overcrowding. Barcelona has a similar number of tourists as the three largest urban tourism destinations in Germany, i.e. Berlin, Munich and Hamburg. The manifestations and protests against visitors, who are regarded as intruders in the living environment of Barcelona's inhabitants, are mirrored by similar tendencies in Berlin. However, Munich and-

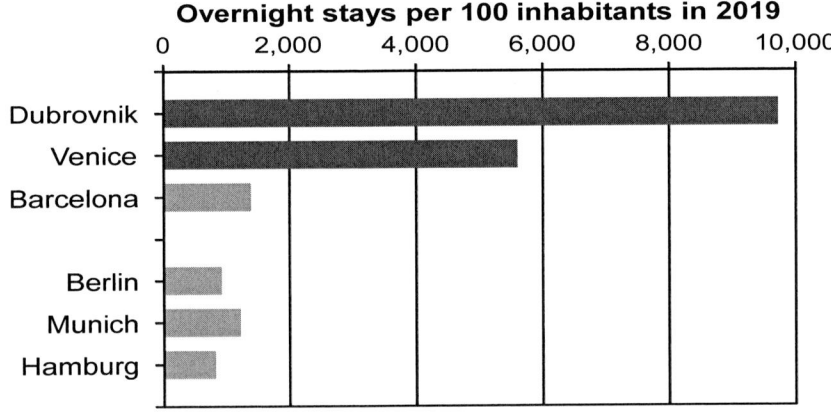

Figure 1 *Tourism intensity in Dubrovnik, Venice and Barcelona as well as Berlin, Munich and Hamburg (overnight stays per 100 inhabitants) 2019. Source: Kagermeier, 2012, p. 5*

Hamburg, which have about the same tourism intensity, have not yet experienced any widespread unease (cf. Kagermeier & Erdmenger, 2019). Despite having almost the same tourism intensity, i.e. exposure to the stimulus of visitors in the city, cities experience very different responses: in Berlin and Barcelona, there have been major protests since 2011, whereas in Munich and Hamburg there have been very few indications of a perception of pressure. This means that the simple indicator of overnight stays per habitant is insufficient to capture this effect. We must therefore take a closer look at the question how overtourism can be characterised. Koens and Postma (2017, p. 9) distinguished three aspects that could lead to the perception of overtourism:

1) A physical carrying capacity limit (crowding): there are simply too many visitors in a given space, corresponding with the perception of overcrowding.

2) Direct negative effects of tourists (encounter): an excessively adverse visitor impact is perceived. Examples include congested infrastructure, noise, disturbance and irritation.

3) Indirect effects (livelihood): perceived structural change due to the tourism economy, as well as competition for use of resources (retail or the housing market aimed at tourists).

Of the 11 recommendations proposed by the United Nations World Tourism Organisation (UNWTO et al., 2018, p. 27 ff.) to tackle the challenge of the overtourism phenomenon, four are associated with the crowding effect:

1) Dispersal of visitors within the city and beyond (crowding)

2) Time-based dispersal of visitors (crowding)

3) Stimulation of new itineraries and attractions (crowding)

4) Review and adaptation of regulation (crowding).

The categories of impact (direct negative effects) and encounter (indirect negative effects) each encompass two proposed management approaches:

5) Enhance visitor segmentation (encounter)

6) Ensure that local communities benefit from tourism (livelihood)

7) Create city experiences for both residents and visitors (livelihood)

8) Improve city infrastructure and facilities (encounter).

Most of the management propositions can therefore be seen as end-of-pipe approaches with an orientation towards the effects and symptoms of visitor presence. Only the last three propositions aim at understanding the process of the causes and development of negative perceptions and feelings, as well as corresponding communication approaches:

9) Communicate and engage with local stakeholders

10) Communicate and engage with visitors

11) Set monitoring and response measures.

Inhabitants are considered as local stakeholders, albeit only at a rather general and superficial level. For example, reference to them is made in recommendations like "organise local discussion platforms for residents" (UNWTO 2018, p. 39). In a nutshell, focusing only on the number of visitors expressed in the indicator of tourism intensity seems to fall short of the mark, given that similar values of tourism intensity result in quite different responses by local populations.

The key factors of vulnerability and resilience

To get a more comprehensive understanding of local inhabitants' responses to the stimulus of tourism intensity, we refer to the concept of vulnerability. According to Tuner (2003), the level of vulnerability (in this case, that of local inhabitants) is influenced by three dimensions:

1) Exposure

2) Sensitivity (tolerance) and

3) Resilience (cf. Fig. 2)

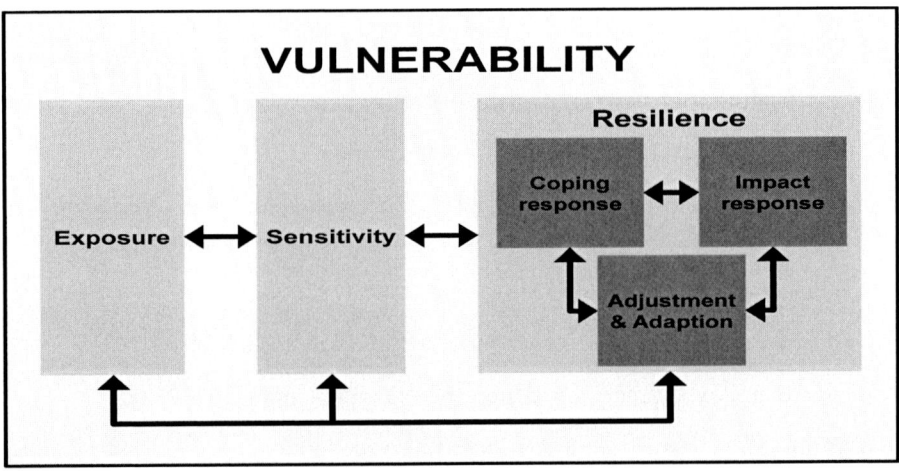

Figure 2 *The concept of vulnerability according to Tuner et al. (2003, p. 8077)*

The dimensions are interrelated and influence each other. Resilience is driven by

a) the capacity to respond to an impact

b) the capacity to cope with a specific situation/hazard and

c) the capacity to adapt and adjust to a specific situation/hazard.

According to this model, a similar stimulus (exposure) may induce different extreme perceptions and implications. A low level of tolerance (sensitivity) among a city's local population may result in one city considering tourism intensity to be more serious than that in another city with the same level of tourism intensity. The level of tolerance is influenced by the level of resilience in a community. As a simple example, a given sea rise level due to climate change affects inhabitants in the coastal regions of Bangladesh or Indonesia much more severely than it does inhabitants of the Netherlands. The Dutch dispose of the necessary means to cope and adapt by raising dykes, meaning that the country is more resilient to the same stimulus. The emphasis on direct exposure reduction in the UNWTO management measures focuses mainly on direct exposure of inhabitants to visitors. It may therefore be necessary to take a more comprehensive look at the specific conditions of an urban society in order to understand the different responses of host communities.

Comparing Berlin and Munich, it can be said that Berlin has undergone intense transformation over the past three decades. As a result, there has been an enormous inflow of new inhabitants who compete alongside longer-term residents on the housing market. At the same time, the housing market in both parts of the city (East and West) was marked by a relative surplus of accommodation with comparatively low levels of rent until the end of the 20th century. Since the turn of the century, intense gentrification and investments by external corporations have caused a drastic and rapid rise in real estate prices, reducing the amount of affordable housing. In the low-cost market segment, housing market demand began to outstrip supply. This situation was aggravated by the fact that the city council sold much of its former social housing to external investors, generating another wave of rent hikes. Munich is accustomed to a quite high, albeit more stable, level of rent prices. Hence the pressure, stress and tensions felt by the local population are much higher in Berlin, owing to the short-term changes that influence their sensitivity to other irritating factors such as a large number of visitors.

Findings in Munich showed that the local population still saw sufficient opportunities to avoid encountering tourists if they wanted to, given that the tourist bubble in Munich is largely limited to the city centre. The locals therefore have other places to frequent as a mechanism of responding to or coping with the large number of visitors. Moreover, the main target group of urban tourism to Munich are relatively traditional cultural tourists who blend in quite easily with the local population (cf. Kagermeier & Erdmenger, 2019). Target groups in Berlin are characterised to a greater extent by tourists seeking unique nightlife experiences in the gentrifying districts of Kreuzberg, Neukölln, Friedrichshain and Prenzlauer Berg. The intrusion of visitors into residential districts not only intensifies the impact of their presence, but also deprives local inhabitants of opportunities to avoid encounters if they feel disturbed by the presence of visitors. Accordingly, the width of the gap between the lifestyles and behavioural patterns of the local population and visitors probably plays a role in the degree of irritation. Hence the local population in Munich can be characterised as being more resilient than Berlin residents as the visitors' behaviour causes less irritation due to its spatial and temporal characteristics.

In its first three management approaches, the UNWTO proposes dispersing visitors throughout the city, trying to establish new itineraries and spreading tourism throughout the year. These measures could be counterproductive because they might lead to the opposite effect: they might deprive the local population of the coping and adjustment options needed in their residential districts to avoid direct encounters with visitors. Reducing the length of quiet periods, when fewer tourists visit the city, could put an end to the rest periods that the local population need to recover and take a deep breath. Since resilience influences the local population's sensitivity, a mono-dimensional focus on mere tourism impact falls short of the mark. To tackle overtourism, we must take the entire environmental framework into account.

Traditional destination marketing and management (DMM)

In recent decades, traditional DMM approaches were mainly designed to promote economic growth of the tourism segment in the regional economy. The main focus was therefore on stakeholders who were directly involved in the economic results of the tourism market. This is mirrored in the rather well-known definition of a destination provided by Bieger and Beritelli (2013)[1]:

"Geographical area (place, region, hamlet) that the respective guest (or a guest segment) selects as a travel destination. It contains all the accommodation, food, entertainment/activities necessary for a stay. It is therefore the competitive unit in incoming tourism, which must be managed as a strategic business unit" (p. 54).

Bieger and Beritelli viewed travel destinations as spatial entities that could be marketed to potential visitors or guests as a product. The condition for becoming a product is the ability for potential guests to see this spatial unit as what they want and need for their stay. Thus, the perceptions of potential visitors dominate the design of a travel destination. This traditional understanding of a destination focuses on the demand and supply sides. The perception of the local population is neglected and ignored. As such, the inhabitants of host communities are more or less excluded from this understanding, given that they are only a minor aspect in the (economic) success and performance of a destination (cf. Fig. 3).

---

[1] Original quotation: "Geographischer Raum (Ort, Region, Weiler), den der jeweilige Gast (oder ein Gästesegment) als Reiseziel auswählt. Sie enthält sämtliche für einen Aufenthalt notwendigen Einrichtungen für Beherbergung, Verpflegung, Unterhaltung/Beschäftigung. Sie ist damit die Wettbewerbseinheit im Incoming Tourismus, die als strategische Geschäftseinheit geführt werden muss". Translation by the author.

In recent decades, traditional marketing and management approaches for destinations were mainly growth-oriented (partly mirroring the general socio-economic and political paradigm), treating destinations as marketable products. Another major focus was on improving quality, which was regarded as a key competitive factor. Identifying and addressing promising target groups was the main concern, implying the commodification of the destination as a consumable product. Until now, then, the DMOs and the tourism policy have mainly focused on potential visitors and stakeholders in the tourism industry.

Figure 3 *Stakeholder relevance in traditional DMM approaches (Source: modified following Koens & Postma 2017, p. 30)*

There was little awareness among those involved in the tourism industry – and certainly among the majority of tourism researchers – that a city is also a living space with limitations. Not only the material cultural heritage of tourist destinations (e.g. monuments, museums and beer gardens), but also the immaterial cultural elements (e.g. festivals and parades), which make up the living environment of the local population, were mainly seen as a local backdrop to increase a destination's attractiveness and hence marketability. In contrast, little attention was paid to protecting the privacy of residents in their living environment. Conflicts between visitors and residents can be interpreted by referring to two different – and sometimes antagonistic – perspectives from which a spatial context is viewed: the use of an urban environment by visitors follows an experiential perspective that conceives this space as a "destination". From the point of view of tourism providers, this customer perspective corresponds to the commodification of a spatial unit and its consideration as a destination. The aim of the economic perspective is to market a destination as an economic product in order to generate income and jobs.

In contrast, residents view their "living space" primarily from a socio-cultural perspective. From the residents' point of view, this spatial unit (which can be a region, a city or simply a neighbourhood) is their living space, i.e. their living environment. The overtourism debate and the challenge to find new comprehensive approaches to address and cope with visitor pressure and its negative effects represent a new paradigm for DMOs and tourism policy (Becken & Simmons, 2019). Inhabitants' interests and their need to ensure their quality of life must be taken into account to the same extent as the interests of the tourism industry and visitors (cf. Fig. 4). Balancing diverging perspectives and interests not only means reaching compromises, but also taking into account the different rationalities behind the perspectives and perceptions.

Abolishing tourism is not an option for economic reasons – and also in view of the continued demand and need for holidays. Since neither individual tourists nor the tourism industry seem to be serious about focusing on the social sustainability of destinations, it is up to the municipal and regional DMOs to identify, consider and respect the interests of the local population in their sphere of influence, just as they have campaigned for tourism interests in the past. Indeed, this means that

Figure 4 *Stakeholder relevance for managing visitor pressure (Source: Koens & Postma, 2017, p. 30)*

the role of DMOs must become much more complex and extensive. This is all the more difficult because it is not just about dealing with the symptoms visible on the surface, as the UNWTO seems to suggest to a certain extent. Ultimately, the overtourism debate is about the tension between understanding a spatial context as a tourist destination and as a living space for the local population. The awareness of the need for balancing the interests of protection and use has already been introduced and elaborated in the context of nature conservation. In destination management, however, the main focus was previously on marketability.

To proactively try to avoid a shift in the mood of an urban society, it is advisable to focus closely on local participation and to take any subjective feelings of unease seriously. The role of DMOs is therefore likely to change in importance in the coming years. Until now, DMOs have seen themselves as players primarily committed to quantitative growth, focusing on the target group of visitors. In the future, it will be at least as important for them to act more as a mediator, taking the perspective of local stakeholders. This certainly poses a central challenge for the fundamental reorientation of tourism governance. At the same time, it may well be that the overtourism debate also introduces a more fundamental paradigm shift in tourism, which has previously always been growth-oriented. The new paradigm in tourism policy must be finding a balance between the interests of citizens with the interests of the tourism industry and visitors.

Challenge: address and involve citizens

Encountering articulations of overtourism seems to be some kind of "silver bullet" in the run-up to its emergence, by strengthening resilience and communication with the population (Boley, Strzelecka & Watson, 2018). However, the ability to influence acceptance among the local population is a complex social construct that will probably not be achieved by running modest image campaigns or taking simple limitation approaches. Instead, it requires a systematic, coordinated approach by all relevant actors in many areas of action, based on well-founded social science analyses. If interaction with the local population is to be successful, the previous perspectives and patterns of action among professional tourism players should also be fundamentally called into question. Communication is not just a one-way street where tourism stakeholders can communicate their positions and views. Successful communication requires multilateral interaction at eye level.

However, achieving participation at eye level is no easy task. Findings from focus group interviews in Munich (Erdmenger, 2021; Erdmenger & Kagermeier, 2021) have shown that there is little interest or willingness among the population to express minor irritation or unease in a structured way (focus groups, workshops, round tables) as long as the situation is regarded as "bearable". The local population would often only express their problems and grievances once a certain threshold had been crossed (tipping point). However, by the time the local population has expressed its initial concerns about the perceived visitor pressure and the negative effects of tourism, the "horse has usually already bolted," i.e. it is usually too late to implement preventive approaches.

On the other hand, residents who do not see their city or neighbourhood as a marketable product, but as their living environment, tend to be very sensitive to changes in their environment. As early as the 1970s, the phenomenon of residents resisting change was described as the NIMBY phenomenon (Not In My Back Yard) (Badger, 2018). Whether new construction projects, infrastructure projects, industrial development or even wind turbines are concerned, almost any change in the familiar and long-established environment can lead to protest. While negative impacts and repercussions are usually – unsurprisingly – at the heart of such arguments and disputes, the discussion is often very emotional and also highly dependent on the perceived impact. Sometimes the objective impact is exaggerated, and protests can also be prompted by a general unease (Borell & Westermark, 2018). To a certain extent, it can even be assumed that any change in a familiar environment will lead to uncertainty and backlash, which is partly independent of the actual expected impact. This means that dealing with the impact of change in a spatial environment is not just about providing facts and arguments, but also, to a large extent, about managing the psychological concerns and sensitivities of individuals in a given community.

In light of the above, stakeholders in DMOs and tourism policy should not make absolute any articulations, but should also look at the general settings of urban society. Protests may also be prompted by a general unease and pressure resulting from other spheres (such as the housing market and economic or social transformation). Early warning approaches with low threshold values must therefore be developed to ensure that the subjective sensitivities of the local population are heard before they become the subject of local governance discourses – which are then often transformed into the aversive rejection of tourists. Two types of interaction with residents seem to be necessary:

1) Identification of the (subjective) perceptions and attitudes of residents and

2) Open and frequent communication with residents.

To keep in touch with sentiment among residents, (traditional) systematic quantitative surveys are needed to detect indications of irritation or unease as an early warning tool (to be repeated at set intervals to detect changes). This could be the first step in helping local policymakers to identify possible future conflicts. However, systematic monitoring of the mood of the local population cannot be done by surveys alone. Simple quantitative surveys are not fully able to recognise emerging potential conflicts at an early stage and explore them in terms of content. The systematic evaluation of letters to the editor in local newspapers or online platforms could be another way of recognising emerging unease before it turns into wider protest. A first step, for example, was taken in Berlin recently. In November 2022, a so-called Citizens' Advisory Board (Bürger:innen-Beirat) was founded there with representatives from all twelve districts (https://du-hier-in.berlin/buergerinnenbeirat). The board invites citizens to a Citizens Forum (https://du-hier-in.berlin/buergerinnenforum), which met for the first time in January 2023. The aim of these activities is to create platforms where citizens, the DMO, urban policymakers and representatives of professional tourism service providers can share ideas, enabling sensitivities to be sounded out. However, far more comprehensive and low-threshold activities are needed to keep track of attitudes in local civil society and to seek intensive contact and interaction.

1) One option could be for representatives of DMOs or local politicians to systematically attend meetings of local NGOs, civic organisations and interest groups. Following such discourses could be another way of discovering unease and displeasure in "statu nascendi" in good time.

2) Participating in local festivities could be another (albeit personnel-intensive and time-consuming) way of establishing informal contacts with inhabitants and keeping track of the mood of the population. Early warning symptoms have rarely been systematically documented and analysed – or even taken into account – up to now. To prevent the "overtourism perception syndrome", such early warning signs must be taken seriously. Local and regional decision-makers must take appropriate action to reduce frustration among residents – sometimes at the expense of visitor interests. Berlin has taken a step in this direction by offering a so-called Kiez-Tour (*Kiez* is the German term for neighbourhood), where representatives of the local DMO "VisitBerlin" set up a stand at highly frequented locations (such as local markets) in the districts. The aim is to engage in relatively informal conversations with citizens on the subject of "Berlin and tourism" in the local neighbourhoods (https://du-hier-in.berlin/kiez-tour).

3) Another approach could be to communicate more information about certain leisure activities to the local population. Showing (and even creating) places and opportunities that are rarely frequented by foreign visitors could constitute alternative options for retreat and privacy. These coping options could offer alternatives to the hotspots in the tourist bubble that are heavily frequented by foreign visitors, helping to improve the coping capacity.

4) Other low-threshold ways to involve the population could be organising idea workshops (perhaps in the context of existing festivities in the neighbourhoods). Incorporating the idea of gamification, specific result-based and benefit-oriented themes must be chosen, because abstract and protracted participation processes are usually not very popular. At the same time, these approaches can communicate and convey the more general picture that local tourism actors care about the interests and benefits of inhabitants – and that they take them seriously, not just viewing them as an internal marketing tool (Moscardo, 2019).

Establishing and maintaining close – and personal – contacts with residents also offers representatives of the public sector and DMOs the opportunity to act as advocates for tourism issues. As has been shown, there is no fixed absolute limit for social carrying capacity (similar to Eisenstein & Schmücker, 2020, p. 36 or Postma, Koens & Papp, 2020, p. 233 ff.). The threshold, at which the mood changes, i.e. a tipping point, also depends on the state of mind in the local community. The level of tolerance towards out-of-town visitors also depends on overall sensitivities among the local community.

The subjective perception of no longer feeling comfortable in one's neighbourhood or the feeling of alienation in one's living environment has a stronger effect than any cognitive knowledge of positive economic effects. When a DMO tries to proactively communicate with the local population in an effort to increase residents' acceptance of the challenge of intensive tourism frequency, it must find more subtle topics for communication. As the Munich example suggests, a more nuanced, indirect way might be to focus on local pride and residents' identification with the city. Promoting approaches that target local pride and identification with the "hometown" of locals could also be seen as an indirect way of increasing the social capital and stability of the urban society (Nijs, 2017; Erdmenger, 2019). This in turn would involve the integration of tourism acceptance into a comprehensive and holistic communication discourse with reference to the well-being and social climate in a city or region.

Conclusions

This chapter argues that it is important to look for ways to reconcile the interests and needs of residents with the promotion of tourism activities as an important economic aspect of the local and regional economy. However, this implies a fundamental paradigm shift in the role played by local and regional DMOs. Moreover, there are no easy ways to accommodate residents' needs. Systematic monitoring of residents' attitudes is necessary. Professional tourism players – above all, the DMO and public stakeholders – must also be willing not only to assess the concerns of citizens, but also to take them seriously. The future challenge will be to strike a balance between the divergent needs of the tourism industry and visitors on the one hand, and the local population on the other. Taking simmering unease seriously also means moving away from a traditional tourism marketing perspective so as not to endanger social peace in an urban society.

Promoting a holistic community discourse also means that focusing on mere (over-)tourism aspects falls short of the mark. Far-reaching tensions in urban society must be taken into account. Stress and pressure in an urban society, e.g. due to transformation processes in other urban economic or social fields, influence resilience. This could refer to the housing market or disruptive changes in an urban society. Sociocultural, economic and demographic frame conditions must be taken into account as part of a holistic, integrative and spatially differentiated urban development policy. A holistic approach must therefore start at the root of an urban society's state of mind. This has a fundamental impact on urban governance. The era of simple sectoral approaches in tourism policy and management seems to be over. The economically sectoral DMOs of the 20th century must transform and merge with the entire urban governance approach if they want to succeed in progressing towards stable (urban) tourism – at whatever level.

Literature

Badger, E. (2018). The Bipartisan cry of 'not in my backyard'. *The New York Times*. [Online]. Available at: https://www.nytimes.com/2018/08/21/upshot/home-ownership-nimby-bipartisan.html

Becken, S. & Simmons, D. G. (2019). Stakeholder management: different interests and different actions. In R. Dodds & R. Butler (Eds.), *Overtourism: Issues, Realities and Solutions* (pp. 234-249). Berlin: de Gruyter.

Bieger, T. & Beritelli, P. (2013). *Management von Destinationen. 8th edition.* München: Oldenbourg.

Boley, B., Mcgehee, N. G., Perdue, R. & Long, P. (2014). Empowerment and resident attitudes toward tourism: strengthening the theoretical foundation through a Weberian lens. *Annals of Tourism Research*, 49, 33–50.

Borell, K. & Westermark, Å. (2018). Siting of human services facilities and the not in my back yard phenomenon: a critical research review. *Community Development Journal*, 53(2), 246-262.

Christ, A. (2017). Tourist go Home! Europas Sehnsuchtsorte in Gefahr. *Programm ARD*. Available at: https://programm.ard.de/TV/arte/tourist-go-home-/eid_28724109736671

Eisenstein, B. & Schmücker, D. (2020). Overtourism?! Zur Tourismusakzeptanz der Bevölkerung in Deutschland. In S. Brandl al. (Eds.), *Tourismus und ländlicher Raum. Innovative Strategien und Instrumente für die Zukunftsgestaltung* (pp. 33-49). Berlin: Erich Schmidt Verlag (ESV).

Erdmenger, E. (2019). Community resilience in urban tourist destinations. How beer garden romance and a hygge localhood boost social capital. *Zeitschrift für Tourismuswissenschaft*, 11(3), 437-450.

Erdmenger, E. & Kagermeier, A. (2021). Participatory destination governance and other pipe dreams. A study of what a host community actually wants – and what it doesn't. *Berichte. Geographie und Landeskunde*, 94(3), 225-245.

Helmes, I. (2016). Ersticken Touristen die schönsten Städte? *Süddeutsche Zeitung*. Available at: https://www.sueddeutsche.de/reise/trend-staedtereise-und-die-folgen-ersticken-touristen-die-schoensten-staedte-1.2909667

Kagermeier, A. (2021). *Overtourism*. Tübingen: UVK Verlag.

Kagermeier, A. & Erdmenger, E. (2019). Overtourism: ein Beitrag für eine sozialwissenschaftlich basierte Fundierung und Differenzierung der Diskussion. *Zeitschrift für Tourismuswissenschaft*, 11(1), 65-98.

Koens, K. & Postma, A. (2017). *Understanding and managing visitor pressure in urban tourism. A study into the nature of and methods used to manage visitor pressure in six major European cities.* Breda/Stenden.

Koens, K., Postma, A. & Papp, B. (2018). Is overtourism overused? Understanding the impact of tourism in a city context. *Sustainability*, 10(4384), 1–15.

Moscardo, G. (2019). Rethinking the role and practice of destination community involvement in tourism planning. In K. Andriotis, D. Stylidis & A. Weidenfeld (Eds.), *Tourism Policy and Planning Implementation. Issues and Challenges* (pp. 36-52). London: Routledge.

Nijs, V. (2017). *Resident attitudes towards tourism – testing the resident empowerment through tourism scale (RETS) in Bruges*. Master Thesis, MODUL University Vienna. Available at: https://www.modul.ac.at/index.php?eID=dumpFile&t=f&f=9387&token=60c0b1d4764f6fcf9090105bec76ddd23c63cab2

Postma, A., Koens, K. & Papp, B. (2020). Overtourism: carrying capacity revisited. In J. A. Oskam (Ed.), *The Overtourism debate: NIMBY, Nuisance, Commodification* (pp. 229-249). Bingley: Emerald.

Turner, B. L. II, et al. (2003). A framework for vulnerability analysis in sustainability science. *Proceedings of the National Academy of Sciences of the United States of America (PNAS)*, *100*(14), 8074-8079.

UNWTO (United Nations World Tourism Organization), CELT (Centre of Expertise Leisure, Tourism & Hospitality), NHTV Breda University of Applied Sciences & NHL Stenden University of Applied Sciences (2018). *'Overtourism'? Understanding and Managing Urban Tourism Growth beyond Perceptions*. Madrid: UNWTO.

Chapter 10 - Overtourism, dependencies and protests: challenging the 'support narrative'

Sebastian Amrhein

Introduction

Global tourism is one of the biggest worldwide industries, provided by a steady growth of yearly 3-4% (World Tourism Organisation, 2020) since the 1950s, accounting for about 10% of worldwide jobs and GDP (World Travel & Tourism Council, 2020). Yet, the triumph also produces negative effects for tourist destinations and their inhabitants. The drawbacks of tourism include environmental pollution and noise disturbance, rising costs for housing and groceries or the modification and commodification of places, to name just a few (Koens et al., 2018; Novy & Colomb, 2019). Such negative effects became popular in recent years under the term 'overtourism', which Koens et al. (2018) define as the "excessive negative impact of tourism on the host communities and/or natural environment" (p. 2). In the years prior to the pandemic, numerous residents of intensively visited destinations took their displeasure with the downside of the tourism industry to the streets. Demonstrations and protest movements against overtourism emerged particularly in Southern European destinations (e.g. Barcelona, Malta, Lisbon or Mallorca) but also in Northern European cities like Berlin or Amsterdam (Milano et al., 2019a; Colomb & Novy, 2016).

The social movements and their demands to stop the sell out of their neighbourhoods raised huge attention in media and tourism scholarship. Research on the topic has accumulated in the years between 2017 and 2019, documenting the impacts on destinations and the daily lives of residents (Butler, 2019; Mansilla, 2018; Milano et al., 2019b). The rapidly increasing popularity of the protests even raised hope among critical tourism scholars that these movements could have the power to transform the current status-quo of growth-driven global tourism (Dodds & Butler, 2019; Higgins-Desbiolles et al., 2019). Yet, the success of the movements has been limited so far. One explanation is undoubtedly the occurrence of the Covid-19 pandemic, the resulting disruption of global travel and with it the interruption of overtourism and the protests against it.

However, we argue that another reason for the lack of profound success of the movements is based on the insufficient pressure exerted on politics and industry, which we attribute to the non-participation and support of large parts of the population. This results in rather small movements with undifferentiated demands, which are easier to delegitimise or ignore by advocates of growth-oriented tourism development. From such perspectives, the absence of many is equated with acceptance/support of tourism - in line with the widely accepted assertion that the more people benefit from tourism, the more they support it (further referred to as the 'support narrative'). Research by critical tourism scholars demonstrates that this assumption is based on a truncated view that reduces people to mere economic subjects (Cocola-Gant, 2023; Boley et al., 2018). At the same time, there is reason to believe that, rather than support, it is a lack of cognitive, physical or temporal capacity that hinders people from protesting (Amrhein et al., 2022a; Jun et al., 2016). We therefore argue that non-participation in anti-tourism protests is not synonymous with acceptance of tourism development and its negative effects for the environment, society and community. Rather, economic dependency and insecurities are important factors that have received too little attention in tourism research to date. In this chapter, we build on sociological approaches and existing research on social movements and their relation to tourism to substantiate our claims and challenge the 'support narrative'. In addition, we illustrate how the Covid-19 pandemic renders these dependencies visible and reinforces insecurities. It is thus an obstacle to profound change rather than a catalyst.

Benefit or dependency?

The attitudes of residents towards tourism have been studied extensively in tourism scholarship since at least the 1970's. Among the most prominent examples of such research is the irritation index, developed by Doxey in 1975. Also Pizam's (1978) investigation of residents' perceptions of tourism on Rhode Island (USA) is a classic study. However, even though research is frequently outlined since decades, determinants of residents' attitudes towards tourism are not yet fully decoded. This becomes evident when having a look at the different results of hitherto research. Andriotis and Vaughan (2003) for instance illustrate a relationship between residents' sense for the environment and their opinion about tourism. In turn, this cannot be confirmed by Deccio and Baloglu (2002) who found no significant relation between these two attributes. McGehee and Andereck (2004) conclude that residents' age is a significant predictor for residents' tourism attitude, which however was rejected in other studies (e.g. Perdue et al. 1990). At the same time, McGehee and Andereck (2004) could not proof a relationship with the education of residents, which was in turn mentioned as a significant variable by Andriotis and Vaughan (2003). Such contradictory results can be documented in many studies. In addition, exogenous influences such as historical tourism development or urbanisation, which are named as important factors by Ko and Stewart (2002), are not taken into account in most investigations.

This brief insight into existing research shows that residents' attitudes and the ways in which they develop is a complex field with numerous (potential) variables that complicates clear statements. Despite all the difficulties, however, there seems to be broad agreement on the 'support narrative', which is confirmed by Boley et al. (2018) when saying: "At the core of the resident attitude literature is the general understanding that the more residents economically benefit from tourism, the more they support tourism" (p. 1). This assumption is reflected in statements of tourism scholars who critic or even delegitimise the above mentioned anti-overtourism movements, describing them as contrived or accusing them of frustration and jealousy because they do not profit economically from tourism (e.g. Buhalis, 2020, Butcher, 2020). The World Tourism Organisation (UNWTO) also considers tourism as an activity whose primary goal is to generate growth, jobs and financial incentives that all people crave (World Tourism Organisation, 2004). When having a closer look at the literature, the strong manifestation of this 'support narrative' is surprising, as many studies raise doubts about its value. Already in 1975, Doxey pointed out that economic benefits of tourism are only considered positive up to a certain threshold (see Fig. 1). Once a critical limit is exceeded after a certain period of time, the negatively perceived effects predominate and residents meet tourism with rejection.

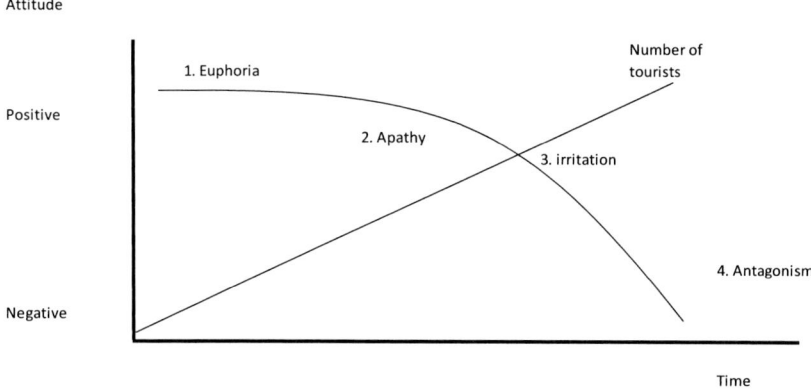

Figure 1 *Doxey's Irritation Index (own illustration)*

Further examples confirm that it is not necessarily peoples' benefit that is decisive for their advocacy of tourism development. Rather, it is often the (economic) dependence/reliance with which a correlation is evident (e.g. Andereck et al. 2005; Andriotis & Vaughan, 2003; Ko & Stewart, 2002; Latkova & Vogt, 2012; Pizam, 1978). Andriotis and Vaughan (2003) list twenty investigations which consider "economic and/or employment dependency in tourism" (p. 174) as affecting residents' attitudes. Madrigal (1993) also states, that "perhaps the most persistent finding over the years has been the positive relationship between perceptions of tourism and economic reliance on the tourism industry" (p. 337). Based on an investigation of residents in Wales, Snaith and Haley (1999) illustrate that economic dependency is a significant predictor of a positive attitude towards tourism. Yet, a rather positive position towards tourism is not the only result of high dependency. When investigating the Turkish destination of Manavgat, Yayla et al. (2023) found that residents' reliance on the tourism industry might also lead to more acceptance of its negative effects. Jun et al. (2016) go down the same line, stating that "when most residents in the Mu Si community [a community living at the entrance of the Khao Yael National Park in central Thailand, information added by the author] heavily rely on tourism development in terms of jobs and income creation, even though they understand negative impacts of tourism or concerns for natural resources protection, they still support for tourism development" (p. 5).

These studies demonstrate that (economic) dependency on the tourism industry influences the attitude towards tourism as well as the acceptance of negative effects severely. Surprisingly, many researchers hardly distinguish between the terms 'benefit' and 'dependency'; both concepts are often used synonymously. McGehee and Andereck (2004) for instance state that "[t]he majority of studies have shown residents who are dependent on the tourism industry or perceive a greater level of economic gain tend to have a more positive perception of tourism's economic impact than other residents" (p. 133). Further examples can be found in Ko and Stewart (2002), writing that "[m]any studies have supported a causal relationship between 'personal benefits from tourism development' and 'perception of tourism impacts' [...] Support for this relationship aligns with common sense that residents [...] who depend upon tourism-based employment would be more favourable toward tourism" (p. 528). Williams and Lawson (2001) cite several studies that regard peoples' financial dependence as an important factor of residents' opinion on tourism. They conclude by stating that "the single consistent (almost always found to be statistically significant) finding is that residents who derive financial benefit from tourism are more in favour of it" (p. 274).

Such ambiguities as well as methodological and interpretative weaknesses in studies investigating residents' attitudes and finally confirming the 'support narrative' have also been revealed by Boley et al. (2018). According to them "tourism researchers and destination managers have taken a somewhat haphazard and nonchalant stance towards the measurement of these perceptions (ibid, p. 18)". Their main critic focuses on:

(1) The application of underdeveloped scales that use only one or two items to measure the latent construct;

(2) The equation of personal benefit with economic benefit – pointing out to "solely treating the relationship between residents and tourists as a function of money" (ibid, p. 4);

(3) The assumption of employment as a proxy for residents' perceptions of economically benefiting, without considering the often precarious working conditions.

The latter aspect has neither been reflected in studies on tourism attitudes (to the best of the authors' knowledge), even though numerous investigations document the often precarious conditions tourism workers are exposed to. Zampoukos and Ioannides (2011) for instance attest tourism labour to be "often low paid, low skilled, temporary and/or part-time" (p. 25). In contrast to the UNWTO - which highlights prosperity and the job opportunities tourism generates for almost all regions of the planet and pointing out the high share of women and young people employed in tourism (World Tourism Organization, 2019) - they see it as a matter of concern that a high share of women and young people is particularly affected by these parlous circumstances (Zampoukos & Ioannides, 2011). Similar findings are made by scholars such as Murray and Cañada (2017), Lacher and Oh (2012) and Cañada (2019) who criticise the precariousness of tourism employment and consider hazardous labour conditions and global tourism to be highly related. Lee et al. (2015) further outline the misconception that these circumstances will change by additional growth of the industry. They even predict a worsening of "structurally driven precarity for tourism workers who are predominantly low paid, low-skilled, and increasingly recruited from overseas" (Lee et al., 2015, p. 194). This leads to tremendous inequalities which are again fuelled by tourism related privatisation and commodification of spaces (Burawoy, 2014; Büscher & Fletcher, 2017). Such circumstances and inequalities can be inflammatory for societal malaise that forms the basis for protest and the creation of social movements (Boltanski, 2011).

As mentioned above, protest movements against overtourism have formed in several destinations. However, the size of the movements is rather modest compared to the total population. In Mallorca for example, there were several hundred people participating in the allegedly biggest protest after the pandemic (Europa Press Islas Baleares, 2022), which corresponds to about 0,1% of the total population. In Lisbon and Porto also a few hundred or only dozens of protesters were reported (France 24, 2018). In a recently published report, Ozden and Glover (2023) argue that the size of the movement is one of the most important factors for its success. Chenoweth (2020) speaks of a threshold of 3,5% of the population, forming a critical mass that is likely to succeed. Such a high level of residents' participation is rarely observed in anti-overtourism protests until now (with the exception of Venice, where the figures approach the 3.5%). As stated above, the answer from proponents of the 'support narrative' is simple: people who benefit from tourism, support or accept its development. We argue that this explanation is too simplistic and does not reflect the complex reality of residents in the tourist destination. We assert that dependencies and insecurities (re)produced by tourism as well as the physical and temporal capacities of tourism workers are of immense importance. In the following section, we build on existing sociological, social movement and tourism research to support our claims.

Movements' dependency on residents' freedom

Sociologists such as Burawoy (2014) consider movements as essential to render inequalities in the world and to give hope for improvement. The famous French philosopher Michel Foucault sees in social movements an important mechanism that distinguishes true from false. He describes them as important forces that, by definition, challenge power (Roose & Dietz, 2016). Karl Marx saw revolutions and the end of oppressive forces as a result of movements formed due to precarious working conditions and inequalities. In the aforementioned pre-pandemic anti-tourism movements, however, most of the participants did not belong to, what Marx called, the proletariat, i.e. the oppressed working class. Instead, there was a large proportion which could rather be classified as the middle class. As Amrhein et al. (2022a) note in their study of social movements on the Balearic island of Mallorca, the protesters are even accused of consisting mainly of academics who formulate their criticism of tourism from the ivory tower (p. 11). This observation is consistent with descriptions by Schmitt (2010). Building on the writings of the French sociologist Pierre Bourdieu, he notes that accustomed suffering in a society rarely breaks ground in emancipatory political activities. Rather, these activities are carried out by educationally privileged actors who express their displeasure (Schmitt, 2010).

For Axel Honneth (2011), a German sociologist assigned to the critical Frankfurt School, there is a direct link between precarious working conditions at the one hand and dependencies and insecurities at the other. He sees the latter as typical symptoms of the increasing precarisation, underpayment and flexibilisation of the labour market in our capitalist system, which in turn affects the autonomy of workers, contributing to an increasing speechlessness of the workforce and hindering them from collective reactions against injustices (Honneth, 2011). The British economist Guy Standing (2011) also views insecurity and precarious conditions as dominant forces of today's labour market. He argues that the Marxian proletariat has been replaced by a precariat. Jack Mezirow (2003), an US-American sociologist, considers dependencies and insecurities as factors that can hinder individuals from critical reflection of self and their environment. According to him, critical reflection and thus the ability to realise the personal situation and surrounding circumstances are key for personal transformation needed for political action. Schmitt (2010) goes down a similar line: "Not everyone has the means to produce a personal opinion. Personal opinion is a luxury. There are people in the social world who are 'spoken for', who are spoken for because they themselves do not speak [...]" (p. 39, author's translation from German language).

Max Horkheimer (1985), another associate of the Frankfurt School, assumes that people have internalised social injustice as a fact, unable to realise injustices or even unable to dream about a different reality. With this statement he comes very close to Bourdieu's concept of habitus, with which Bourdieu describes internalised limits and possibilities. Habitus includes deeply ingrained habits, dispositions and ways of thinking that shape an individual's perception and behaviour within a given social context (Bourdieu, 1992). It is characterised by the circumstances of growing up and the social environment, including factors such as family background, education, and the norms and values of the culture they inhabit (Bauer & Bittlingmayer, 2014). Habitus plays a crucial role in the reproduction of social inequality as it is very unlikely that people will revolt against. The reason is that in their habitus, the tool of protest does not exist (Roose & Dietz, 2016). In addition to these effects, there are several groups of people who simply do not have the temporal or physical capacities to take their displeasure to the streets. Cocola-Gant (2023) mentions for instance elderly or handicapped people, pregnant women or single working parents. At the same time, as he attests, are these groups most seriously impacted by the negative effects created by tourism and the commodification of spaces, through e.g. crowding, complication to meet daily needs, lack of recreation opportunities and places to socialise (ibid.). In short, dependencies, uncertainties and disadvantageous situations of people can have considerable effects on the formation and expression of their opinions and their ability to protest against those circumstances. In the following paragraph we will specifically address the pandemic situation and illustrate how the subsequent shut-down of international travel has further strengthened dependencies, respectively rendered them even more visible.

Covid-19 as a catalyst for dependencies

The dependencies of destinations as well as individuals working there became obvious during the years 2020 and 2021 when global mobility was shut down due to the coronavirus (Milesi-Ferreti, 2021). Especially in destinations where the economy traditionally has been very much reliant on tourism and social systems do not cushion unemployment, people were affected severely. For example in Cancun, a popular beach destination in Mexico, in which tourism workers live from hand-to-mouth, the consequences were dramatic. For example, people were not able to pay their bills for basic needs such as water and food (Frye, 2021; Lopez, 2021). While most of the world was still in strict lockdown, Mexico was forced to open its borders and allow travel to mitigate the impact, despite low vaccination coverage and high risks of infection. In a TV show, former Mexican tourism secretary Enrique de la Madrid justified the decision by saying it is not just the coronavirus that kills, but also poverty (Frye, 2021).

Strong dependencies were but not only evident in low- and middle-income countries. On the Spanish island of Mallorca, where the tourism industry's direct and indirect effects account for approximately 85% of the economy (Balearic Islands Tourism Board, 2017), the Spanish government decided to impose strict travel restrictions in 2020 and 2021 to ban tourists from the island and condemn the dispersion of the Covid-19 virus. These measures resulted in an immense increase of unemployment among the tourism workforce, which could only partly be compensated by government's deficiency payments. Consequently, people were forced to seek alternative employment to pay their bills. As it was easier for qualified personal to find work in other sectors, the tourism industry has experienced a kind of 'brain drain' during the pandemic (Jackson, 2022; Sigala, 2021). Others who did not have the opportunity to leave the sector or the island felt the effects of dependency once again, as illustrated by the sharp increase in foodbank dependents on the Island of Mallorca (Martiny, 2021).

At the beginning of the pandemic, there were voices that saw the Covid-19 caused disruption of international travel as a break in rapid tourism growth and an opportunity for profound change (Amrhein et al., 2022b; Higgins-Desbiolles, 2020).

At the same time, there was scepticism about this optimistic stance. It seems that the latter will be proved right. The measures taken from politics and the tourism industry to tackle overtourism mainly focused on a more evenly distribution of tourists across the destination, smart solutions such as apps to avoid crowding and the implementation or the increase of tourist taxes (McKinsey & Company, 2017; Peeters et al., 2018; Redazione ANSA, 2020). Regulations such as the limitation of cruise ships to a maximum of three big vessels per day in the port of Palma de Mallorca have been taken, but were called a "missed opportunity" by the movement Platform Against MegaCruises (Kassam, 2021, n.p.). Another measure is the requirement for four and five star hotels on the island of Mallorca to implement height-adjustable beds, in order to facilitate the daily business of the cleaning staff. But, according to Milagros Carreño, spokesperson of the Kelly's - an association of cleaning workers on the Balearic Islands - this is only a "plaster", which does not address the real needs of the workers (Onda Cero Mallorca, 2022, n.p.). Mansilla and Milano (2019) claim that the measures taken are not focused on the core of the problem, which they, like other scholars as well as movements, see in the capitalist, growth-oriented, profit-driven system (Büscher & Fletcher, 2017; Higgins-Desbiolles et al., 2019). Rather, the measures implemented serve to maintain this system. Far-reaching effects have indeed not been observed so far. On the contrary, the travel industry recently expressed optimism that 2023 could be a new record-breaking year (Bartlitz, 2023).

Building on our earlier argumentation, we argue that the pandemic reinforces dependencies and reduces the potential for change through protests. On the one hand, the loss of jobs and revenue due to the breakdown of international mobility is grist to the mill of all those who advocate a back to business as usual. On the other hand, as we see it, the pandemic and the often insufficient political reactions to condemn the economic challenges for affected people have severely increased fears and uncertainties among tourism workforce. People who found no alternative employment during the pandemic have once again become very aware of their dependence. Additionally, the mentioned brain drain leads to a higher share of relatively new and low-skilled, young workforce (probably also a higher share with a migration background). According to Bourdieu's concept of habitus, it is unlikely that this group will join movements against the negative impacts and injustices that is (re-)produced by tourism. As Hadjisolomou et al. (2022) put it, "People who need jobs don't complain" (p. 20). It is more likely that they will accept the conditions and try to climb up the "symbolic ladder", supporting the industry to reproduce the existing circumstances (Roose & Dietz, 2016, p. 66).

Conclusions

In this chapter we have suggested that global tourism is not exclusively an economic activity – it has also a strong impact on societies. People in much travelled areas are particularly affected. Usually, these often negative effects are justified with reference to job-related and income opportunities for residents. As we have demonstrated, this approach is one-dimensional and truncated. Likewise, the assumption that a lack of protest against tourism is equivalent to acceptance or support is a misconception that we have tried to refute in this chapter. To do so, we outlined the often precarious conditions tourism workforce is exposed to and revealed strong evidence for residents' (economic) dependencies on tourism and its impact on their attitude towards the tourism industry. We further drew on approaches from social movement research to verify the profound impact of dependencies/insecurities on the formation and expression of people's opinions. Using the example of anti-overtourism movements, we identified a typical pattern, namely the emergence of a vicious circle that can result from tourism (re-)producing dependencies, which in turn prevent people from protesting against the negative effects. The resulting reduced number of protesters is subsequently used by proponents of traditional, growth-oriented tourism development to question the legitimacy and the will of the movements.

In our chapter, we tried to highlight these interactions. However, so far, our analysis has been based exclusively on desk research and the processing of literature. A conclusive examination of the theses raised, based on empirical data, is still missing (to the best of the authors' knowledge). In our view, empirical research is urgently needed in order to examine the interactions between tourism and the (economic) dependencies it (re-)produces and the resulting consequences for residents and social movements. As previous studies are almost exclusively quantitative in nature and often unable to analyse the complex social processes at stake, we plea to set up a qualitative study, focussing on the situation of tourism workers. A detailed examination of their opinions and the underlying reasons would provide answers to the questions of benefit, acceptance and dependence and would thus help to differentiate these terms and their effects more clearly and finally challenge the detaining 'support narrative'.

The results obtained might support social movements to better address the needs of residents in their demands towards policy makers, to increase their participation in movements and to reduce workers' insecurities, dependencies and structural inequalities. All in all, the challenges for and produced by global tourism are enormous. The year 2023 could again break records in international tourist arrivals. We consider it crucial for tourism research to recognise the outlined dimensions. At the same time, it is necessary to take into account that global tourism is a practice that follows capitalist defaults. In order to better understand these dimensions and develop solutions, we see it as essential for tourism research to broaden its perspectives and, as in our example, to consider tourism in a broader social context rather than seeing it primarily as an economic activity.

Literature

Amrhein, S., Hospers, G.-J. & Reiser, D. (2022a). Transformative effects of overtourism and COVID-19-caused reduction of tourism on residents: an investigation of the anti-overtourism movement on the island of Mallorca. *Urban Science*, *6*(1), 25.

Amrhein, S., Hospers, G.-J. & Reiser, D. (2022b). Impact of overtourism on residents. In D. Gursoy & S. Celik (Eds.), *Routledge Handbook of Social Psychology of Tourism* (pp. 240–250). London, New York: Routledge.

Andereck, K. L., Valentine, K. M., Knopf, R. C. & Vogt, C. A. (2005). Residents' perceptions of community tourism impacts. *Annals of Tourism Research*, *32*(4), 1056–1076.

Andriotis, K. & Vaughan, R. D. (2003). Urban residents' attitudes toward tourism development: the case of Crete. *Journal of Travel Research*, *42*(2), 172–185.

Balearic Islands Tourism Board (2017). Balearic Islands Regional Context Survey. [Online]. *Balearic Islands Tourism Board*. Available at: https://projects2014-2020.interregeurope.eu/fileadmin/user_upload/tx_tevprojects/library/file_1508251726.pdf

Bartlitz, J. (2023). Tourismus: darum könnte 2023 zum Rekordjahr werden. *tagesschau.de*. [Online]. Available at: https://www.tagesschau.de/wirtschaft/verbraucher/reisetrends-2023-itb-101.html

Bauer, U. & Bittlingmayer, U. H. (2014). Pierre Bourdieu und die Frankfurter Schule. In U. Bauer, U. H. Bittlingmayer, C. Keller & F. Schultheis (Eds.), *Bourdieu und die Frankfurter Schule: kritische Gesellschaftstheorie im Zeitalter des Neoliberalismus* (pp. 43–82). Bielefeld: transcript.

Boley, B. B., Strzelecka, M., & Woosnam, K. M. (2018). Resident perceptions of the economic benefits of tourism: toward a Common Measure. *Journal of Hospitality & Tourism Research*, *42*(8), 1295–1314.

Boltanski, L. (2011). *On Critique: A sociology of Emancipation*. Cambridge: Polity Press.

Bourdieu, P. (1992). *Die verborgenen Mechanismen der Macht. Schriften zu Politik und Kultur 1*. Hamburg: VSA.

Buhalis, D. (2020). *There is no overtourism - only badly managed tourism*. [Online]. Available at: http://buhalis.blogspot.com/2020/02/there-is-no-overtourism-only-badly.html

Burawoy, M. (2014). Facing an unequal world. *Current Sociology*, *63*(1), 5–34.

Büscher, B. & Fletcher, R. (2017). Destructive creation: capital accumulation and the structural violence of tourism. *Journal of Sustainable Tourism*, *25*(5), 651–667.

Butcher, J. (2020). The construction of 'overtourism': the Case of UK media coverage of Barcelona's 2017 tourism protests and their aftermath. In H. Séraphin, T. Gladkikh, & T. Vo Thanh (Eds.), *Overtourism: Causes, Implications and Solutions* (pp. 69–88). London: Palgrave Macmillan.

Butler, R. W. (2019). Overtourism in rural settings: the Scottish highlands and islands. In R. Dodds & R. Butler (Eds.), *Overtourism: Issues, Realities and Solutions* (pp. 199–213). Berlin: De Gruyter.

Cañada, E. (2019). Trabajo turístico y precariedad. In E. Cañada & I. Murray (Eds.), *Turistificación global: perspectivas críticas en turismo* (pp. 267–287). Barcelona: Icaria.

Chenoweth, E. (2020). *Questions, Answers, and Some Cautionary Updates regarding the 3.5% Rule*. Boston: Harvard University, Carr Center for Human Rights Policy - Harvard Kennedy School.

Cocola-Gant, A. (2023). Place-based displacement: touristification and neighborhood change. *Geoforum*, *138*.

Colomb, C., & Novy, J. (Eds.) (2016). *Protest and Resistance in the Tourist City*. London: Routledge.

Deccio, C., & Baloglu, S. (2002). Nonhost community resident reactions to the 2002 Winter Olympics: the spillover impacts. *Journal of Travel Research*, *41*(1), 46–56.

Dodds, R. & Butler, R. (2019). Conclusion. In R. Dodds & R. Butler (Eds.), *Overtourism: Issues, Realities and Solutions* (pp. 262–276). Berlin: De Gruyter.

Doxey, G. V. (1975). A causation theory of visitor–resident irritants, methodology and research inferences: the impact of tourism. *Travel Research Association, 6th Annual Conference Proceedings*, 195–198.

Europa Press Islas Baleares (2022). Cientos de personas protestan ante el Consolat de Mar contra la "masificación turística" en el Mediterráneo. *Europa Press Islas Baleares.* [Online]. Available at: https://www.europapress.es/illes-balears/noticia-cientos-personas-protestan-consolat-mar-contra-masificacion-turistica-mediterraneo-20220927192039.html

France 24 (2018). Portuguese protest over rising short-term tourism rentals. *France 24*. [Online]. Available at: https://www.france24.com/en/20180922-portuguese-protest-over-rising-short-term-tourism-rentals

Frye, M. (2021). Risky business? Balancing Mexico's pandemic response with tourism. *CNN*. [Online]. Available at: https://edition.cnn.com/travel/article/mexico-pandemic-tourism-health-balance/index.html

Hadjisolomou, A., Booyens, I., Nickson, D., Cunningham, T. & Baum, T. (2022). *Fair Work for All?: A Review of Employment Practices in the Scottish Hospitality Industry*. Glasgow: University of Strathclyde.

Higgins-Desbiolles, F. (2020). Socialising tourism for social and ecological justice after COVID-19. *Tourism Geographies*, *22*(3), 610–623.

Higgins-Desbiolles, F., Carnicelli, S., Krolikowski, C., Wijesinghe, G., & Boluk, K. (2019). Degrowing tourism: rethinking tourism. *Journal of Sustainable Tourism*, *27*(12), 1926–1944.

Honneth, A. (2011). *Das Recht der Freiheit: Grundriß einer demokratischen Sittlichkeit*. Berlin: Suhrkamp.

Horkheimer, M. (1985). Zur Soziologie der Klassenverhältnisse. In M. Horkheimer (Ed.), *Gesammelte Schriften 12* (pp. 75-104), Frankfurt/Main: S. Fischer.

Jackson, M. (2022). Challenge for industry to beat the "brain drain'". *Tourism Update*. Available at: https://www.tourismupdate.co.za/article/challenge-industry-beat-brain-drain

Jun, S. H., Pongsata, P. & Noh, J. (2016). An examination of residents' support for tourism development in Thailand. *Travel and Tourism Research Association: Advancing Tourism*, *15*.

Kassam, A. (2021). Palma to limit cruise ships after environmental concerns. *The Guardian*. Available at: https://www.theguardian.com/world/2021/dec/27/mallorca-port-cruise-ship-limit-palma-spain

Ko, D.-W. & Stewart, W. P. (2002). A structural equation model of residents' attitudes for tourism development. *Tourism Management*, *23*(5), 521–530.

Koens, K., Postma, A. & Papp, B. (2018). Is overtourism overused? Understanding the impact of tourism in a city context. *Sustainability*, *10*(12), 4384.

Lacher, R. & Oh, C.-O. (2012). Is tourism a low-income industry? Evidence from three coastal regions. *Journal of Travel Research*, *51*(4), 464–472.

Látková, P. & Vogt, C. A. (2012). Residents' attitudes toward existing and future tourism development in rural communities. *Journal of Travel Research*, *51*(1), 50–67.

Lee, D., Hampton, M. & Jeyacheya, J. (2015). The political economy of precarious work in the tourism industry in small island developing states. *Review of International Political Economy*, *22*(1), 194–223.

Lopez, O. (2021). Tourists are returning to Cancún. But workers' fears about COVID-19 never went away. *Time*. Available at: https://time.com/5921756/mexico-tourism-coronavirus/

Madrigal, R. (1993). A tale of tourism in two cities. *Annals of Tourism Research*, *20*(2), 336–353.

Mansilla, J. A. (2018). Vecinos en peligro de extinción. Turismo urbano, movimientos sociales y exclusión socioespacial en Barcelona. *Pasos. Revista e Turismo Y Patrimonio Cultural*, *16*(2), 279–296.

Mansilla, J. A. & Milano, C. (2019). Becoming centre: tourism placemaking and space production in two neighborhoods in Barcelona. *Tourism Geographies*, *18*(2), 1–22.

Martiny, J. (2021). Mallorca without tourists - an island at the limit. *Deutsche Welle*. [Online]. Available at: https://www.dw.com/en/mallorca-without-tourists-the-impact-of-the-coronavirus-pandemic/a-56282403

McGehee, N. G. & Andereck, K. L. (2004). Factors predicting rural residents' support of tourism. *Journal of Travel Research*, *43*(2), 131–140.

McKinsey & Company & World Travel & Tourism Council (2017). *Coping with Success: Managing Overcrowding in Tourism Destinations*. McKinsey & Company & World Travel & Tourism Council.

Mezirow, J. (2003). Transformative learning as discourse. *Journal of Transformative Education*, *1*, 58–63.

Milano, C., Cheer, J. M. & Novelli, M. (2019a). Overtourism: an evolving phenomenon. In C. Milano, J. M. Cheer & M. Novelli (Eds.), *Overtourism: Excesses, Discontents and Measures in Travel and Tourism* (pp. 1-17). Abingdon: CABI.

Milano, C. Novelli, M. & Cheer, J. M. (2019b). Overtourism and degrowth: a social movements perspective. *Journal of Sustainable Tourism*, 27(12), 1857–1875.

Milesi Ferretti, G. M. (2021). The travel shock. *Hutchins Center on Fiscal & Monetary Policy*. [Online]. Available at: https://www.brookings.edu/research/the-covid-19-travel-shock-hit-tourism-dependent-economies-hard/

Murray, I. & Cañada, E. (2017). *Global Labour Column*. Johannesburg: University of the Witwatersrand.

Novy, J. & Colomb, C. (2019). Urban tourism as a source of contention and social mobilisations: a critical review. *Tourism Planning & Development*, 16(4), 358–375.

Onda Cero Mallorca (2022). Más de uno Illes Balears 18/01/2022. *Onda Cero Mallorca*. [Online]. Available at: https://www.ondacero.es/emisoras/baleares/mallorca/audios-podcast/mas-de-uno/mas-uno-illes-balears-18012022_2022011861e6d5f104912a0001d3ee1d.html

Ozden, J. & Glover, S. (2023). What makes a protest movement successful? *Social Change Lab*. [Online].

Peeters, P., Gössling, S., Klijs, J., Milano, C., Novelli, M., Dijkmans, C., Eijgelaar, E., Hartman, S., Heslinga, J., Isaac, R., Mitas, O., Moretti, S., Nawijn, J., Papp, B. & Postma, A. (2018). *Research for TRAN committee - Overtourism: Impact and Possible Policy Responses*. Brussels: European Parliament.

Perdue, R. R., Long, P. T. & Allen, L. (1990). Resident support for tourism development. *Annals of Tourism Research*, *17*(4), 586–599.

Pizam, A. (1978). Tourism's impacts: the social costs to the destination community as perceived by its residents. *Journal of Travel Research*, *16*(4), 8–12.

Redazione ANSA (2020). Venice readies visitor counting system - lifestyle. *ANSA*. [Online]. Available at: https://www.ansa.it/english/news/lifestyle/travel/2020/02/ 07/venice-readies-visitor-countingsystem_50c51fd2-f952-47af-9334-4c374b219350.htm

Sigala, M. (2021). Rethinking of tourism and hospitality education when nothing is normal: restart, recover, or rebuild. *Journal of Hospitality & Tourism Research*, *45*(5), 920–923.

Snaith, T. & Haley, A. (1999). Residents' opinions of tourism development in the historic city of York, England. *Tourism Management*, *20*, 595–603.

Standing, G. (2011). *The Precariat: The New Dangerous Class*. London: Bloomsbury Academic.

Roose, J. & Dietz, H. (2016). Social Theory and Social Movements. Wiesbaden: Springer Fachmedien Wiesbaden.

Schmitt, L. (2010). *Bestellt und nicht abgeholt: soziale Ungleichheit und Habitus-Struktur-Konflikte im Studium*. Wiesbaden: VS Verlag für Sozialwissenschaften.

Williams, J. & Lawson, R. (2001). Community issues and resident opinions of tourism. *Annals of Tourism Research*, *28*(2), 269–290.

World Tourism Organisation (2004). *Indicators of Sustainable Development for Tourism Destinations: A Guidebook* (English version). Madrid, Spain: World Tourism Organization (UNWTO). [Online]. Available at: https://www.e-unwto.org/action/showBook?doi=10.18111%2F9789284407262

World Tourism Organisation (2019). World Tourism Day 2019. *World Tourism Organization*. [Online]. Available at: https://www.unwto.org/world-tourism-day-2019

World Tourism Organisation (2020). International tourism growth continues to outpace the global economy. *World Tourism Organization*. [Online]. Available at: https://www.unwto.org/international-tourism-growth-continues-to-outpace-the-economy

World Travel & Tourism Council (2020). Travel & Tourism Economic Impact. *World Travel & Tourism Council (WTTC)*. [Online]. Available at: https://wttc.org/research/economic-impact

Yayla, Ö., Koç, B. & Dimanche, F. (2023). Residents' support for tourism development: investigating quality-of-life, community commitment, and communication. *European Journal of Tourism Research*, *33*, 3311.

Zampoukos, K. & Ioannides, D. (2011). The tourism labour conundrum: agenda for new research in the geography of hospitality workers. *Hospitality & Society*, *1*(1), 25–45.

Chapter 11 - Unveiling the implications of digital platforms in platform-mediated overtourism: a call for comprehensive research

Sina Hardaker

Introduction

Digital platforms are increasingly influencing and mediating our daily lives as well as our economy (Hardaker, 2021; Kenney & Zysman, 2019; 2020), including the tourism sector (Celata & Romano, 2022; Sigala, 2022). The far-reaching disruptions that digital platforms bring about in society have led to the term 'platform urbanism' (e.g. Fields, Bissell & Macrorie, 2020; Richardson, 2020b), which falls within the area of geography and urban studies. In these disciplines the concept is used as a means to describe the intensifying link between technologies and cities as well as the accompanying growth of digital platforms (Sadowski, 2020; Richardson 2020b).

While tourism studies recently started to more directly discuss the platform economy (Capineri &Romano, 2021; Munasinghe et al., 2022; Sigala, 2022), a clear focus on the implications of digital platforms in the accommodation sector, in particular Airbnb (e.g. Guttentag, 2015; 2019; Oskam & Boswijk, 2016; Pastor & Rivera-García, 2020) has already been observed for several years. Studies on Airbnb address inter alia the socio-spatial inequalities (Morales-Pérez, Garay & Wilson, 2020) as well as population displacement and gentrification (Cocola-Gant & Gago, 2019). Only recently, the negative consequences resulting from digital platforms have been directly linked to overtourism[1]. Celeta and Romano (2022) for instance, argue that the spread of short-term rental platforms in Italian cities is not merely a coincidental factor, but rather essential for understanding contemporary overtourism in terms of how and where it occurs. Platforms like Airbnb not only increase the accommodation capacity of urban areas, but also fundamentally reshape the morphology of Italian tourist cities. Thus, the concerns

---

[1] Celata and Romano (2022) point out in regard to overtourism that "Despite the relevance of the issue and its effects, there is still lack of conceptual clarity about what overtourism is, how contemporary concerns about it differ from earlier worries, what are its causes and consequences and, consequently, how it should be investigated and managed". In this chapter the term is used rather broadly, indicating negative effects for the local population as well as nature due to a too large number of tourists.

surrounding overtourism are not solely attributed to the sheer number of tourists, but to their growing intrusion into residential areas (Celeta & Romano, 2022).

In this chapter I argue that research on the platform economy's impact on the tourism industry is still in its infancy, concentrating mainly on single phenomena, such as Airbnb (e.g. Roelofsen, 2022; Stabrowski, 2017; Wilson, Garay-Tamajon & Morales-Perez, 2022; Yao et al., 2019). Yet, the mechanisms through which digital platforms potentially contribute to overtourism are complex and multifaceted, requiring a thorough investigation of their impact. Hence, research on digital platforms can shed light on the role of technology in shaping travel behaviour and decision-making and how these behaviours can lead to overtourism.

The chapter bridges the divide between tourism, (economic) geography as well as platform studies, arguing that the digital platform economy should be included more widely in the discussion of overtourism and studies should look more closely at the impact of platforms on the scale of the city due to their considerable power in mediating large tourism streams. It is important to note that there is more than Airbnb that deserves attention. Also platforms whose (spatial) implications might not be visible at first sight are relevant. This chapter aims to identify the specific features of digital platforms that potentially contribute to overtourism. Ultimately, it argues that research on overtourism and digital platforms can inform the development of policies and practices that balance the economic benefits of tourism against its negative impacts and promote sustainable and responsible tourism. Against this backdrop, I argue for the establishment of a research stream focussing on platform-mediated overtourism.

The remainder of the chapter is structured as follows. After a brief introduction on digital platforms, their pivotal role and current research on them in tourism studies is discussed. Subsequently, some examples will be given. Finally, I propose directions for future research regarding platform-mediated overtourism.

Digital platforms and the tourism sector

In economics, digital platforms are understood as two-sided/multisided matchmakers (Rochet & Tirole, 2004), enabling multiple actors to find each other and to connect (Schwarz, 2017). They progressively dictate the way the economy is organized (Hardaker, 2021; Kenney & Zysman, 2016; 2020) by continually reforming spatial representations, controlling interactions between users, workers, capital and information (Graham, 2020) as well as reorganizing urban interactions and operations (Richardson, 2020a; 2020b). This includes the economic and social fabric of essential aspects of our everyday lives (van Dijck, van Poell & de Waal, 2018), such as work (Anwar & Graham, 2020), housing and travel (Celata, Capineri & Romano, 2020) and consumption/shopping (Bissell, 2020; Hardaker, 2022). The enormous impact of digital platforms can be observed at a variety of different segments that have experienced radical market changes such as accommodation (e.g. Airbnb; see Zervas, Proserpio & Byers, 2017; Ferreri & Sanyal,

2018; Aguilera, Artioli & Colomb, 2019; Cocola-Gant & Gago, 2019; van Doorn, 2019), mobility (e.g. Uber and Lyft; see Hall & Krueger, 2017; Fan et al., 2019; Walker, 2020; Wells, Attoh & Cullen, 2021) as well as search, social media and content creation (e.g. Google, Facebook and YouTube; see van Dijck, van Poell & de Waal, 2018; Zuboff, 2019; Kenney & Zysman, 2020a). While these segments are part of the touristic value chain, the tourism industry has also been disrupted on a more general note by platforms, such as Booking.com and TripAdvisor, as they are "impacting on demand and supply and more generally on tourism practices" (Capineri & Romano, 2021, p. 1). In this regard, studies so far took on Lefebvre's spatial triad theory (Farmaki, Christou & Saveriades, 2020), logistical approaches (Jansson, 2022) as well as the relationship of tour operators to tourism platform services such as Airbnb (Pompurová, Sebova & Scholz, 2022), pointing out new platform tourism services competition with traditional businesses, while simultaneously arguing that they can potentially benefit all subjects from the opportunities generated. For instance, Salet (2021) focusses on authenticity in online travel writing, which emphasizes much on re-imagination and re-discovery, arguing that platformisation fuels fast production and a competitive approach to authenticity.

In particular the sharing economy has been identified as a disrupting force within the tourism industry (Celata, Hendrickson & Sanna, 2017; Dolnicar, 2021; Eckhardt et al., 2019), as it "has changed why and where we travel (TripAdvisor); how we travel to and within a destination (Uber, Ofo, Lyft, sharing bicycles, motor houses, and private jet platforms); where we stay (Airbnb, HomeAway); where and what we eat (Deliveroo, Uber Eats, Eatwith, Feastly, VizEat); what we see/do and how we experience destinations (Airbnb experiences, ToursByLocals, travel2change, Meetup, Vayable); where and how we work even while on holidays (Airtasker, Amazon Mechanical Turk); and with whom we share travel experiences" (Sigala, 2022).

Sigala (2022) points out a variety of alterations brought about by digital platforms. For example, in the sharing economy they have induced changes in tourists' preferences, lifestyles as well as consumption patterns. Digital platforms have also contributed to the redefinition of value and distribution chains, because they have resulted in intensified competition between traditional and sharing providers. Furthermore, the supply side of tourism has been altered due to the emergence of new tourism entrepreneurial ventures, business models as well as microentrepreneurs. Simultaneously, existing markets have been transformed and new markets have been created, while (tourism) institutions, socioeconomic systems and laws have been challenged. By way of example, think of changing definitions and labour legislation for gig workers (Sigala, 2022).

Particularly the platforms Airbnb and Uber have attracted much scholarly attention. By augmenting, substituting and reorganising physical spaces, Airbnb and Uber have reterritorialized existing infrastructures. A Special Issue in the *Journal of Sustainable Tourism* on peer-to-peer service platforms in tourism by Minoia and Jokela (2022) also focuses on Airbnb, as it is recognized as the leading digital platform specializing in short-term property rental. Indeed, Airbnb represents an outstanding case study regarding spatial implications mediated by a digital platform (Celata, Capineri & Romano, 2020; Cocola-Gant & Gago, 2019; Roelofsen & Minca, 2018; Schor, 2017; Semi & Tonetta, 2020; Spangler, 2020; Törnberg & Chiappini, 2020). Cocola-Gant and Gago (2019) highlight the increasing insecurity and displacement concerns for tenants to which the Airbnb business model contributes, while it simultaneously acts as an instrument that fosters the financialisation of housing and gentrification of communities.

Several studies even argue that Airbnb should be understood as a new urban institution that is transforming relations between market, state and civil society actors (Ferreri & Sanyal, 2018). Airbnb has developed into a significant player in urban governance (Aguilera, Artioli & Colomb, 2019; Semi & Tonetta, 2020) turning citizens into "place entrepreneurs" (Törnberg & Chiappini, 2020). As in the case of Uber drivers or Airbnb entrepreneurs, the risk is continuously moved towards the 'independent' contractor, while simultaneously transforming intimate personal space, such as a private home or a private car, into a business asset. In a similar vein, Uber can be seen as an "interstitial platform infrastructure" that relies on pre-existing infrastructures such as road networks, sidewalks, and other public spaces often funded by the public sector (Stehlin, Hodson & McMeekin, 2020). Although digital platforms do not own the underlying assets that enable performance of the economic activity they stimulate (for example, Uber owns no taxis, Airbnb owns no rentable real estate), they can dictate and reorganise value creation and territorialise the link between the spatial and temporal coordination of two actors in form of "the delivered meal, the hailed ride, the space to sleep", which "are not in any simple sense "objects", but rather are materializations of the flexible spatio-temporal arrangements that occur through the calculated coordination of the different actors", as Richardson (2020b, p. 461) puts it.

However, apart from distinguished examples, such as Airbnb in the accommodation sector and Uber in the transport industry, there is a lack of understanding with regard to the platform economy's concrete influence upon value transfer away from the local economy to the platform and with regard to the reorganising institutional logic of the tourism sector. More and more businesses are somehow integrated into platform ecosystems, yet, localness remains an important pillar. What unites the vast majority of these studies is their emphasis on platform-mediated challenges that are associated with negative spatial and/or social consequences. Yet, digital platforms have only recently been linked to overtourism (Celata & Romano, 2022), which will be discussed in more detail below.

Overtourism and digital platforms

A great deal of geographical and tourism-related research in recent years has focused on the dynamics of the sharing economy and the accompanying configuration of work as well as its spatial implications. What most studies share is the focus on inequalities (e.g. Roelofsen & Minca, 2018; Spangler, 2020) in the sharing economy that has opened up new avenues for extracting value (Semi & Tonetta, 2020). As Stehlin, Hodson and McMeekin (2020) argue, it is about the intersection of platformisation with persistent socio-spatial inequalities and the potential for a more equitable approach to platform urbanism. While Schor (2017) highlights its misconception regarding its supposed novelty, all studies have in common that the sharing economy has sparked controversy regarding inequality, particularly because of its impact on wages and labour conditions. Sigala (2022) highlights the controversial discussion around the sharing economy's impacts, pointing out the positive impacts on the one hand (including the democratisation of travel/tourism – i.e. lower cost of traveling and affordability for tourism by more people – and a better distribution of tourism revenues; e.g. Mody, Cheng & Hanks, 2019) as well as negative impacts on the other hand (including the predatory, exploitative, illegal, under-organised, and under-regulated repercussions of the sharing economy).

Negative impacts on residents have been discussed broadly within overtourism studies (Amrhein, Hospers & Reiser, 2022). Contemporary overtourism is not, moreover, simply due to congestion or overcrowding; the concern is about how touristification affects and interacts with the social fabric of the destination and what the consequences are for its residents. Consequently, numerous social movements have arisen in opposition to platforms such as Airbnb (Cócola-Gant & Pardo, 2017; Wilson, Garay-Tamajon & Morales-Perez, 2022), resulting in policy responses (Aguilera, Artioli & Colomb, 2019; Nieuwland & van Melik, 2020) throughout a number of cities around the globe.

One noteworthy study undertaken by Celata and Romano (2022) clearly links Airbnb's potential contribution to overtourism, suggesting that the diffusion of short-term rental platforms is not merely a concomitant factor, but crucial to understanding the how and where of contemporary overtourism. They argue inter alia that Airbnb not only contributes to an increasing accommodation capacity of urban areas, but radically changes the morphology of the tourist city: "The growing concerns about overtourism are not due to the rising number of tourists per se, but to their increasing penetration into the residential city." Consequently, they suggest that overtourism should not merely be conceived as "overcrowding" (Celata & Romano, 2022). Arriving at similar results, yet, not linking them specifically to overtourism, Morales-Pérez, Garay and Wilson (2020) assert that the spatial expansion and growing professionalisation of Airbnb-mediated rentals in Barcelona serve as the foundation for the platform's contribution to capital accumulation, property speculation as well as socio-spatial inequality. In the case of the Spanish cities of Barcelona and Madrid, Benítez-Aurioles (2018) similarly reveal that greater sensibility of demand with respect to distance to the centre can be observed. This also leads to a so-called 'shrinkage of space', increasing overtourism in tourist centres.

In short, reviewing critical studies regarding overtourism, a large number of research can be associated to platform-mediated overtourism already (Bouchon &

Rauscher, 2019; Goodwin, 2017). However, it is important to note that this very link is rarely the main focus of the analysis. Thus, the last section will discuss the need and the potential of research regarding platform-mediated overtourism.

Platform-mediated overtourism: discussion and future research

Digital platforms have transformed the way we travel, enabling travellers to access information and book trips more easily than ever before. This has led to a surge in tourism that has strained infrastructure and damaged local ecosystems and cultures. In some destinations it has created also social and economic inequality. By matching different actors and enabling new forms of value creation, digital platforms have become a powerful actor. They are able to provide unprecedented logistical affordances to people to navigate, influence and manage various (tourist) flows. As pointed out by Jansson (2022), the platform economy rests on logistical accumulation causing a situation in which human behaviour is not merely predicted but actively guided to generate lucrative digital data flows. Consequently, tourism is understood as a logistical intersection, where the operational mechanisms of the platform economy intertwine with the requirements and capabilities of travellers in terms of navigation, coordination and organization.

Focusing on the conceptualisation of digital platforms, this chapter aims to link the platform economy to overtourism. Yet, I argue that digital platforms often represent an intangible, yet highly influential and powerful actor when it comes to (over-)tourism. As argued by Hardaker (2021), there are mainly three key reasons why conducting research on digital platforms is difficult, namely unawareness, unaccountability and non-transparency. This is probably one possible reason for the intense focus on Airbnb in previous studies. The consequences of the platform are relatively obvious and can - at least in some areas such as the number of apartments, etc. - be quantified. This is significantly less straightforward in the case of Google or Instagram. How many tourists are actually clearly influenced by Instagram images to go and see the Tower of Pisa, the rice terraces in Bali or the royal palace in Thailand? To what extent does Google actively shape perceptions and guidance through a city when we rely on Google Maps and thereby 'shrink' the city to certain stores and services, while certain providers do not exist in Google's digital world? And how does one of their key features and advantages – the generated network effects – potentially lead to the further shrinking of space, thus presenting an influential factor for overtourism? Further, as digital platforms repeatedly operate at a different spatial scale (Graham, 2020; Hardaker, 2023-forthcoming) local responsibility is avoided.

So far, the implications of the platform economy have been studied in a large variety of contexts. Consequently, several terms have emerged, such as 'platform economy' (e.g. Kenney & Zysman, 2016; Kenney, Bearson & Zysman, 2020), 'platform capitalism' (e.g. Langley & Leyshon 2017a; Srnicek, 2017), platform logic (e.g. Schwarz, 2017), platform power (e.g. Culpepper & Thelen, 2019) as well as platform society (e.g. van Dijck, van Poell. & de Waal, 2018). Within the discussion of platform urbanism (e.g. Barns, 2020; Fields, Bissell & Macrorie, 2020; Hardaker 2021; Richardson, 2020a; 2020b; Sadowski, 2020) tourism-related studies have recently emerged and, as shown earlier, have been debating the implications of major players such as Airbnb within the context of platform-mediated tourism (Minoia & Jokela, 2022; Supaporn et al., 2023) for several years. This chapter makes a plea for establishing a framework of platform-mediated overtourism, which is still in the early stages of development and can greatly benefit from the existing body of research.

It is argued that digital platforms often represent an intangible, yet highly influential actor in the field of (over-)tourism. Profiting from network effects these platforms potentially lead to the further shrinking of space, thus enabling overtourism. Further, as they repeatedly operate at a different spatial scale, they remain a largely unaccountable factor. Future research to better grasp the impact of digital platforms on the tourism industry and the challenge of overtourism in particular could therefore focus on the context of the shrinkage of space (Harvey, 1990; Kirsch, 1995) and look further than the frequently used example of Airbnb (e.g. on Booking.com as well as on Google) as well as popular European cities.

More research should be conducted to examine the effects of digital platforms on overtourism. In this respect, a focus on destinations in the Global South might be promising. As pointed out by Mody, Cheng and Hanks (2021), research concerning the sharing economy in tourism is dominated by western-situated researchers and studies, although the sharing economy is booming in countries like China and India, since in these places this phenomenon is generally a governmental priority to quicken regional development. Further, limited theoretical engagement and the utilisation of a limited range of methods and perspectives (disciplinary, stakeholders and sectors) can be criticized. So far, several studies mainly draw on qualitative methods, such as in-depth interviews and media screening (e.g. Bissell, 2020). In order to interrogate the implications of sharing economies that are difficult to grasp, Frenken et al. (2020) suggest the application of experimental autoethnographic, participatory or digital/visual methods. In my view, it makes sense to carry out further research on the following topics:

Increased accessibility: Digital platforms have made it easier for people to find and book travel experiences, from flights and accommodation to guided tours. This has led to an increase in the number of tourists visiting popular destinations, potentially resulting in overcrowding and overtourism.

User-generated content: Social media platforms have allowed travellers to share their experiences and photos, often creating a "buzz" around a limited number of destinations. This can potentially lead to more people wanting to visit those destinations, thus further contributing to overtourism.

Real-time information: Digital platforms such as Google Maps and TripAdvisor provide real-time information on tourist destinations, including ratings and reviews. This might lead to a concentration of tourists in certain areas, potentially resulting in overtourism.

Personalized recommendations: Digital platforms use algorithms to recommend destinations and experiences based on a user's interests and past behaviour. This might create a domino effect where certain places become 'hotspots' and attract a large number of tourists, which increases the risk for chance of overtourism.

Reduced costs: Digital platforms have made it easier and cheaper for people to travel, leading to an increase in the number of tourists. This can result in overcrowding, strains on infrastructure and damage to the environment.

Increased marketing: Digital platforms allow travel companies to market their destinations and experiences to a wider audience, which often creates a hype and rising demand for certain destinations. This can lead to a concentration of tourists in those areas and increase the risk that overtourism occurs.

Shorter booking windows: Digital platforms allow travellers to book their trips at the last minute, often resulting in a sudden influx of tourists to a particular place. This can lead to overcrowding and other issues associated with overtourism.

Influencer culture: Digital platforms have created a culture where so-called 'influencers' and celebrities promote certain destinations, leading to a surge in popularity and a concentration of tourists in those areas.

Lack of regulation: Digital platforms often operate outside of traditional regulatory structures, allowing for an unchecked and unbalanced growth in the tourism industry. This can result in the exploitation of local communities and the environment, exacerbating issues associated with overtourism.

Lack of education: Digital platforms may not provide adequate information about the negative impacts of tourism on local communities and the environment. This can result in tourists unknowingly contributing to overtourism and other negative effects of tourism.

Conclusions

In this chapter I have shown how important it is to analyse the link between research on overtourism and that on digital platforms. After all, digital platforms are having a big impact on overtourism. By better considering the ways in which digital platforms contribute to overtourism, we can develop a more nuanced understanding of the broader socio-economic and environmental impacts of tourism and develop effective strategies to manage and mitigate its negative impacts. This will require interdisciplinary research that considers the interplay between technology, tourism and the environment as well as the perspectives of different stakeholders, including local communities, tourism operators and policymakers. Identifying the specific features of digital platforms that potentially contribute to overtourism, such as personalized recommendations and user-generated content, should also be explored further. Lastly, research should examine the potential of digital platforms as tools for managing overtourism, such as by providing real-time data on tourist flows and facilitating sustainable tourism practices.

Literature

Aguilera, T., Artioli, F. & Colomb, C. (2019). Explaining the diversity of policy responses to platform-mediated short-term rentals in European cities: a comparison of Barcelona, Paris and Milan. *Environment and Planning A*, *49*(6), 1308-1323.

Amrhein, S., Hospers, G.J. & Reiser, D. (2022). Impact of overtourism on residents. In D. Gursoy & S. Celik (Eds.), *Routledge Handbook of Social Psychology of Tourism*. London: Routledge.

Anwar, M. A., & Graham, M. (2020). Hidden transcripts of the gig economy: labour agency and the new art of resistance among African gig workers. *Environment and Planning A*, *52*(7), 1269-1291.

Barns, S. (2020). *Platform Urbanism: Negotiating Platform Ecosystems in Connected Cities*. New York: Palgrave Macmillan.

Bissell, D. (2020). Affective platform urbanism: changing habits of digital on-demand consumption. *Geoforum*, *115*, 102-110.

Benítez-Aurioles, B. (2018). The role of distance in the peer-to-peer market for tourist accommodation. *Tourism Economics*, *24*(3), 237-250.

Bouchon, F. & Rauscher, M. (2019). Cities and tourism, a love and hate story; towards a conceptual framework for urban overtourism management. *International Journal of Tourism Cities*, *5*(4), 598–619.

Butler, R. W. (2019). Tourism carrying capacity research: a perspective article. *Tourism Review*, *75*(1), 207–211.

Capineri, C. & Romano, A. (2021). The platformization of tourism: from accommodation to experiences. *Digital Geography and Society*, *2*, 100012.

Celata, F. & Romano, A. (2022). Overtourism and online short-term rental platforms in Italian cities. *Journal of Sustainable Tourism*, *30*(5), 1020-1039.

Celata, F., Capineri, C. & Romano, A. (2020). A room with a (re)view: short-term rentals, digital reputation and the uneven spatiality of platform-mediated tourism. *Geoforum*, *112*, 129-138.

Celata, F., Hendrickson, C. Y. & Sanna, V. S. (2017). The sharing economy as community marketplace? Trust, reciprocity and belonging in peer-to-peer accommodation platforms. *Cambridge Journal of Regions, Economy and Society*, *10*(2), 349-363.

Cocola-Gant, A. & Gago, A. (2019). Airbnb, buy-to-let investment and tourism-driven displacement: a case study in Lisbon. *Environment and Planning A*, *53*(7), 1671-1688.

Cocola-Gant, A. & Pardo, D. (2017). Resisting tourism gentrification: the experience of grassroots movements in Barcelona. *Urbanistica Tre, Giornale Online di Urbanistica*, *5*(13), 39-47.

Culpepper, P. D. & Thelen, K. (2019). Are we all Amazon primed? Consumers and the politics of platform power. *Environment and Planning B*, *53*(2), 288-318.

Dolnicar, S. (2021). Sharing economy and peer-to-peer accommodation – a perspective paper. *Tourism Review*, *76*(1), 34-37.

Fan, Y., Xia, M., Zhang, Y. & Chena, Y. (2019). The influence of social embeddedness on organizational legitimacy and the sustainability of the globalization of the sharing economic platform: evidence from Uber China. *Resources, Conservation and Recycling*, *151*, 104490.

Farmaki, A., Christou, P. & Saveriades, A. (2020). A Lefebvrian analysis of Airbnb space. *Annals of Tourism Research*, *80*, 102806.

Ferreri, M. & Sanyal, R. (2018). Platform economies and urban planning: Airbnb and regulated deregulation in London. *Environment and Planning B*, *55*(15), 3353-3368.

Fields, D., Bissell, D. & Macrorie, R. (2020). Platform methods: studying platform urbanism outside the black box. *Urban Geography*, *41*(3), 462-468.

Frenken, K., van Waes, A., Pelzer, P., Smink, M. & van Est, R. (2020). Safeguarding public interests in the platform economy. *Policy and Internet*, *12*(3), 400-425.

Goodwin, H. (2017). The challenge of overtourism. *Responsible Tourism Partnership Working Paper 4*, October 2017.

Graham, M. (2020). Regulate, replicate, and resist: the conjunctural geographies of platform urbanism. *Urban Geography*, *41*(3), 453-457.

Guttentag, D. (2015). Airbnb: disruptive innovation and the rise of an informal tourism accommodation sector. *Current Issues in Tourism*, *8*(12), 1192-1217.

Guttentag, D. (2019). Progress on Airbnb: a literature review. *Journal of Hospitality and Tourism Technology*, *10*, 814-844.

Hall, J. V. & Krueger, A. B. (2017). An analysis of the labor market for Uber's driver-partners in the United States. *Environment and Planning B*, *71*(3), 705-732.

Hardaker, S. (2023, forthcoming). A critical perspective on the increasing power of digital platforms through the lens of conjunctural geographies. In Vale, M., Ferreira, D., Rodrigues, N. (Eds.), *Geographies of the Platform Economy: Critical Perspectives*. Heidelberg: Springer.

Hardaker, S. (2022). More than infrastructure providers - digital platforms' role and power in retail digitalization initiatives in Germany. *Tijdschrift voor Economische en Sociale Geografie*, *113*(3), 310-328.

Hardaker, S. (2021). Platform economy: (dis-)embedding processes in urban spaces? *Urban Transformations*, *3*(12).

Harvey, D. (1990). Between space and time: reflections on the geographical imagination. *Annals of the Association of American Geographers*, *80*, 418-434.

Jansson, A. (2022). Guided by data: a logistical approach to tourism in the platform economy. *Digital Geography and Society*, *3,* 100040.

Kenney, M. & Zysman, J. (2016). The rise of the platform economy. *Issues in Science and Technology*, *32*(3), 61-69.

Kenney, M. & Zysman, J. (2020). The platform economy: restructuring the space of capitalist accumulation. *Cambridge Journal of Regions, Economy and Society*, *13*(1), 55-76.

Kirsch, S. (1995). The incredible shrinking world? Technology and the production of space. *Environment and Planning D*, *13*(5), 529-555.

Langley, P. & Leyshon, A. (2017a). Platform capitalism: the intermediation and capitalisation of digital economic circulation. *Finance and Society*, *3*(1), 11-31.

Langley, P. & Leyshon, A. (2017b). Capitalizing on the crowd: the monetary and financial ecologies of crowdfunding. *Environment and Planning A*, *49*(5), 1019-1039.

Minoia, P. & Jokela, S. (2022). Platform-mediated tourism: social justice and urban governance before and during Covid-19. *Journal of Sustainable Tourism*, *30*(5), 951-965.

Mody, M., Cheng, M. & Hanks, L. (2021). Sharing economy research in hospitality and tourism: a critical review using bibliometric analysis, content analysis and quantitative systematic literature review. *International Journal of Contemporary Hospitality Management*, *33*(5), 1711-1745.

Morales-Pérez, S., Garay, L. & Wilson, J. (2020). Airbnb's contribution to socio-spatial inequalities and geographies of resistance in Barcelona. *Tourism Geographies*, *24*(6-7), 978-1001.

Munasinghe, L. M., Gunawardhana, T., Wickramaarachchi, N. C. & Ariyawansa, R. G. (2022). Platformization of travel and tourism real estate: a study on the operation of online tourist accommodation booking platforms in Sri Lanka. *Tourism and Sustainable Development Review*, *3*(2).

Nieuwland, S. & van Melik, R. (2020). Regulating Airbnb: how cities deal with perceived negative externalities of short-term rentals. *Current Issues in Tourism*, *23*(7), 811-825.

Oskam, J. & Boswijk, A. (2016). Airbnb: the future of networked hospitality businesses. *Journal of Tourism Futures*, *2*, 22-42.

Pastor, R. & Rivera-García, J. (2020). Airbnb and tourism intermediation: competition or coopetition? Perception of travel agents in Spain. *Revista Empresa y Humanismo*, *23*(2), 107–132.

Pompurová, K., Sebova, L. & Scholz, P. (2022). Reimagining the tour operator industry in the post-pandemic period: is the platform economy a cure or a poison? *Cogent Business & Management*, *9*(1).

Richardson, L. (2020a). Coordinating office space: digital technologies and the platformization of work. *Environment and Planning D*, *39*(2), 347-365.

Richardson, L. (2020b). Coordinating the city: platforms as flexible spatial arrangements. *Urban Geography*, *41*(3), 458-461.

Rochet, J.-C. & Tirole, C. (2004). Two-sided markets: an overview. *Working Paper Massachusetts Institute of Technology MIT* [Online]. Available at: https://web.mit.edu/14.271/www/rochet_tirole.pdf

Roelofsen, M. & Minca, C. (2018). The Superhost: biopolitics, home and community in the Airbnb dream-world of global hospitality. *Geoforum*, *91*, 170-181.

Roelofsen, M. (2022). *Hospitality, Home and Life in the Platform Economies of Tourism*. Heidelberg: Springer.

Sadowski, J. (2020). Cyberspace and cityscapes: on the emergence of platform urbanism. *Urban Geography*, *41*(3), 448-452.

Salet, X. (2021). The search for the truest of authenticities: online travel stories and their depiction of the authentic in the platform economy. *Annals of Tourism Research*, *88*, 103175.

Schor, J. B. (2017). Does the sharing economy increase inequality within the eighty percent? Findings from a qualitative study of platform providers. *Cambridge Journal of Regions, Economy and Society*, *10*(2), 263–279.

Schwarz, A. J. (2017). Platform logic: an interdisciplinary approach to the platform-based economy. *Policy and Internet*, *9*(4), 374-394.

Semi, G. & Tonetta, M. (2020). Marginal hosts: short-term rental suppliers in Turin, Italy. *Environment and Planning A*, *53*(7), 1630-1651.

Sigala, M. (2022). Sharing and platform economy in tourism: an ecosystem review of actors and future research agenda. In Xiang, Z., Fuchs, M., Gretzel, U., Höpken, W. (Eds.), *Handbook of e-Tourism*. Heidelberg: Springer.

Spangler, I. (2020). Hidden value in the platform's platform: Airbnb, displacement, and the un-homing spatialities of emotional labour. *Transactions of the Institute of British Geographers*, *45*(3), 575-588.

Stabrowski, F. (2017). 'People as businesses': Airbnb and urban micro-entrepreneurialism in New York City. *Cambridge Journal of Regions, Economy and Society*, *10*(2), 327-347.

Stehlin, J., Hodson, M. & McMeekin, A. (2020). Platform mobilities and the production of urban space: toward a typology of platformization trajectories. *Environment and Planning A*, *52*(7), 1250-1268.

Supaporn, C. A., Nongrat, S., Siripat, C., Jirayuth, C. & Chompunoot, D. (2023). Digital platform-mediated tourism system in small-town destination. *International Journal of Interactive Mobile Technologies*, *17*(5), 143-161.

Törnberg, P. & Chiappini, L. (2020). Selling black places on Airbnb: colonial discourse and the marketing of black communities in New York City. *Environment and Planning A*, *52*(3), 553-572.

Van Dijck, J., van Poell, T. & de Waal, M. (2018). *The Platform Society: Public Values in a Connective World*. New York: Oxford University Press.

Van Doorn, N. (2019). A new institution on the block: on platform urbanism and Airbnb citizenship. *Environment and Planning B*, *46*(10), 1808-1826.

Walker, M. (2020). Uber and the problem of regulatory arbitrage. In Dundon, T., Wilkinson, A. (Eds.), *Case Studies in Work, Employment and Human Resource Management*. Cheltenham: Edward Elgar Publishing Limited.

Wells, K. J., Attoh, K. & Cullen, D. (2021). Just-in-place labor: driver organizing in the Uber workplace. *Environment and Planning A*, *53*(2), 315-331.

Wilson, J., Garay-Tamajon, L. & Morales-Perez, S. (2022). Politicising platform-mediated tourism rentals in the digital sphere: Airbnb in Madrid and Barcelona. *Journal of Sustainable Tourism*, *30*(5), 1080-1101.

Yao, B., Qiu, R. T., Fan, D. X., Liu, A. & Buhalis, D. (2019). Standing out from the crowd – an exploration of signal attributes of Airbnb listings. *International Journal of Contemporary Hospitality Management*, *31*(12), 4520–4542.

Zervas, G., Proserpio, D. & Byers, J. (2017). The rise of the sharing economy: estimating the impact of Airbnb on the hotel industry. *Journal of Marketing Research, 54*, 687-705.

Zuboff, S. (2019). Surveillance capitalism and the challenge of collective action. *New Labor Forum, 28*(1), 10-29.

Conclusions - Learning to live with overtourism in Europe?

Sebastian Amrhein & Gert-Jan Hospers

With this edited volume, we intend to illustrate that overtourism in post-pandemic Europe has far more pronounced effects than merely full roads and streets, environmental pollution, damage to cultural heritage and rising housing prices. It is a multi-faceted phenomenon that poses complex challenges for a lot of stakeholders, be it residents, policymakers, the tourism industry and academia.

The chapters in the book discuss a number of aspects related to overtourism. It does not provide a complete overview of the issues at stake, but maps a part of the wide spectrum of facets that are relevant in overcrowded tourist destinations. Some contributors to this book identify research fields that have received little attention in tourism scholarship so far. Take the emotional levels on which overtourism influences those who are affected by it. Based on empirical data collected in Copenhagen and Munich, it becomes apparent that negative feelings of residents may occur subliminally and can only be attributed to tourism on closer examination. However, such feelings are not only influenced by direct contacts with travellers or by crowding effects, but also by the atmosphere of the location in question. The elusive aura of a place can have an impact on the experience of overtourism, while simultaneously being influenced by too many visitors. This 'invisibility' is crucial, but hardly quantifiable on a personal or spatial level. Perhaps this is also the reason why researchers have little attention for it.

However, this invisible level is not only relevant for the personal and spatial aspects of areas confronted with overtourism. Also the more obvious impacts of overtourism are strongly related to the particularities of time and place of a destination. Depending on factors like the geographical location, level of urbanisation, socio-economic conditions and time of the year, the impact of tourist activities and situations on a place and its inhabitants (and vice versa) may vary from case to case. This makes it difficult to come up with universal analyses and generic solution approaches. The development of effective solutions is also complicated by the diversity of interests and interdependencies of people who play a role in the ins and outs of a tourist destination. A good illustration is Amsterdam's 'tourism table': it demonstrates the complexity of involving different stakeholders in developing measures to manage or mitigate overtourism. Or take the DMOs or related tourism institutions that have focused on growth and the well-being of travellers since decades: they clearly have different interests than, say, residents who protest against overtourism. Changing the rationale and strategy of these institutions and the mindsets of their employees will take time.

The long-standing success of a growth-oriented perspective on tourism matters has been further fuelled by the platform economy. Digital platform companies like Airbnb and Uber typically have no geographical or emotional connection to a place and its inhabitants. At the same time, they are suspected of increasing the concentration of travellers in particularly popular locations through their algorithm-driven approach. Platform companies usually justify their share in the negative effects of overtourism on destinations and their inhabitants by referring to the creation of jobs and income for the local population. However, in this portrayal, the precarious working conditions, which can be very pronounced in the tourism sector, are disregarded. In turn, the tourism industry may create insecurity and dependency among those working in it – which hinders the free formation of opinion and possible protests against the adverse circumstances. Ultimately, this may lead to an acceptance of the negative effects of tourism.

If only because of the far-reaching consequences of overtourism for the places and people involved we see that concrete, creative and partly progressive governance measures play a role in the considerations of tourism scholars as well as decision makers. These are presented in the book at hand on the basis of various mini-cases and more extensive case studies coming from all over Europe, be it urban areas, coastal and island destinations as well as rural and mountain territories. The necessities, chances and risks of these strategies are discussed as well. Interestingly, even identity-creating approaches such as Cittaslow or holistic concepts like degrowth are worth considering in this respect. However, like the more mainstream policy interventions discussed, these alternative approaches require sound planning, communication and addressing of the needs of the people who suffer most from the conditions of current tourism practices.

Obviously, this book cannot provide a definitive answer to the question of whether we have to learn to live with overtourism. Taking into account the complexity of the challenges as well as the necessity of cooperation between different institutions that have various and partly opposing interests, a pessimistic scenario emerges. However, given the growing knowledge on overtourism, the creativity of solution approaches and the commitment of many participants, a more optimistic view comes to the fore. Expanding the knowledge on overtourism enables us to better understand the phenomenon, its mechanisms and possible touchpoints for intervention. In any case, it is important to look at overtourism from different perspectives, to act at eye level with those affected and to include them both in the research of the effects and in the development of solutions. We also plea for an open mind for promising research fields (e.g. the study of affective and emotional aspects of places), supposedly progressive approaches (such as degrowth) as well as concepts that have been applied already successfully (for example Cittaslow). If anything, all of these contributions show that tourism as we experience it today is based on human-made structures that are not irreversible.

Regionen in Europa/European Regions
hrsg. von Prof. Dr. Helmut R. Ebert (Universität Bonn), Prof. Dr. Karl Eckart (Universität Duisburg), Prof. Dr. Gert-Jan Hospers (Radboud Universität), Prof. Dr. Hartmut Kowalke (TU Dresden)

Karl Eckart; Thorsten David
Die Entwicklung des berufsbildenden Schulwesens in der Emscher-Lippe-Region 1830 bis 2019
Die vorliegende Untersuchung ist ein weiteres Ergebnis des komplexen Forschungsprojektes zum berufsbildenden Schulwesen im Ruhrgebiet. Erfasst worden sind die Struktur und Entwicklung in einer Teilregion des Ruhrgebietes, der Emscher-Lippe-Region, von 1830 bis 2019, also knapp 190 Jahre. Von den Sonntagsschulen über die gewerblichen Fortbildungsschulen und Berufsschulen bis zu den Berufskollegs werden mit einer Gliederung nach den historischen Epochen die wirtschaftlichen, sozialen und schulpolitischen Rahmenbedingungen, die Brüche und Umbrüche dargestellt. Zahlreiche graphische Darstellungen, Diagramme, Karten, Dokumente und Fotos zeichnen dieses vierfarbige Werk aus. Es ist ein Grundlagenwerk für alle Studierenden der verschiedenen Lehrämter, für Geographen, Pädagogen und Historiker sowie für alle am Bildungswesen interessierte Personen, Kommunen, Bibliotheken und Archive.
Bd. 6, 2020, 824 S., 64,90 €, br., ISBN 978-3-643-13965-8

LIT Verlag Berlin – Münster – Wien – Zürich – London
Auslieferung Deutschland / Österreich / Schweiz: siehe Impressumsseite

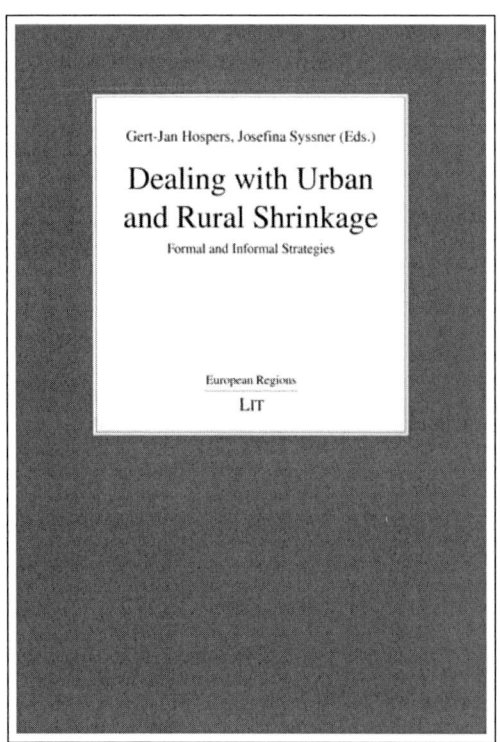

Gert-Jan Hospers; Josefina Syssner (Eds.)
Dealing with Urban and Rural Shrinkage
Formal and Informal Strategies
More and more places across the world are confronted with demographic shrinkage. This edited volume discusses how local communities in city and countryside have responded to the challenge of population decline. It is argued that formal strategies based on political and public sector decisions are only one way to deal with shrinkage. Informal adaptation strategies developed by civil society play an important role as well. To illustrate this, the book brings together a variety of theoretical perspectives, case studies and policy lessons from both urban and rural areas.
vol. 5, 2018, 146 pp., 55,90 €, pb., ISBN-CH 978-3-643-90822-3

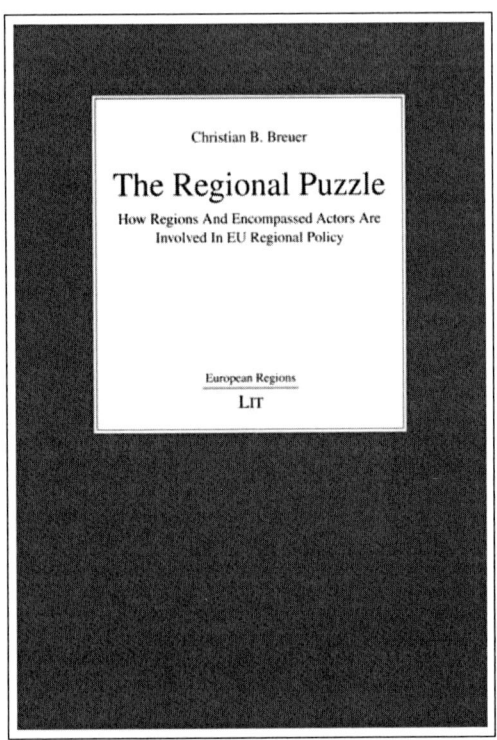

Christian B. Breuer
The Regional Puzzle
How Regions And Encompassed Actors Are Involved In EU Regional Policy
Regions have increasingly broke ground in the European sphere. For decades, they have been subject to forces both influencing them from above (regionalisation) as well as from below (regionalism). In the European Union, the regions and their actors have mainly manifested themselves via EU Regional Policy. Besides a closer look at the rationales behind this trend (see e.g. multi-level governance) and the brought along changes in the decision-making process, three case regions have thoroughly been addressed – Latvia, Scotland and Saxony. This book highlights pitfalls, possibilities and the position of regions and its actors in both the domestic and the European setting in a clear and structured way.
vol. 4, 2012, 408 pp., 44,90 €, pb., ISBN-CH 978-3-643-90094-4

Paul Benneworth; Gert-Jan Hospers (Eds.)
The Role of Culture in the Economic Development of Old Industrial Regions
In this edited volume scholars coming from all over Europe discuss the extent to which high- and low-culture can contribute to the economic development of Europe's old industrial regions. Including case studies from areas in the United Kingdom, Germany, the Netherlands, Sweden, Finland, Poland and Russia, the book demonstrates that culture can play a role in regenerating old industrial regions, but rather as an image booster than as a job machine.
vol. 3, 2009, 216 pp., 29,90 €, pb., ISBN 978-3-8258-1006-1

LIT Verlag Berlin – Münster – Wien – Zürich – London
Auslieferung Deutschland / Österreich / Schweiz: siehe Impressumsseite